THE LAND OF
ALE AND GLOOM

Discovering the Pacific Northwest

PHILLIP HURST

What is there for the soul to understand?
The slack face of the dismal pure inane?

Theodore Roethke, "A Walk in Late Summer"

Just look around you in any public barroom and you will quickly see: Bad people drink bad beer.

Hunter S. Thompson

CONTENTS

THE LAND OF ALE AND GLOOM

Discovering the Pacific Northwest

ALL THAT DAVID COPPERFIELD CRAP OR: HOW I LEARNED TO STOP WORRYING AND DRINK MORE BEER

In the fall of 1979, President Carter's national security adviser, Zbigniew Brzezinski, was awoken at three a.m. with a report that the Soviets had launched a massive nuclear strike against the United States. Knowing the Soviets had subs armed with ballistic missiles off the Atlantic seaboard, Brzezinski calculated the administration had just a few minutes to decide whether to press the button and retaliate, thereby incinerating and irradiating the entire northern hemisphere. In the logic of the arms race, the United States was winning the Cold War because the Soviets possessed only enough thermonuclear warheads to kill every man, woman, and squirrel in America five-thousand times over, whereas America had enough to kill all the Soviets ten-thousand times over, with the only way to maintain this delicate peace being the pointing of all these weapons at each other. Such was Brzezinski's dilemma.

Lucky for civilization, it was a false alarm. A training video somehow mistaken for live fire. Brzezinski never even bothered to wake up President Carter, instead leaving the Commander in Chief to sleep on more important matters—such as his decision to legalize homebrewing, which had been banned since Prohibition. Carter's wisdom cleared the path for states to allow the opening of brewpubs for the selling of these newly legit "microbrews," as craft beers were known back then.

I was born in the spring of 1979, and such was the world I found myself dropped into: one with a lot of bizarre and frightening things, alongside some enlightened and pleasant things. Skip forward a few decades—past a storied college basketball career that saw me set the school record not for assists or three-pointers, but torn ACLs, stints as an honest used car salesman, a night-blind pizza delivery man, and a narcoleptic security guard, the eventual return to school for a few graduate degrees of dubious practicality, all topped off with approximately 30,000 miles of brooding and aimless car travel throughout the American West—and I awoke one day in the spring of 2016 not to a phone call heralding Armageddon, but to a pair of melancholy realizations.

First, thanks to all that higher education soaked up while avoiding the workaday world, I'd ended up working in higher education myself (if as that lowliest of intellectual serfs, the community college adjunct instructor), and the academic year was winding down, which reminded me of my own student days and how I'd cherished summer's freedoms. But this only served as a reminder that I was no longer quite so young—in fact, the paired digits of my numerical age suggested in no uncertain terms that I was about halfway dead.

This is no epiphany, of course. Everybody gets older, everybody over the age of approximately seven knows this, and we all must eventually come to grips with our own mortality. So why should I be any different? Who awarded me a patent on gloom? But sometimes it's the obvious things that strike the deepest chord, and I'm hardly the first guy to squirm when confronted with this particular thought.

Take Jack Kerouac, a writer who I discovered young (when you're supposed to discover him) and whose books I've loved ever since. In *Desolation Angels,* having spent the summer of 1956 high on a desolate mountaintop in the North Cascades, half-mad from writing Buddhist poems and killing innocent mice, Jack catches a reflection of himself in a darkened window and thinks how the deepening lines on his face indicate he's come to the halfway point of his life, to middle age, to "the decay and the strife all to come" when an old fart like himself will no longer find any girls willing to take him to bed. That's the sort of mood I found myself in.

Better yet, consider the experience of Captain Meriwether Lewis. In the summer of 1805, the explorer celebrated a birthday while camped near the Bitterroot Range along the Salmon River, known today as The River of No Return. The Corps of Discovery had just reached the Continental Divide and realized there was no such thing as the Northwest Passage which President Jefferson had sent them to find. Lewis was a close friend of Jefferson, and had lived and studied with him before departing on his great journey. During this period, Jefferson reflected that Lewis was plagued by "sensible depressions of mind" which seemed to run in his family. Sure enough, reflecting on his failure to find the all-important water route, Lewis's journal strikes a mournful tone: "I had in all human probability now existed about half the period which I am to remain in this . . . world," he wrote, "that I had as yet done but little, very little indeed . . ."

Meriwether Lewis was thirty-one when he wrote those words.

Jack Kerouac had been thirty-four when he wrote his.

I was thirty-seven.

My second realization was perhaps even less insightful: I wasn't a very happy guy. In fact, I couldn't quite recall what true happiness even felt like, as if the whole notion was a con, a scam, like the get-rich quick schemes on late-night TV. I supplemented my meager teaching income by bartending, and awoke most days shrouded in a bluish fog. A strong pot of coffee would perk me up just enough to drag my brain to the classroom, so as to deliver pithy remarks to bored teenagers, whereas a second pot saw my weary bones to the gym, so as to forestall the inevitable heart attack (that most cliché of American deaths), before I either changed into a uniform and headed to the bar to stir martinis and shake gimlets, or came home to the couch and my four best friends, the walls.

If this all sounds a bit depressing, that's because it really was. Blame the usual suspects: a half-baked career after a few false starts at other careers, all of which sounded like glorified jail sentences; family and friends whom my lack of overt success underwhelmed and disappointed; and frustrated artistic ambitions in the form of a couple books I'd written that weren't exactly generating a buzz in the publishing world ("Dear Author, thank you so much for querying. While we read your submission with great interest, we've decided to pass. Best of luck finding a home for this manuscript, and in all your future endeavors in the restaurant industry"). Add to this a girlfriend recently lost under distressing circumstances, a beloved but very dead tomcat, and I was left with a question: Was there anything out there that still brought me joy?

Thankfully, the answer was yes.

The answer was beer. Cold, delicious, hoppy beer.

For better or worse and absurd as it might sound, beer was the one thing left that still made me happy. You know the sort of happiness I mean. The unthinking, spontaneous kind. Christmas morning. Riding a bike on a warm April day. A contentment that isn't earned by some labor, or by endlessly delaying gratification, or by plotting and executing some clever plan, but just falls from the sky like manna. On its face at least, beer is a simple substance with a simple purpose, and amidst the dark swells of life's inevitable confusions and anxieties, simple things have a way of shining through the murk and buoying us when we most need buoyed.

The above should not be taken to imply all was misery, though. I knew some good people and had my health, and the terrified and defensive sarcasm of my teens and the bitter black humor of my late-twenties had mellowed into an irony that consoled me through much disappointment. But that's not quite the same thing as happiness, and so it seemed a change was in order. While I sensed an embrace of beer was part of this change, drinking myself stupid held little appeal, as I'd already thoroughly explored that route (with beer being just the tip of the iceberg in terms of mind-altering substances) and it'd led more or less nowhere.

Instead, I asked myself what it was about beer that'd retained this joy-giving potential when so much else had fallen away. After all, beer is just a soup of water and grain, spiced with hops and fermented with yeast. In all probability, beer or something like it has been around since the domestication of plants and the resulting agricultural revolutions throughout the ancient world. Beer predates the wheel. Beer predates literature. In fact, beer predates nearly everything we call civilization. In *The Myth of Sisyphus,* Camus famously points out that all of Western thought boils down to just one basic philosophical problem—that after suicide there would be no more beer. So surely it wasn't just the substance itself, or the fuzzy-headedness brought about by having too much of it, that I was drawn to.

Also, I asked what it meant for a guy hailing from a central Illinois cow town to have spent a decade bouncing around the big cities of the West Coast—Portland, San Diego, Seattle— which happen to be where the craft beer revolution was born and remain where the majority of America's best beer is made. Being from a rural place, I was naturally curious about urban life, and I liked it well enough, having come to know those cities and their beers intimately. But what about the places I'd so far overlooked—places as small as my own hometown, even—were they making wonderful beers, too? Might I find a pilsner or a person or some strange vision out there? A clue of some kind, a trail back to the guy I'd been before life had quietly bled out its color.

So come June, the long rainy season having finally passed, I decided to hit the road. The terrain of my explorations was the home of craft beer, the Pacific Northwest, and while geographical boundaries for this region vary greatly—from the thin slice of wet ground between the Cascades and the Pacific, to the entire region between Alaska and San Francisco Bay, stretching clear east to the Rockies—for our purposes, as in all things, beer will be the guide. Thus, the entirety of Washington and Oregon feels about right, as Canada wasn't really part of the craft beer revolution and California's beer scene merits a book all its own.

In the back of my mind, however, I realized I wanted to explore the Northwest for reasons that ran deeper than beer. Though not a native son, I'd felt an emotional kinship with the landscape from the moment I first saw it: with its leaden skies and low gray clouds and the cold and pounding surf, with the dripping and eerie forests and that sense of damp green gloom which seeps, like the constant rain, into the minds and hearts of those who call the region home. But the Pacific Northwest is also a strikingly beautiful place—perhaps the most sublime America has to offer—and so I suspected I'd find arresting scenery, the sort of adventuresome people such scenery attracts, and (of course) the adventurous ales such people like to drink, no matter where I traveled and no matter how backwater the locale. For a half-dead guy this alone seemed reason enough to go, there being so much to taste but so little time to savor it.

Rallying from his melancholy, Jack Kerouac came down from the mountaintop and resolved to embrace the pleasures and pains of his life, along with those mad and wonderful friends "who never yawn or say a commonplace thing."

Rallying from his melancholy, Meriwether Lewis's birthday resolution was "to live for *mankind*, as I have heretofore lived *for myself*."

Rallying from my own melancholy, my resolution was "to go drink some beer."

After all, the clock was ticking—*is* ticking—and that's a fact we've all got to live with somehow.

THE HUMOURS OF A BEER SNOB

The community college was located in Everett, Washington, an old mill town thirty miles north of Seattle. Everett was blue-collar and a little rough around the edges, and this from a guy who knows whereof he speaks, as my central Illinois hometown had just twelve-hundred people, zero stoplights, and only one bar serving only one style of beer: American light lager (alternately, American *lite* lager).

Unlike small-town Illinois, however, Everett had a few craft breweries. One of them, Scuttlebutt, sat near the water on Port Gardner Bay Marina. Port Gardner was named by the intrepid George Vancouver, who landed his *Discovery* near a village of the Snohomish tribe in 1792. Vancouver promptly planted a flag and claimed the area for England, fired off his cannons at nothing in particular, issued his crew a round of grog in celebration, and then—as the Snohomish watched and scratched their heads—raised anchor and sailed away once again. Soon other white men followed from the Hudson Bay Company, then prospectors and homesteaders fresh off the Oregon Trail, who brought with them guns and smallpox and a tendency to dam the rivers and cut down all the trees.

But as far as Everett's breweries went, I couldn't find one that suited my taste. To borrow a term from the oenophiles, perhaps the *terroir* of Everett, Washington simply disagrees with me? My beer snobbery is a venial sin at worst, though, and to be dubbed a "beer geek" is actually an honorific of the highest order. The only real downside to loving craft beer is that craft beer gets a tad spendy, at least insofar as beer-drinking goes. Then again, my teaching gig paid so little that I felt curiously obliged to rid myself of whatever pittance might've otherwise remained. As Young Werther puts it, most of us work away our lives just trying to make a living and are so troubled by whatever freedom remains that we quickly find a way to be rid of it.

Hence, Everett's best little craft beer taphouse: Brews Almighty.

#

To get there, I left the college and drove south down Rockefeller Avenue—named after Standard Oil's very own, the magnate who'd bankrolled the town of Everett back in the late nineteenth century. Mr. Rockefeller was convinced by some optimistic land speculators that the deep waters of Port Gardner Bay would become the terminus of railroad tycoon Jim Hill's Great Northern, the second of the transcontinental lines linking the agricultural, mineral, and timber wealth of the Midwest with the Pacific. Everett, Washington would become the New York City of the West was the thought, or at least another Boston.

Then I reached Hewitt Avenue, the main drag. Henry Hewitt Jr. was the speculator most responsible for Rockefeller sinking his millions into Everett—a shantytown the historian Norman H. Clark describes ever so delicately as "a mud-drenched community of idiots." Henry Hewitt's dream didn't pan out, of course. Jim Hill named Seattle the terminus of his railroad, and Rockefeller soon launched a series of cutthroat legal maneuvers to get his money back. Afterward, Everett became a resource town beset by vicious class warfare, and Hewitt Avenue became a din of drunken timberman, last-chance prostitutes, and ten-card stud. It got so seedy that the tent show evangelist Billy Sunday (a charismatic former pro baseball player turned religious entrepreneur) came to preach his righteous brand of teetotalism to the rowdy millworkers. As a counter measure, the esteemed lawyer Clarence Darrow (of Scopes Monkey Trial fame) was brought in by the local taxpayer's association to argue for keeping Everett wet, mostly so that the working class would continue subsidizing city government with their bar tabs.

Port Gardner Bay sparkled down the hill as I waited out a long stoplight. Just then, a middle-aged white dude entered the crosswalk. He carried a sack of groceries. He also sported a garish red baseball cap advertising another white dude—one who fancied himself a modern-day Rockefeller. For whatever reason, halfway across the street and dead even with the Honda's windshield, this pedestrian paused to give yours truly a truly dirty look.

MAKE AMERICA GREAT AGAIN, his cap read.

Donald Trump had recently been named his party's presumptive nominee, and along with everyone else, I'd been seeing that slogan more and more often—on hats, on shirts, on yard signs and roadside billboards. Still hadn't quite gotten used to it, though. Nonetheless, I smiled politely at the man and shook off the unaccountable weirdness of our little staring match. After a quick left, I was soon parked outside Brews Almighty.

19

Inside was a well-curated tap list. Beer people tend to be thoughtful people, and to the owner's credit there's rarely a dull keg. While deciding what to have, I informed the reliably surly woman tending the taps that it was important I choose just the right beer, as I was celebrating.

"Is it a boy or a girl?"

"Better," I said. "It's the end of spring quarter."

Then she asked if I was a student up at the college, and I admitted to actually teaching English courses there.

"No wonder you need a beer," she said.

I explained that today had been my last class until September; I was officially a free man.

"Must be nice," she said, "cashing those state paychecks all summer long."

I agreed with her that it surely would've been nice, but for the fact that Washington State didn't see fit to pay me over the summer. When she asked how I meant to live with no income, I explained that I'd managed to squirrel away a few pennies and also planned to bartend a couple of nights a week. I'd recently filed a deferment on my high-interest student loan payments, as well. I told her about this, too, adding that—in my humble opinion—Uncle Sam was in the extortion racket.

"Makes me glad I never got enough education to go into education," she said.

"Funny, I give my students that exact same advice."

Then she asked how I planned to spend all my free time, and I said some traveling and a little writing—and that, more importantly, I intended to drink all the craft beer I could find.

"Well you've come to the right place for that."

In addition to the aforementioned worthy pursuits, I also planned to finally read the book I'd brought along, Robert Burton's *The Anatomy of Melancholy*. The brick-thick volume had more pages than my hometown has people. My copy was so heavy that I sat it atop the bar to give my hand a rest. The cover depicted the sepia-toned human skull and dwindling hourglass from Philippe de Champaigne's *Vanitas* (1671), an example of *memento mori*, an expression meaning: "Remember that you too must die." The idea traces back to ancient Greece, appears throughout various religions, and pops up frequently in art. Think Hamlet chatting with Yorick's skull, or those little skeletons on Dia de Los Muertos.

"Looks like you got yourself a beach read there," the bartender said.

Then I admitted that I'd been lugging old Burton around shamefully unread for the last fifteen years (though I'd never before brought him to a bar). I'd purchased the book shortly after graduating college, compelled by the curious perfection of the title, but more so by my own feelings of melancholy, which had cropped up from time to time. A strange way of self-medicating, perhaps, but I'd wondered if reading the longest, oddest, and most famous tome on my affliction might provide some insight.

But the *Anatomy* is the densest of books. Burton, a cloistered Oxford academic, added successive editions over the decades, expanding, explaining, compounding (and confounding) his life's work until it spiraled into thorny brambles of labyrinthine ideas and ancient scholarship and sheer verbal gush with such eye-straining regularity that I'd only managed to read bits of it—tasty if puzzling snippets—here and there.

"Let me see if I got this straight," the bartender said. "You're done with school, but now you're gonna read *that?*"

She had a point. Pouring over the gloomy musings of an English Renaissance scholar probably isn't the most relaxing way to spend one's leisure time, but Burton is both learned and ironic. For example, he explains by way of justifying his Sisyphean attempts to both perfect his treatise and to simultaneously cure himself of the titular disorder, that idleness must be avoided at all costs. "I write of melancholy," he declares, "by being busy to avoid melancholy." And while he occasionally had his priorities out of whack—Burton was a self-professed *"aquæ potor"* or water-drinker—he rightly shoots down those who would malign beer-drinking. Quoting assorted long-forgotten philosophers, he asserts that brew, "'tis a most wholesome and a pleasant drink" that's "more subtle and better for the hop that rarefies it" and has "an especial virtue against melancholy."

Notably, this follows an extended formal digression[1] which summarily denounces virtually every food one might feasibly consume. Pork is overly moist and packed with humours, and thus likely to cause a quartan ague (recurring fever), while rabbit

---

[1] *The Anatomy* itself reads like a 1,300 page, single-spaced, nine-point-font digression. Aesthetically, Burton was a kitchen sink guy. Even the book's title digresses. Consider Burton's preferred version: *The Anatomy of Melancholy, What it is: With all the Kinds, Causes, Symptomes, Prognostickes, and Severall Cures of it: In Three Partitions, with their Severall Sections, Members, and Subsections: Philosophically, Medicinally, Historically, Opened and Cut-up.*

meat is dark and hard to digest and tends to cause nightmares, whereas "all venison is melancholy, and begats bad blood" much as cheeses and curds only serve to increase one's incipient melancholy; furthermore, Rhasis and Magninus "discommend all fish" as fish are nutritionally slimy and "breed viscosities." As for vegetables, Crato and company find few if any fit to eat, but cabbage is most troublesome of all, with Galen writing that cabbage makes for a heavy soul; and you can forget about parsnips and potatoes, because none other than the esteemed Bruerinus declares all roots windy and "troublesome to the head." Finally, beans and peas are for naught, as they fill the brain with gross fumes, or so saith Isaac.

But perhaps most indicative of the whole mad book is Burton's take on carp.

"Carp," Burton writes, "is a fish of which I know not what to determine." He then proves this by weighing at excruciating length the opinions of learned carp experts such as Franciscus Bonsuetus, who derides carp as a "muddy fish," and Hippolytus Salvianus, who in his *New York Times* and Amazon.com bestselling classic on carp, *de piscium natura et præparaione,* criticizes carp for its slimy meat. On the other hand, Paulus Jovius approves of carp, as so doth Messieurs Dubravius and Freitagius, who "puts it amongst the fishes of the best rank."

In this way, Burton manages to wax philosophical on carp—and every other subject under the sun—without ever quite stating a definitive conclusion. So it's refreshing when, after rambling on and on like this until his reader is left in a glassy-eyed daze, Burton finally recommends a food that experts from the Classical Period through the Dark Ages and up into the Renaissance can agree is unlikely to cause melancholy: beer.

"Not to judge a book by the cover," the bartender said, "but that looks like a downer."

When I told her the book's subject was in fact the oldest downer known to mankind— depression—she wanted to know if it was like a medical book, or if I meant the fella who wrote it was depressed himself.

"A bit of both," I said, and fanned the impossible clump of pages. "If that makes sense?"

"He should've gotten himself some of that Prozac. I hear it works wonders."

"I used to pop those things like Certs," I said, but the bartender merely smirked and asked if I thought it'd helped any.

This was actually hard to say, though. Looking back, it's possible the pills had helped a little, at least at first, although that might've just been me *hoping* they would help. "These days I stick to what I know works," I said. "Like beer and books."

"Well, I'm still not sure about that book of yours, but I can definitely pour you a beer."

I pointed out the ale I'd been eyeing, and as the bartender filled my glass I considered that her skepticism of Burton was understandable. Because while encyclopedic on matters of the human condition, the *Anatomy* remains a product of its pre-Enlightenment time. This shows most clearly via Burton's penchant for quotation. There's nothing he loves more than to quote some dusty old sage, even when those sages say things like if a pregnant woman sees a rabbit her child will be born with a hare-lip, or that depressed old grandmas are actually witches who fornicate with the devil. Nevertheless, the book was long enough to at least keep me busy.

Moments later, beer in hand and sunken comfortably into a booth, I angled the lamp just so and began to read. Burton, like most educated people of his day, ascribed to the ancient theory of humours that arose with Hippocrates in Classical Greece and clung to men's imaginations until anatomists fully mapped the course of blood throughout the body. Melancholy, which is the fluid largely responsible for our disposition, counts as one of these humours (the others are blood, phlegm, and choler), and derives etymologically from the Greek *melaina chole,* or black bile. In what's surely no coincidence, this theory originates with the liver. According to Burton, the liver is a "shop of humours" that produces these mysterious fluids which determine everything about us—health, mood, proclivities, even our fate.

With summer finally here, my own liver had some work to do, and Brews Almighty was a good place to get started. Brewery posters from Ninkasi and Elysian and neon signage from Firestone-Walker and Widmer adorned the walls, while the bottle coolers were decorated with Seahawks stickers, and the stereo played Zeppelin's "Going to California" at a volume low enough that nobody had to shout.

As for my beer, it was rusty orange, headless, legless, and sour. Think ripe apricot cut with lemon. It was brewed in Bend, Oregon, a town in the central Cascades known as "Beer Town, USA." I hoped to visit Bend, and maybe even visit the maker of this beer—10 Barrel—although the brewery had recently been purchased by Anheuser-Busch InBev, a Belgian-Brazilian transnational conglomerate prone to making offers which simply cannot be refused—not the severed heads of horses, but long strings of zeros and commas. Regardless of what their press releases might claim, AB-InBev's goal is to one way or another stop talented craft brewers, such as the folks at 10 Barrel, from carving any deeper into the market share. Such buyouts were a business decision, pure capitalism, and so tend to leave a few victims in their wake. This isn't just true of beer, either. Nor is it just true of today.

Consider the Everett Massacre, for example.

The events occurred just shy of a century before, back in November of 1916, at the height of industrial tensions between mill owners and striking workers, when the Seattle branch of the International Workers of the World (the "Wobblies") sent a contingent of loyalists to Everett to support the picketers. Once arrived, the Wobblies were taken to a field, stripped nude, and made to run a gauntlet of deputies who beat them bloody with clubs. Undaunted, a week later the IWW sent more men. The Everett police force was in the pocket of the monopolists and spread rumor that these un-American Wobblies planned to burn the mills and loot the town, when the worst they had in mind was a few soapbox polemics along Hewitt Avenue. By the time the IWW boat reached the dock, hundreds of local men had gathered to ward them off. This being America, everyone brought guns. Somebody inevitably lost his temper and fired a shot. This was quickly followed by everyone firing shots, and soon the Wobblies were bullet-riddled and dying.

The Everett Massacre earns a mention not only in the history books, but in a few of the Northwest's prominent novels: notably, Ken Kesey's *Sometimes a Great Notion,* and Jack Kerouac's *The Dharma Bums* and *Desolation Angels.* In Kesey's novel, which is curiously unsympathetic to the labor movement, considering its author would later become an icon of the counterculture, one of the dead was the grandfather of a local union rep; while for Kerouac, who always identified with the downtrodden, having grown up amidst the greasy soot of another mill town—Lowell, Massachusetts—the dead are "oldtime heroes."

But whatever one's politics, the shooting on Port Gardner Bay made clear that efforts to unite workers in collective bargaining for reasonable safety standards simply would not fly in the freedom-loving mills of Everett, Washington. Perhaps it's overreaching to see a connection between such historical events and the modern auguries of beer-drinking, but then again maybe not. After all, AB-InBev had recently launched a summer advertising campaign titled "America is in Your Hands," which swapped the trademark "Budweiser" on its cans and bottles with the word "America." The campaign was set to run through the November election, and thereby inspire red-blooded Americans to hold a cold sweaty can of good old-fashioned patriotism in their hands—and hopefully not think too hard about the fact that the beer inside that can was no longer brewed by an American-owned company.

Despite the callousness of such a marketing ploy, and while I remain wary of the motives of mega-corporations like AB-InBev, the company hasn't (at least to my knowledge) had anyone shot for exercising their free speech rights, and the 10 Barrel ale's tangy brightness was a relief after the cold drip of the rainy season. The souring owed to lactobacillus, a form of bacteria commonly found in the human vagina, amongst other places less conspicuous, such as sourdough bread. But while sours now reside on the frontier of American craft brewing, they're actually kin to the oldest beers known to exist.

Wild-fermenting ales were being made around today's Belgium upwards of 5,000 years ago. Thus, back before anyone had any clue how yeast functioned, long before Pasteur and his *Etudes sur la bier,* brewers were throwing open the attic doors in the knowledge that *something* would happen to the sugary wort they'd cooked up—something not unlike magic. In fact, those early brewers referred to this frothy and mysterious bubbling as "God is good." And so it was fitting to drink a sour at Brews Almighty, with its angelic theme, as those first brewers of wildly fermented ales viewed the transformation as nothing short of a divine blessing.

The beer was so tasty that I was considering having another, except just then a pair of local Everett guys entered with their scary-looking tattoos, muscle-tees, shin-length shorts, and—inevitably—their pit bulls. What is it with men expressing their inner-macho via pooch? Because those dogs never asked to be paraded around like loaded pistols, and they didn't choose to have fire hydrants for necks and jaws like hippopotami, but were born and bred that way, much as I was born at the tail end of Generation X and therefore missed the ingrained millennial knowledge that all things of value necessarily have interactive screens and Wi-Fi, and thus lacked the foresight not to invest in a degree in literature and creative writing.

I watched the newcomers try to order from the bartender.

"Sorry, boys," she said, "but we don't serve Bud Light. Our beer actually tastes good. Maybe you should try an IPA?"

I thought of these guys as Thug Life Kowalskis, because they put me in mind of a young Marlon Brando if Brando had been into Tupac and traded Tennessee Williams for Tennessee whiskey. Kowalskis usually don't hang around craft beer spots for long, though, as they prefer bars which serve six-dollar pitchers of the aforementioned American light lager, as opposed to six-dollar pints of India Pale Ale. But cost isn't the only factor at work here. There are elements of nationalism and class pride, as well, as American macrobrew is seen by many as the drink of real hard-working blue-collar Americans, sort of like those millworkers who misplaced their loyalties and shot up the Wobblies on Port Gardner Bay.

If beer really is the drink of the working class, though, it needs be said that corporate lager such as Bud Light isn't even really beer, at least not as history has defined the beverage. Because even before the usage of hops, bittering agents were added to temper the sweetness of the grain, whereas American corporate lagers employ so miniscule an amount of hops that the bitterness is undetectable upon the tongue. The saccharine wateriness of such barley pop appeals to those who've never been properly exposed to real beer, which is by necessity bitter as well as sweet, a balance which Robert Burton writes is foundational to the human experience. He quotes Solomon to show that even amidst our laughter is sorrow, and notes how all good and prosperous things also hath some bitterness; seen in this light, it's patently absurd for mortal man to deny the various miseries which spice his life. But Burton doesn't lament. Instead, he argues that whether one finds life's bitterness pleasant or painful, it is simply the habit of man, and thus the habit of this world.

Sure enough, confronted with real beer in all its complexity and mystery, the Kowalskis dragged their pit bulls right back out the door. And here was one of the great ironies of beer-drinking: the more rebellious and dangerous-looking the clientele, the more likely they are to have a rap sheet, the more apt to ride Harley-Davidsons and overvalue their Second Amendment rights, the greater the likelihood of their drinking characterless beers with multi-billion dollar marketing schemes devised by shark-suited corporate overlords who would no sooner tip a Bud with one of these working-class guys than cease busting unions and lobbying to enable the exportation of manufacturing jobs to Mexico and China.

Perhaps I'm as bitter as an IPA, or as sour as that 10 Barrel ale, but maybe what we drink matters more than we care to admit. Maybe ignorance of one aspect of culture—even beer culture—is a bellwether of neglect for all the rest.

BEER NEAR ME: A JOURNEY TO MIDDLE-EARTH (AND MOUNT VERNON)

A couple of days later, I awoke in my cozy little (daylight) basement studio with what was either a hangover or a head cold. Regardless, the treatment protocol was the same.

Skookum Brewing lay in the town of Arlington, another old mill town near the forks of the Stillaguamish River. It should've been a short drive north, but short drives are rare as suntans in the Puget Sound basin. Bottlenecked between the saltwater and Cascades, Seattle's population explosion has resulted in world-class gridlock. This endless stop-and-go is frustrating enough to make Seattleites contemplate quitting their upwardly mobile careers to go live someplace far, far away, like Iowa or Nebraska, places they've never even visited and assume are ugly and boring—so much so that there might not be much traffic.

Sure enough, eleven a.m. on a Saturday and I-5 was totally stalled. So I swigged my coffee, palmed the Honda's horn, and swerved onto the exit for route 9, where I proceeded to zoom up the turn lane and then cut back into the other lane— serenaded by a chorus of outraged honking—at every stoplight. In this way, I passed hundreds of stalled passenger vehicles and soon followed a roundabout to my destination.

Inside Skookum's tasting room, the sour biscuit smell of cooking wort cut through my sinus congestion. Ten and twenty-barrel fermentation tanks filled one end of the space, while wood-lined copper boilers took up the other. A serene-looking brewer dude in green rubber waders sampled a little morning beer while hosing out kegs.

"Skookum" is a Chinook word meaning monstrous or very powerful, but it reminded me of something I might roll up and smoke with that mellow brewer. Having recently lifted the prohibition on marijuana, Washington was enjoying a Green Revolution. Pot shops have blossomed everywhere. Considering I came of age in the '90s Midwest, where marijuana still carried a taboo, it felt odd to see these shops in suburban strip malls. McDonald's, Jiffy Lube, Starbucks, and Slow Yo Roll Recreational Marijuana. They even hire teenagers to drum up business by twirling big green signs out by the curbs. It's weird. I doubt I'll ever get used to it.

One good thing about legalization is now breweries feel free to use weed terms to describe their beer. On Skookum's draft board was an India Pale Ale called the Cont(r)act High, which promised the "dank" flavor of "Sticky icky!" But this doesn't necessarily mean Skookum's brewers were toking up behind the kettles (although it doesn't necessarily *not* mean that, either). No, the terms are simply accurate, as pot and hops are close cousins. If you like the smell of the one, you'll probably enjoy the taste of the other. But while I love hops, I'm not a particularly talented smoker of marijuana. Being introverted by nature, a couple puffs of that legal Seattle weed leaves me huddled in a corner, counting my heartbeats and mourning something cruel I may or may not have actually said to a classmate back in seventh grade.

My stuffy nose would've ruined a beer like the Cont(r)act High, though, as much of the pleasure lies in the hop aroma.

Instead, I needed something rich and sweet on the tongue, so I ordered an imperial stout called the Murder of Crows. It was conditioned with oak chips soaked in Old Crow bourbon. Beer and bourbon makes sense together, as the laws of bourbon-making require the spirit only be aged in new charred oak barrels, leaving distillers with a bunch of perfectly good barrels which they can't use again. Scotch and tequila makers buy them up, and brewers are following suit.

Next came a Belgian-style saison aged in cabernet barrels. It was light, tart, dry, and rustic—although not nearly so rustic as the older couple at the next table over. In addition to their both being dressed head to toe in denim, rather like Wood's *American Gothic*, they'd been watching me jot my notes with unabashed curiosity. Writing in bars can seem pretentious, so unless the young woman pulling taps is in particular need of impressing, I try to keep a low profile. If a stranger should ask what I'm up to, which strangers sometimes will, I admit to being an English teacher, which typically wilts their interest and discourages any further questions.

"Excuse me, young man," the woman said. Her husband smiled at me expectantly, as if he'd put her up to it. I laid aside my pen and asked how I might be of assistance.

"We need to pay for these beers"—and then I noticed she'd pulled a rubber-sleeved bank book from her denim purse—"but do you think they'll take our personal check?"

I inquired as to whether they were by chance residents of lovely and bucolic Arlington.

"We are," the husband said, still smiling.

"We most certainly are," agreed his wife, still holding the rubber checkbook.

"And do you two come to this brewery a lot?"

"We visit when we can," the wife said. Then she leaned in close to whisper. "We like the beer, but it's awfully expensive."

Her husband nodded, as if she'd conferred a great truth, and then I recalled the Thug Life Kowalskis back in Everett, who wouldn't drink in a place like Brews Almighty because pints of craft beer cost a little more than Bud Light. And now here were these two retirees, pinching pennies so they could enjoy locally made Skookum beer. Unbeknownst to them, they'd warmed my heart. "Well this is my first time here," I said, "but I'll bet if you show them your bank book"—I pointed at the bulky thing—"they'd be happy to accept your check."

The denim-clad duo thanked me with real sincerity. Over the husband's shoulder, taped to the walk-in cooler, was a notice: "KEEP YOUR CLOTHES ON! Indecent Exposure WILL NOT be tolerated. Anyone involved will be banned from the premises."

On my way out, I settled my tab. "See grandma and grandpa over there?" I said to the bartender. "I'd like to pay for their beers, too."

The bartender said no problem, and then asked if they really were my grandparents.

"May as well be," I said.

#

I've always felt a healthy dose of chance is good for the soul and that too much planning inhibits discovery, and so, hoping to give fate a whirl and ward off the melancholy of the predictable,

I typed a singular query into my iPhone's magic GPS thingamajig: *beer near me . . .*

A number of cute little red pins showered the map and I followed one toward Whiskey Ridge Brewing. Upon finding the tiny place, the owner-bartender-brewer greeted me with an apology: "We've only got three beers on tap today, unfortunately."

The one I tried was pretty good, though. While sipping, I discovered the owner-bartender-brewer was also a –writer. "I used to study English . . ." she began.

But more words weren't necessary. I understood. She'd opened the classifieds the day after graduation only to discover that four years' of pondering the baroque history of Yoknapatawpha County and the bespectacled symbolism of Dr. T. J. Eckleburg's looming peepers barely qualified one to drop sliced potatoes into a vat of burbling oil. After that, she worked a few years at menial tasks, keeping hope alive by writing her novel at night. Maybe she even finished it. But the world, as it's prone to do, responded with silence. Thus, brewing.

"I studied English and creative writing, too," I said.

She looked at me in a state of barely contained alarm, clearly hoping I'd given up and become a teacher, but terrified I might announce I'd published a novel or a collection of stories.

But then I put her mind at ease, and described how I'd spent the last decade bartending up and down the West Coast, writing whenever I found the time and teaching a few composition courses here and there, but not getting much accomplished by way of publishing.

"Do you think the book is dying?" she asked, and while this was probably a valid question, I felt hesitant to provide the answer she seemed to want. Instead, I told her about a guy I'd gone to graduate school with—a poet—who'd ended up brewing for Ska out in Durango.

"Is that a good thing?"

"Good enough."

"Maybe books are more like the undead"—she poured me a taster of another of her beers, without my having asked—"like animate corpses."

"The *Twilight* series did pretty well."

"Oh god, I know. Shiny vampire boyfriends with washboard abs. It's sad, isn't it? Talking about it makes me need a beer."

"I hear you," I said, "but to be honest, most of life makes me feel that way."

After promising to visit again soon—though I never will, because lamenting the death of literature is something I prefer to do alone so as to preserve the fantasy that I might yet beat the odds—I took a stroll down Olympic Avenue. A bowling alley served cheeseburger lunches out of a gutted Cadillac ingeniously converted into a bar, while across the street was a thrift shop with the inscrutable name of Fog and Butter. But then I came upon a tall building with a sign in woodland green calligraphy declaring it the Mirkwood & Shire Café.

Sure enough, a few daytime beers had led me to the fabled land of magic and dragons known as Middle-earth. For those who somehow missed the Hollywood adaptations, Mirkwood is a haunted forest in J.R.R. Tolkien's fantasy realm, and the Shire is the greenly English burrow where Hobbits dwell, a

Hobbit being a pint-sized humanoid with hairy feet and pointed ears.

Up the steps and past a few gargoyles I went. The place had three levels. Upstairs was Mordor Tattoo parlor, Mordor being the Third Reich-style land where orcs and evil wizards conspire to make mincemeat of Hobbits. Another sign advertised the Rivendell (magical elven city) Hair Salon, but Rivendell had recently gone out of business. The ground floor was a restaurant decorated with murals of scary eyeballs and medieval knights. I headed downstairs to a dungeon of blood red walls and awful music. The table rocked to and fro as I unfolded my laptop. Soon I was greeted by a daffy but sweet barmaid with a badly infected septum piercing.

"Hail and well met, fine lass. Perchance might a weary traveler trouble you for a flagon of your finest ale?"

"Whoa!" she said, blinking at me. "That was pretty sweet."

"What's this place called, anyway"—I glanced around at the subterranean décor—"the Mines of Moria?"

She confessed it was her first day, but offered to go ask somebody if I was really curious, which I assured her I was not. "I'll just take a beer," I said.

"Wait," she said, and only then did I realize how monumentally stoned she was, the Green Revolution apparently not being lost on the employees of the Mirkwood & Shire. That, or she had the world's worst case of pink eye. "They," she said, smacking her cottony lips, "I mean somebody—like the owners or maybe that chick who trained me—I mean, they told me something about this. Like what we call it down here."

"I saw the Misty Mountains beer garden outside."

"Oh yeah?" She wore a smock that might've almost passed for period garb at your local Renaissance fair. Or maybe she just shopped at Fog and Butter. Then she told me I was in the Ouija bar, or something like that. It was kinda hard to say.

Thankfully, Middle-earth had one very good beer on tap: the Johnny Utah citrus pale ale from Georgetown Brewing. Georgetown is located in the Seattle neighborhood of the same name. Their beer is fresh and unfiltered and consistently excellent. But when the waitress stood the pint on a coaster, the table wobbled and beer sloshed near my laptop. She looked at me as if some mystery had occurred. I moved it—the computer, not the pint—slowly away.

"So what's the story with all the Middle-earth stuff?"

"The owners are nerds," she said, and giggled.

"It's cool. I like it."

"Me too. I think working here's gonna be pretty rad."

She was right. Middle-earth was pretty rad. In fact, this wasn't my first journey there, as between the ages of ten and fourteen, my friends and I embarked upon many heroic quests together, not only braving the horrors of Mirkwood Forest (huge spiders, hungry trolls) and the goblin armies of Mordor, but also the social ostracization of our peers.

MERP was fun, though. Middle-earth Role Playing. Swords-and-Sorcery. A game of paper and imagination, a pre-Xbox, stegosaurus of a hobby. The rule books alone were hundreds of pages long and contained the improbably complex lexicons of Middle-earth, such as Elvish (think flute music and wind whistling through the forest canopy), Dwarvish (consonants, breaking bricks), and Entish (Ents are tree people, thus wooden moaning), which my friends and I dutifully

PHILLIP HURST

struggled to pronounce. Things only complicated from there. Numerical tables denoted various possibilities for encountering dramatic weather high in the mountain passes or while crossing rain-swept moors, and the likelihood of detection at given visibilities while exploring dreary tunnels deep in the goblin-haunted underworld, or better yet, while piloting a sloop across a dark tarn boiling with hungry krakens. Add to this the many and varied formulas for dealing with all possible combinations of sword strike vs. armor type, fireball vs. dragonscale, and other fantasy whatnot, and MERP moved at an Ent's pace. Looking back, the amount of math we willingly subjected ourselves to seems astounding.

The cliché is that boys play games like MERP because they haven't yet discovered girls, but in my experience that's off the mark, as my friends and I quit playing right around the time we began getting our hands on illicit cases of beer. Like Frost says, nothing gold can stay.

Then again, who needs twelve-sided dice when you've got a twelve-pack?

\#

On the drive up to Mount Vernon, things got odd (or maybe *odder,* considering I'd just drank a beer in Middle-earth) when I passed an Adopt-A-Highway sign sponsored by ANGEL OF THE WINDS CASINO. Thus, a federal highway lovingly maintained by Native Americans who'd had the very land it ran across stolen from them, only to build a casino that fleeced the descendants of those who'd ripped off their ancestors.

Better yet, a few miles later another Adopt-A-Highway sign read: LARC NUDISTS. This was the Lake Associates Recreation Club, a family-oriented club for those who appreciate a clothing-optional lifestyle. According to their website, while escaping the daily grind of clothes-wearing, visitors to LARC often encounter wildlife such as hawks or eagles. Perhaps predictably, members also enjoy volleyball. The club rules are more or less standard, but for two exceptions: first, whenever nude, club members must always sit upon their own towel; and second, absolutely no swimsuits are allowed in the hot tub.

I was busy scanning the woods for nudists when I saw yet another sign—CANNAREX, a local recreational marijuana dispensary, had apparently decided to adopt some highway. Taken together, this trio stuck me as more than a little unlikely. Dispossessed Native American casino-operators and stoned nudist do-gooders maintaining the same stretch of I-5? Nobody back in the Midwest would've ever believed such a thing.

Once in Mount Vernon, however, I visited Skagit (pronounced like *gadget*) River Brewery, where Helen the bartender poured me a whooping six-sample taster tray. First up was the ESB, or extra-special bitter, which wasn't actually bitter at all. This raises the question of why the English, who bequeathed us this style, named a malty, crackery ale "bitter"— especially considering they knew darn well their pales and IPAs were the bitter ones? ESB, like brown or amber ale, is an easy drinking beer of moderate ambition. I get why people like them: they want to have three or four without exhausting their taste buds or falling off their barstool. But for me, beer isn't just a drink to wash down a burger. Beer is the main course. Beer is the whole point. So I wasn't particularly excited to sample

Jenny's Scottish Ale, because—like ESBs—Scottish ales are of little obvious distinction. While there's evidence of brewing in Scotland going back thousands of years, today's Scottish ales resemble their English cousins, although less estery due to colder fermentation temperatures. But then I noticed something interesting. The menu claimed Jenny's was brewed to complement Mount Vernon's Annual Highland Games.

I asked Helen why Mount Vernon, Washington had a Scottish-themed celebration.

"I'm not sure," Helen said, "but we do it every year." She smiled and went back to pouring pints. She had a motherly vibe.

"So it's kilts and bagpipes?"

Helen seemed surprised I would question something as well-known as the Mount Vernon Highland Games. "Oh sure. People really get into it."

I sipped the Jenny's. It tasted like liquid caramel. "Local guys toss around the big log?"

"You betcha," she said, and then walked away. Unfortunately for Helen, she had to keep passing by me to pour certain beers.

"But you have no idea *why* this festival exists?"

"Well . . ." She was having trouble with a foamy keg.

"Were there Scottish immigrants here?"

Helen spun around, hands planted firmly on her hips. "It's just the way it's always been."

I turned to the guy on the next stool over and asked a few similar questions. "It's just what folks do around here," he said, and sipped an inch off his pint.

Here was small-town life in a nutshell: a group of people related by locality, custom, and often by blood, who've reached an unspoken agreement not to worry too much about why they did the weird things they do. Oh, how I remember this mentality. The metropolis of Windsor, Illinois had no Highland Games, but we did have Bessie Bingo. Bessie was a cow. The bingo card was a grid spray-painted on Maple Street. The chips you can imagine. People placed bets, sometimes winning, most times losing, but nobody ever questioned the tradition, or stopped to wonder at the light in which such a practice cast the town.

Anyway, there was nobody else to quiz about the Highland Games, so I reached for a book—a coffee table beer encyclopedia, no less—which stood just down the rail. The introduction sketched how brewing dates back at least 5,000 years, although the practice likely goes back further than that. Residual alcohols from crude beer have been found in Mesopotamian vessels dated to at least 5,000 BC, and evidence of fermented beverages was detected on pottery unearthed from gravesites in northern China dated to 7,000 BC. Not much of a stretch then to imagine our ancestors sipping wildly fermented beer-like beverages upwards of 10,000 years ago. The book also mentioned the Sumerian beer goddess Ninkasi—who was immortalized in a hymn which outlines an ancient brewing recipe—as well as the *Epic of Gilgamesh,* the oldest written story known to exist, and one that's heroes enjoy tipping a pint.

The author then dusted off that most cherished saw of the beer book—the claim that civilization itself owes to brewing. The basic argument goes like this: fermentation was discovered accidentally, when grains gathered by hunter-gatherer societies got damp enough to germinate, then got rained on and forgotten about long enough for ambient yeasts to do their work. Although an accidental discovery, fermentation's benefits were many: first, a use for extra crops, which helped transition communities to farming; then domestic and regional trade economies developed around fermented drink—a drink which promoted marriage, debate, cooperation, and submission to governance; and, finally, intoxicating beverages encouraged religion by making people loopy enough to swallow ghosts and miracles.

More interestingly, the author noted how the rise of Islam in the seventh and eight centuries led to a drastic reduction in brewing. This got me thinking. What set of circumstances were required for a people to embrace such a prohibition—or at least embrace it clear into the modern day, and not (like Americans) for a lousy thirteen years? Luckily, beer-making had already spread out of the Fertile Crescent into Western Europe prior to Mohammad, and so while sampling Skagit River's IPA, I read about the drink's more recent history. The writer covered his bases: Trappist monks brewing in the monasteries, Louis Pasteur finally explaining the role of yeast in fermentation, and immigrants carrying European beer styles to the New World. It was good to have books like this around. The more you know about what you drink, the more it means, and the more it means, the better it tastes.

I tabbed out and tipped Helen hugely as compensation for all my nosy questions. A couple blocks from the brewery, meandering along 1st Street, I saw a little green bench just across from the handsome marquee of the 1926 Lincoln Theatre. There, bathed in twinkling lights, I sat and scribbled a few notes and felt almost content for once—and I wasn't even buzzed. To idle well is an acquired skill. Taking your time is the key.

Basking in observation. These are the pleasures of the senior citizen, I suspect: sitting on a bench and watching the world pass by. Had I somehow slipped into premature old age? And if so, would that really be so bad?

But I still wanted to know about the Highland Games, so instead of continuing on to the northerly city of Bellingham as planned, I headed into Epic Ales. Scanning the tap list, my decision to overnight in Mount Vernon felt vindicated by the inclusion of Silver City Brewing's Fat Scotch Ale. This is a separate species from the *Scottish* ale I'd had back at Skagit River. While the Scottish ale shares a lineage with the milder strains of English ale, the Scotch ale is an American invention that can be hard to distinguish from barleywine. Craft brewers take the popular idea of Scotland—whisky, peat, salty gales lashing Hebridean isles—and try to bring that to life via smoked malt, potent ABVs, heavy fruit esters, and wood-aging.

"Did you go the Highland Games last year?" I asked the bartender, as he poured the wee heavy ale. But he hadn't, and from there our conversation devolved into a mutual lamentation over how we really should've invested all the money we'd ever spent on Microsoft and Apple products in the companies' stock.

"Denver just got too expensive," he said. "But a year later I couldn't afford Seattle, either."

"So Mount Vernon?"

"It's okay up here."

A long-haired old man to my right chimed in, apropos of nothing. "I'm from the town of Sunburst, Montana."

I told him that sounded like a fine place to be from and that I was from the town of Windsor, Illinois.

The old man grimaced. "Illinois? Don't they have . . . tornadoes there?"

Sure do, I said, smack in the heart of Tornado Alley, next town over got torn to splinters, and with each word the man grow paler. Finally, I asked if he'd had the misfortune to experience a tornado himself. But the old fellow just shook his head, whipping his yellowed hair about his skull, and said how he'd once heard tell of a twister coming to Sunburst, Montana. Feeling equal parts exasperated and entertained, I asked whether he might know the story behind Mount Vernon's Annual Highland Games—but he didn't. Instead, he kept on talking about those imaginary Rocky Mountain tornados. Had he perchance enjoyed a few wee heavies?

"It was the mayor," said a woman to my left, who I hadn't realized was listening. "He was really into Scottish stuff, so he started it. People thought it was fun. Now it's tradition."

"Was the mayor Scottish?"

"Don't think so."

Then I asked her the same question I'd asked the bartender.

"I was in Kuwait," she said, "so I didn't have the pleasure."

We fell into a long conversation about the years she'd worked as a secretary for a Kuwaiti oil company, with the old Montanan chiming in something off-topic but oddly poignant every so often, while the bartender idly watched us and shook his head at his mediocre luck: if only he'd invested more wisely, he wouldn't have to spend his nights listening to oddballs discuss the finer points of choosing a dentist in Kuwait and how best to avoid killer cyclones in the Rockies—bar talk that, quite frankly, made even less sense then staging a yearly Scottish

Festival in a small town in Washington State with no connection whatsoever to Scotland.

Later, as I closed my tab, the young woman said something else. "Living in the Middle East taught me not to judge."

"You had problems with the culture?"

"I did at first—it was a shock for sure—but that's not really what I mean."

What she meant was the foreignness of day-to-day life in the Middle East had forced her to change her manner of thinking. To stop gauging and rating everything, which had been her habit back home. Instead, she'd learned to try to see and appreciate new experiences, even—or maybe especially—if they weren't experiences she'd have normally enjoyed. "It wasn't just a defense mechanism, either," she said, "but a real evolution in how I approach life."

"I guess sometimes it helps to leave the familiar behind for a while."

"My only regret is that it took going halfway around the world to learn something so simple and basic."

"This life," the old Montanan said, "is full of woe. But that's not the end of us."

The bartender rolled his eyes and walked away.

"Good or bad is a judgment," the woman said, "but interesting or *un*interesting is a perception. Life went a lot smoother over there once I figured that out. A lot smoother here, too."

I smiled and pondered this humble wisdom she'd seen fit to share. Then I looked down at the treacly dregs of my Scotch ale, an American beer with European roots that's ancestry, like most all beers, could be traced back to the Middle East, the place where my new acquaintance had learned to think differently and thereby find happiness in things she might otherwise have rejected. Here was a beer style I'd long-ago written off as cloying, but taken on its own merits the absence of bitterness was offset by the alcohol's warmth, and the subdued hopping allowed for an array of malt-born flavors— roasty, caramelly, licorice flavors—I otherwise might've missed. Who cares that I didn't particularly *like* it. What did such a notion even really mean? More importantly, how much of our discontent in this life owes to having divvied up the world along the lines of our own preconceived notions?

"Mount Vernon's a nice little town," the old fella from Sunburst said, when I rose from my stool. "Come back and see us again sometime."

I thanked him for the conversation and said it'd been a real pleasure to meet everyone, but he merely stared at the gleaming taps as if hypnotized. Just before I reached the door, he offered up a final nugget of advice. "Don't forget to keep an eye out for tornadoes," he said.

THE BEERY SERIAL KILLERS OF BELLINGHAM

The next morning found me, laptop humming and tasters ready, at Stone's Throw Brewing on Larrabee Avenue in Fairhaven, a quaint little village now incorporated into greater Bellingham. Stone's Throw had three distinct levels: the sunken beer garden where I relaxed beside a cozy fire pit, a main level with picnic tables spilling out front and back, and the brewing operation upstairs beside a seating area eye-level with the rooftops of the surrounding homes.

In short, it was a fantastic little brewery, and later, while walking a dusty footpath fronting Bellingham Bay, I discovered two equally fantastic bookstores: Eclipse and Village Books, both of which were packed with friendly locals. Out on the main drag, a double-decker bus was imaginatively converted into a fish 'n' chips shop, while the historic district was full of red brick buildings that captured a bygone era when the coming of the Great Northern had given communities like Fairhaven hopes of becoming the rail's terminus, and therefore the next Seattle—which, of course, would've made Fairhaven crowded, expensive, and unlivable.

But that hadn't happened. In fact, Fairhaven was so unremittingly pleasant that there wasn't much to say about the place. It was an ideal Pacific Northwest community. Handsome people smiled as I strolled past, no one looked twice at my backpack, and I enjoyed a delicious brunch from sustainably-sourced local fare. Priuses idled politely as I wandered through the intersections, and the dogs never barked once.

No, Fairhaven was fodder for a travel *guide*, whereas a travel *book* seemed to require a little misery to make it tick.

Onward to Bellingham proper. With any luck, it'd be awful. Bellingham was a college town, though, so I worried it too might be pleasant—especially considering Western Washington University's refreshing 2009 decision to cull its football team. When it comes to budget cuts, football really should be the first thing to go. Yes, it can be fun to watch young men of a certain persuasion knock heads, and while I understand a collective release valve is needed for the tribal impulse, if colleges insist upon training their student body in the finer points of jingoism, why not just let them play ping-pong? That way, hostilities could still be unleashed upon the opposing school, kegs could still be tapped before noon, but student-athletes' brains wouldn't get beaten to pudding. Also, fielding a ping-pong team is cheap, so university funds could be allocated to things previously considered unimportant, like paying teachers.

The drive into downtown delivered stunning views of the bay—but Bellingham Bay, not Boundary Bay, which was the name of the first brewery I visited. Boundary Bay isn't actually visible from Bellingham, though. It's to the north up the Strait of Georgia, mostly in Canadian waters. Apparently, Bellingham Bay Brewing just didn't have the same ring to it. Regardless, Boundary Bay Brewing was doing a healthy business, the bar full of smiling, hemp-wearing, Caucasian-dreadlock-sporting Bellinghamers, and every beer I sampled was exceedingly pleasant, which left me (as feared) without much to say.

Up sunny Chestnut and Forest streets, however, was a much newer brewery, Aslan, which featured a noteworthy ale called I Am Gruit!

Hundreds of years ago, before the rise of hops and before Robert Burton wrote his first word on melancholy, brewers spiced beer with an herbal mixture known as gruit—think rosemary and bog myrtle, yarrow and mint, even tree bark—anything to balance the sweetness of the cereal grain. The old gruit recipes remain mysterious, though. Use of gruit was required by law, so that brewers could be taxed by the *gruithuis,* which retained exclusive rights to sell the stuff. So brewers and the *gruithuis* were at odds, with brewers buying the least amount of gruit they could get away with, paying their tax, and then spicing their beer clandestinely. But regardless of how Aslan recreated its recipe—or whether they were screwing the Washington State taxman on the sly—we're talking Dark Ages brewing here, so I wasn't sure what to expect. Sipping, it tasted a bit like ginger beer, and might've paired nicely with a shot of bourbon. Although what *doesn't* pair nicely with a shot of bourbon?

Then my phone rang. I mention this only because my phone never rings. This is most likely because I never call anyone, and if anyone calls me, I make a point of not answering or calling back. But the mystery caller left a voicemail. Turns out it was the community college offering me another class to teach in the fall—could I please get in touch soon? Taking on another class was a commitment, though. It meant weeks of focused reading and assignments and syllabus-writing, and a roomful of larval personalities in the souls of whom I would find myself obliged to kindle an interest in literature, which is no small feat in a world where everyone carries around Facebook and Instagram in their pockets.

Clearly this was a prospect to ponder over a few beers, and so I ambled up Holly Street to Chuckanut Brewery, a specialist in German-style lagers and mild English ales, styles rarely emphasized in the hop-crazed Northwest. The owner had been making beer since I was in kindergarten, from Washington to Colorado to Philadelphia and D.C. In fact, a plaque along the bar recognized his contributions in starting "the first ever Brewery and Restaurant in Istanbul, Turkey." Quite the C.V., and one bolstered by not one, not two, but *six* framed diplomas from the likes of UC Davis's program in brewing science and brewery engineering, and the Siebel Institute's program in brewing microbiology and microscopy, as well as a big rack of medals. And this praise was well-deserved, as every taster I sampled, from Vienna lager to kölsch, from helles to smoked porter, was elegantly executed.

The view, however, was somewhat less than elegant. Beyond the window, across Chuckanut's deck and Whatcom Creek, a ramshackle building stood on pilings over the water. A side door hung open dark as a missing incisor, the walkway cordoned off by sagging chain-link. On the moldy white wall hung a banner: BUD LIGHT HAPPY HOUR, it read, 8AM – 1PM & 4PM – 7PM EVERYDAY! A pair of hateful eyes glared down from this banner, like a nightmare version of Dr. T. J. Eckleburg. It took a moment to realize these were the eyes of the Seahawks mascot, as the team colors had bled away in the coastal weather.

This tavern—the Waterfront—has long been a serial killer hangout. Prior to his career as a murderous necrophiliac, the handsome and charismatic Ted Bundy was a regular there while attending classes at Western Washington. Kenneth Bianchi was another regular, although he was better known down in L.A. as the Hillside Strangler. More recently, a loner by the name of John Allen Muhammad—a.k.a., the D.C. Sniper—began coming in to drink morning Budweisers and watch *The Price is Right.*

Inside, the Waterfront was a dungeon of pool tables and electronic dart boards and the air smelled like the sole of a rotten loafer. The locals might've been confused for colorful old fisherman, but upon closer inspection were Thug Life Kowalskis gone to seed. Behind the bar was a wall of Pull-Tabs, Washington's official bar lottery game whereby intoxicated people spend twenty dollars to win back three. A codger with a few long silver hairs sprouting from his chin sat at the rail before a blue plastic carton full of discarded tabs. A fedora was tilted down over his face and the ice had melted in his whiskey. Only the old man's fingers showed any sign of life, mechanically opening and discarding one losing ticket after another.

My goal, however, was to pass as the Waterfront's newest serial killer, so I took a seat and gave the lady bartender an acrylic smile, one that didn't quite make the climb to my wolfish eyes. I opened my creepy black backpack, placed *The Anatomy of Melancholy* in plain view, and began scribbling cryptic notes. I actually fit the profile pretty well: thirtysomething white male, travels alone, with nondescript clothes and manner. I even had something in common with Ted Bundy, as we both attended law school but neither of us practiced law—unless you count Bundy's stint acting as his own attorney in his murder trials. If you think about it, the Northwest is a prime spot to launch a career in serial murder.

The people tend to keep to themselves, but they're welcoming enough (mostly for fear of seeming xenophobic), a combination which would allow a predator to pass unnoticed. And, of course, there's all that dark, wet forest. A million acre compost bin where things left behind soon go soft and sink into the moss.

"I would like a *Budweiser*, please," I said, pronouncing the beer's name in the breathy and lascivious way that Bundy might've asked for ligatures and panty-hose masks.

But the bartender was unimpressed. She didn't even blink at the toothless skull on the cover of the *Anatomy*. Instead, she pointed at a sheet of paper tacked to the wall behind me, which read: ALL BACKPACKS MUST BE CHECKED BEHIND THE BAR NO EXECPTIONS. But the bartender did make an exception. In fact, after pouring my beer, she didn't pay the slightest attention to me or my backpack. With so many serial killers hanging around the place, what was one more?

Then something I almost could've predicted: my $2.75 Budweiser was served in a *cheater pint*. These look like normal glassware, but hold two ounces less due to a deceptively thick base. Cheater pints will skim sixteen or seventeen beers from a half barrel, which even at the Waterfront's prices would rob the clientele of fifty bucks on every keg tapped. The Babylonian Code of Hammurabi punished overcharging tavern keepers with death by drowning, which seems reasonable enough, so what should the punishment be for cheater pints—fileting? Rotisserie basting? Or maybe just having to spend time in the Waterfront Tavern?

The contrast with Chuckanut Brewing couldn't have been starker. Here on Holly Drive in Bellingham was dispositive evidence that Dr. Thompson was right and craft beer people are good people while bad people drink bad beer. On the one hand, award-winning ales and lagers consumed by gentle souls in a clean and tidy brewpub; on the other, Bud and Bud Light consumed by serial killers and their barfly-victims in a filthy box beside the tracks.

#

Wander Brewing was next, but it was a hike—a hike made to feel even longer by my backpack digging into my shoulders. Burton's *Anatomy* was the problem. I'd been lugging its gloomy weight around not just that summer, and not just for the fifteen years I'd owned the book, but for as long as I could recall. While I was determined to finally finish it, there's little practical reason for a modern person to read Burton. Excepting Ph.D. students too proud to use Cliff Notes and particularly unlucky reedition book reviewers, I'd wager only a handful of people on the planet read the entirety in any given year. It's an anachronism, many opaque pounds of Renaissance esoterica. Still, I'd never quite given up on the idea of reading it: that if I could make some sense of the *Anatomy*, maybe I could also finally make some sense of myself and my longstanding affliction. But summer had only just begun, and much of the book remained unread, much as many beers remained undrunk—hence, Wander.

The brewery lay in an industrial complex a couple doors down from a Crossfit-style gymnasium, wherein a shirtless guy sporting a Civil War-era beard tossed around dumbbells and leapt atop boxes and vaulted into handstands. Amidst all of this, he grunted and bellowed and flexed the swollen slabs of man-breast hanging from his ribcage. While he was certainly an impressive athlete, he also reminded me of a cult member deep into a particularly heated bout of self-flagellation. There's nothing wrong with exercise, of course. I struggle to keep fit as much as the next beer-drinker. But should you ever find yourself strutting half-nude around a glorified adult jungle gym with your ankles taped and chalk dust in your nineteenth century beard, flexing your muscles in a floor-to-ceiling mirror, bleeding from the calluses on your palms and shooting threatening looks at mellow passersby, it may be time for a bout of self-reflection.

"You should try drinking some beer, dude," I suggested. "It really helps."

But good advice is rarely appreciated these days, and his guttural barrage of barbarian nonsense trailed me into the brewery. The place was packed with wooden barrels, as Wander specializes in aged beer and mixed fermentation, meaning not wild fermentation but a mix of yeast cultures and other fun bacteria. I asked the bartender to pour me a few of her favorites and then settled down in the lively garden with a handful of perfect little bulb-shaped tasters. These tulips collected and condensed the pungent aroma of Wander's beers, all of which were yeast-dominant and ripe. But the best of them was Sossusvlei.

A Flanders-style red in the vein of Rodenbach Grand Cru or Verhaeghe's Duchesse de Bourgogne (or closer to home, New Belgium's La Folie), the Sossusvlei was soured with lactobacillus and aged eighteen months in red wine barrels. A swirl, sniff, and sip revealed a musty balsamic acidity just *barely* balanced by dark cherry notes. Because most American brewers lack the huge wooden vats (called foudres) that are used in

Belgium, the Flanders red is tough to get right in any quantity. Maybe I was just in the mood to be wowed, but Sossusvlei seemed a vinous beer worthy of wood-aging, a beer to spur the imagination into a reckoning with ancient European traditions transplanted to the far corner of Washington State.

While paying up, the bartender suggested I visit Kulshan Brewing. The walk there was long and relaxing. People on the sidewalks bid me hello. The marijuana shops blasted Bob Marley, and motorists braked for me in the street. With the notable exception of the Waterfront Tavern, Bellingham was disappointingly, frustratingly pleasant—until I got to Kulshan, that is.

Not that the brewery wasn't perfectly fine. It was. But somehow I managed to sit beneath a big red umbrella at the only picnic table in the only beer garden in all of Bellingham that housed a truly miserable soul. His name was Karl, and he wore a cap with the Caterpillar logo. He was about fifty, short, bearded, white, and pissed.

"Progressives have ruined this town," Karl said. He'd ordered a steak sandwich from the nearby food truck and was now checking his watch and glaring at the girl working the counter. The red umbrella lent his features a murderous cast. I asked what exactly these ruinous progressives had done, but conversing with Karl was something a one-way street.

"Used to be," he said, "we had a nice town here. But then the *Californians* came."

This was an old gripe throughout the Northwest. Everything was great before the Californians spoiled it. Crowded it. Drove up the cost of it. I don't have much sympathy for this particular whine, though, as it's predicated upon a notion that things shouldn't change, and things do nothing but change. People who can't or won't accept that are free to move to whatever region of the country they naively imagine as frozen in time, like a snow globe.

"Used to be," Karl said again, developing his theme, "you could work and live here and do just fine. Now though . . ." He shook his head and rubbed his palms together. Curiously, while his torso was regular-sized, his legs were short as a boy's.

"Migrating Californians drove up the property values?"

"They sell their houses down there and then buy *two* up here."

"Heard Montana's the same way. An old-timer down in Mount Vernon told me all the Hollywood types saw *A River Runs Through It* and decided to become fly fisherman."

Karl snorted. "Hollywood."

"But he was optimistic the tornadoes will blow them all away."

Karl stared down the dead space between us, as if his eyes rested on some image that sat atop me, in my lap. It was unsettling. I wondered if he'd ever had a drink in the Waterfront.

"You'd know better than I would, Karl, but Bellingham seems pretty great to me. I'm traveling around the Northwest this summer. I haven't gotten very far yet, but it's hard to imagine too many places cleaner or friendlier than right here."

Still looking at me in that odd way, Karl asked how I could afford to just bum around. Was I a student? No wife, no kids, no real job. I looked a little old for that sort of thing.

"I'm a teacher," I said.

"Must be nice, sucking up that state money all summer long."

Sometimes this assumption, such as when made by the surly yet lovable bartender at Brews Almighty, is forgivable. But coming from Karl I found it deeply irritating.

"Actually, I don't get paid over the summer," I explained, "so don't worry—your tax dollars aren't funding my bar tabs."

Karl ignored this and resumed bad-mouthing California, then transitioned to a critique of Western Washington University. "Those liberal professors have their heads so far up their asses they can smell their breakfast," he said. "I can't even open up the damn newspaper without having to hear how working people are the real problem."

Still, I insisted, Bellingham seemed like a nice enough place to live.

"Well, sure," Karl said, "Bellingham is nice"—now he finally looked square at me, really fixed me with his dark button eyes—"except for the sort of people it attracts."

Leaving Kulshan that evening, I wondered about grumpy old Karl—the only miserable man in all of Bellingham, Washington, serial killers included—and it occurred I'd finally found the grain of sand in the oyster. As Burton paraphrases Demetrius via Seneca, it's paradoxically misfortunate to live a life without enough misfortune, because then you don't have much to philosophize about. So perhaps meeting Karl was a blessing in disguise? But I wasn't traveling the Northwest only to catalogue minor discomforts. I was trying, via beer and the flavor of the communities which brewed it, to cut through the melancholy so firmly rooted in my life. And Burton says there's nothing better than a little peregrination to charm the senses.

He pities the man who from cradle to grave beholds the same old same old, and points out how the sun and moon and planets keep in constant motion, much as the air blows along as wind and tides ebb and flow, which should be a lesson to us all. So I resolved not to waste another moment worrying about Karl. Instead, walking through the long shadows, I decided to accept that extra class come fall. Handled properly, it seemed travel writing could make a fine subject.

THE CASCADE LOOP - PART ONE: NAUGHTY AMERICANOS, PHONY SAUERKRAUT, AND 9/11

This time, I awoke in my cozy little (daylight) basement studio with what was *definitely* a hangover. While it may sound peculiar to the sober-minded, I'm normally inclined to savor this particular malady. I won't rise until late morning, for instance, until it becomes despicably roman to lay around in my boxer shorts even a moment longer. I dose liberally with anti-inflammatories, up to a full gram depending on the severity, and then—once the joints have stopped creaking and the headache abates—I visit the gym for a long and cleansing run, leaving a penance of yeasty sweat dripping from the treadmill. By the time I've had my shower, I feel restored and the locker room is redolent with the aroma of malted barley.

There was no time for such pleasures, though, as I'd made plans to tour Washington's Cascade Loop, a scenic route that runs for hundreds of miles over the mountains into the high desert and back again to the islands of Puget Sound. And so I crawled out of bed in a hazy fugue, washed my teeth and brushed my face, drank a scalding cup of water and a large bottle of coffee, then chased 800 milligrams of beer with a few sips of warm Ibuprofen. But once on the road, my hangover insisted upon itself. It rode beside me in the passenger seat like a shadowy doppelganger, showing its horsey teeth and guffawing at my futile attempts to ignore it. There was only one possible fix. I needed more coffee: more potent coffee.

In this desperate state, I pulled into Hillbilly Hotties, a nearby bikini barista stand.

Everett is home to a number of these places, wherein young women serve drive-thru lattes in their skivvies. The shops have cheeky names like Naughty Chai, Nubile Beans, Caffeine Cuties, and Java Juggs. A not-so-surprising number of them have been busted in prostitution stings. In fact, one local Snohomish County coffee stand owner reportedly laundered over two million bucks before the heat came down. While I'd never actually stopped at Hillbilly Hotties before, I passed it on my way to the community college and it'd always seemed a classier-than-average bikini barista stand. In line ahead of me was an idling Mercedes-Benz. Through the back window, the driver's comb-over flapped in the breeze. Five minutes passed. What could possibly be taking so long? I was about to give up when the barista—who wore what appeared to be a V-shaped length of neon green dental floss—leaned out and gave me a hearty smile and wave.

Now I was stuck. Guilted into enduring the long wait while she chatted up the man in the Mercedes. After he finally drove away, I rolled forward.

"Thank god you showed up," the barista said. "He was trying to show me his *penith.*"

"His what?"

"His *penith!*"

Then I noticed the picture of a dachshund taped to the window. DON'T TRY TO SHOW US YOUR WEINER, it said, YOU'RE ON CAMERA!

I immediately glued both hands to the steering wheel and stared straight ahead.

"What'll it be, sugar?"

The impediment only surfaced with certain words, apparently. Regardless, I asked for a double Americano with no milk.

"But milk makes it taste *good*," she said, wiggling her hips in rhythm to the tamping espresso whilst tossing a highly-caffeinated come hither look over her shoulder. I felt compelled to say something, and so I asked if she were worried the man in the Mercedes might come back.

"Oh, they always come back. He's probably circling the block right now."

I asked whether she ought to call the police.

"The pigs? Not hardly. They're worse than the pervs. Think just because they got a badge and a gun they can stare all day for free."

I nodded and kept my eyes on the passing traffic.

"We like to keep things mellow around here. My hours are great, seven to two—who can beat that? I got kids, you know, and considering what daycare charges, there's no sense working when they're out of school."

"Thanks for the coffee," I said, and dangled a ten dollar bill out the window. I drove away without waiting for change, glancing nervously in the rearview all the while, half-expecting a squadron of gun-toting pigs with cappuccino mustaches to run me down like the dog I was, as if the whole thing were some bizarre sting. What would I possibly say to my students after they'd read the details of their instructor's seedy arrest in *The Daily Herald?*

To the east, nestled against the foothills of the Cascades, lay the town of Monroe. Signs advertised drag racing and rodeo, and after parking along Main Street I strolled past a place called Sam's advertising SPECTACULAR SALES ON DOG FOOD. This reminded me of the journals of Lewis and Clark, which feature so many references to dining on dogs that the document could almost be mistaken for a canine cookbook. William Clark stuck to fish and potatoes ("all the Party have greatly the advantage of me" he complained in October of 1805, "in as much as they all relish the flesh of dogs"), but Meriwether Lewis seemed to consider dog meat a delicacy. Camped on the wet and miserable Oregon coast in January of 1806, he writes of just how deeply the Corps of Discovery had come to appreciate the culinary potential of man's best friend. For his part, Lewis had "become so perfectly reconciled to the dog" that he actually preferred its taste to that of wild game, and on their return journey he threatened to tomahawk a young Nez Percé who'd tossed a puppy onto his plate by way of ridiculing his eating habits. Though he owned a Newfoundland named Seaman which accompanied the Corps across the continent and back again, considering the hundreds of dogs he ate, it's safe to assume that Meriwether Lewis was really a cat person at heart.

He was also a drinker. In fact, prior to the Corps of Discovery, Lewis was court martialed after drunkenly challenging a fellow soldier to a duel. But the duel was never fought, the court martial dropped, and what ultimately caught my eye that day was the Route 2 Taproom. Because the ache of a bad hangover, like the ache of young love, can sometimes only be assuaged by drinking deeply of the very font from which the pain springs. After parking on the street, however, I realized that to reach the taproom I'd have to cross a set of tracks that were once part of the Great Northern Railway, but were now embedded in an intersection full of enormous pickup trucks coughing exhaust.

It's been my experience that small town people often enjoy hobbies which strike outsiders as a touch peculiar. Bessie Bingo, for example. Or fishing, a pastime no amount of beer can make interesting. Another small town hobby is the homicidal resentment of pedestrians. In certain corners of rural America, the pedestrian is no better than a deer—a dumb animal to be run over and lashed to the bumper—and Monroe proved no exception. I waited for the WALK sign only to step off the curb and find myself menaced by engine-revving trucks vying for the honor of cutting me down in the turn lanes. Like a game of *Frogger,* I stumbled to a halt, hurried forward, backpedaled, and spilled naughty Americano all over my shirt. Seattle drivers may run you over in the crosswalk because they're too busy Tinder-swiping or taking their startup public, but small town drivers will do it just for fun. Or maybe they assume if you're walking it means you're too poor to own a big truck, thus making it a mercy kill.

The Route 2 Taproom proved surprisingly modern, though. Instead of the usual chalkboard, or even a paper menu, the waitress brought an iPad which listed the available beers and specs. Beside each selection, in addition to IBUs and ABV and tasting notes, was a little glowing keg. Some full and green. Others half-full and orange. The red ones about to pop.

"This is pretty high-tech," I said.

"Everything's on the website, too," the waitress said. Then she pulled out another device and fastened it to her wrist. Her fingers hovered over the touch screen, waiting.

I hesitated. "You've got a lot on tap . . ."

"Next time, decide at home—online—before you come in."

"Well, I—"

"Everything's on the website."

But what wasn't on the website were the actual kegs of beer, and the one I finally selected—Hop a Wheelie IPA from Boneyard Brewing, another Bend brewery—was from a greenly virgin keg. I half-expected the beer to materialize on my table amidst little squiggly lines, a la *Star Trek*. Pleasantly surprised, I found myself revising my feelings about Monroe with each citrusy sip. What's most intriguing about beers like Hop a Wheelie is that the fruitiness comes not from the addition of actual citrus, but from combining different varieties of hops. Most examples are dry-hopped (meaning hops are added after the wort is boiled, throughout fermentation) with Citra hops which, as the name suggests, lend a certain flavor. You'd swear you're drinking an infused ale, but all those bright tropical notes come from a little green climbing plant that's normally associated with bitterness. It's magic, really.

Although the beer helped my hangover even more than the coffee, I couldn't indulge much so early in the day. Foot firmly on the brakes, I read the *Anatomy* for an hour between sips. When I finally asked for my tab, the waitress punched some buttons on her wrist teleporter and then stuck my debit card halfway in. The whole works kind of shimmered.

#

PHILLIP HURST

Remember those clothing-optional highway cleaner-uppers known as the LARC nudists? Well, in the town of Sultan was a stretch of roadway adopted by the LAKE BRONSON FAMILY NUDIST PARK. This was no hallucination. I wasn't *that* hungover. Sure enough, in quick succession, on separate stretches of Washington State highway, I'd come across public-spirited nudists. I might've even pulled a U-turn and tracked down the Bronson Family to ask a few delicate questions, except I had a long drive ahead of me.

Passing through the old logging villages of Startup and Gold Bar, I was half-afraid of what the roadside signs might have to offer, but then civilization, such as it was, spit me out. Mist hung like smoke in the Cascades as the road ascended to Stevens Pass. The wiper blades beat back a steady drizzle and the trees were bearded in moss so green their branches seemed to almost glow from within. After coasting down the eastern slope, the gloom lifted and the temperature instantly leapt fifteen degrees, revealing a glorious day alongside the Wenatchee River. At the turnouts, kayakers worked up the nerve to tackle whitewater churn rough as boiling milk. But it was a fine day to pointlessly risk death, and soon enough I saw a welcome sign for the scenic village of Leavenworth: *Willkommen!*

The town (pop. 2,000) resembles a Bavarian village from times past. Think *The Sound of Music* and spätzle. Think cheesemonger's shoppes, glockenspiels and edelweiss, and scallop-trimmed hotels that call themselves *pensions*. Think also of busty fräuleins with dusky upper lips who carry frothing steins as well as mysterious European venereal diseases named after long-forgotten explorers, such as the infamous Captain Scuzzlecock's Searing Black Vaginitis.

67

Beyond Heidelburger Drive-in and the Der Ritterhof Motel was a 76 Station straight from the Alps. The storefronts had hand-painted signs sprinkled with German words. Wooden balconies overlooked the street, flowerboxes adorned the windows, and the steep roofs were covered with thick, round shingles. All very Bavarian, except for the occasional building that's exterior was painted to just look sort of vaguely Continental. Fleur-de-lis here. Doric column there. Lots of hastily stenciled vines and water-spouting cherubs. You can imagine the owners debating just exactly how little faux-authenticity might satisfy the Bavarianization review board.

I'd heard Leavenworth was odd, but I'd also heard it had a brewery, and assumed that even if said brewery was total scheisse, there'd still be some decent German ales and lagers. But a quick stroll down the main strasse revealed a number of worrisome incongruities. Take Bavarian Starbucks. Inside it was mostly just a regular Starbucks—dull interior, bad music, uncomfortable chairs, all designed to get you to buy your $4 coffee and leave—but the outside was pure alpine chateau, complete with murals of sturdy peasant folk leading draft horses loaded down with wooden kegs. Or how about Bavarian Wells Fargo? Or the Bavarian tequila bar next door to the Bavarian Sushi joint. Although mildly intrigued by the thought of Bavarian Pad Thai, I came across two stores that made me forget all about lunch: the Nutcracker Museum, and Kris Kringl [sic].

According to the free literature, the Nutcracker Museum constitutes the largest such collection on the planet, with 5,000 specimens residing atop its dark and foreboding staircase, including one nutcracker supposedly unearthed from ancient Rome. Being a mostly sane and generally reasonable person, however, I wasn't about to pay good money to tour such a place, but the place I *did* tour—Kris Kringl (*Where it's Christmas All Year Long!*)—made the Nutcracker Museum seem almost normal.

To get a sense of it, imagine all the Christmas tchotchke you've ever seen, all the lights and ornaments, every ceramic reindeer, and a lifetime's worth of Santas and sleighs, crammed willy-nilly into a shotgun house. The St. Nick statues were half off (now only $1,200) because their lights didn't work, while in the back was the Dickens Village, a series of costly ceramic dioramas awash in English charm: gentlemen in waistcoats and ruddy-cheeked children in boots and mufflers, trotting hounds and warm little houses all aglow. The only problem was that this wasn't actually Dickensian. After all, where was crippled Tim or the long-suffering Bob Cratchit? The flea-bitten orphans and heartless profiteers upon child labor?

On my way out, I bumped into Sven the Singing Reindeer. A more or less life-sized fellow, the tag dangling from Sven's ear said he cost $6,590 and suggested I kindly refrain from touching him.

"Would you like to hear him sing?"

The proprietress who'd spoken—Mrs. Claus—was pleasantly plump. Clearly a method actress. But when I told her no thanks, she insisted. "He really belts out a tune," she added.

I looked at her sternly and reiterated that under absolutely no circumstances was I even remotely interested in hearing the reindeer sing.

"Okay, great," she said.

Then Mrs. Claus reached around Sven's backside and touched him in a private spot, and the poor ungulate came slowly to life. He began to carol ("*Have a holly jolly Christmas!*")

in a voice not unlike James Earl Jones crossed with Bullwinkle. A circle soon formed. Without a graceful exit available, I had little choice but to stand there with my hands jammed in my pockets, grimacing like I'd taken an antler to the kidney. The Kris Kringl shoppers smiled at me and at Mrs. Claus and made comforting and wholesome sounds. I was afraid for a moment they might actually join hands. This was holiday magic, after all.

When the song finally ended and Sven drooped inanimate once again, I slunk away, feeling as if I'd been wrangled into an unsavory conspiracy. Thankfully, only a few steps down the block (just past Kristallnacht Bakery) was Icicle Brewing. The décor was Bavarian, but the tap list not so much. Just the typical pales, ambers, and porters. Where were the famous German lagers? The dopplebocks? The marzens and maibocks? The rauchbiers?[2] There actually was a dunkelweizen, but the keg had run dry, leaving only one remotely Teutonic option: the Crosscut Pilsner.

The difference between lagers (like the Crosscut) and ales (like Hop a Wheelie IPA) is that lager yeast ferments at cooler temperatures. This came about due to Bavarians of the Middle Ages storing beer in caves they cooled with ice harvested from nearby lakes. After a few months, this beer poured crystal clear and was pleasantly dry. Over time, the yeast adapted to the cooler temperatures to produce a less fruity drink, one which

---

[2] Rauchbier is smoked beer, meaning the grains used are dried over a fire, not with warm air. Smoky beer may sound off-putting, but it grows on you. Although I once tried an Icelandic Rauchbier, only to realize Iceland is short on trees and therefore often uses animal dung for fuel. Sheep Shit IPA, anyone?

required a period of cold aging to mature—"lagering" as it's known, courtesy of the German *lagern,* to store.

In modern times, lagers have gotten a bad name thanks to the use of money-saving adjuncts (usually rice or corn) that result in washed-out beers like Budweiser and Coors Lite. These are the bastard children of those venerable lagers brought across the Atlantic by German immigrants. Prior to Prohibition, lagers were as varied and well-made as ales, but the Volstead Act scarred the American beer landscape deeply. Thirteen dry years later, when the 21st Amendment finally repealed the 18th, almost ninety-percent of the nation's breweries had closed, and those big enough to remain afloat found they were now able to peddle cheap-ingredient lager to a public that could barely remember what quality beer even tasted like.

The Crosscut Pilsner wasn't mass-produced, though. It was a craft lager, and a good one at that, with a dry bite of hops and a clean malt bill. Nevertheless, it wasn't the rich and bready Bavarian-style beer I'd anticipated while driving over the mountains. So I pulled out my phone and punched in a *beer near me . . .* and was soon in the biergarten of Doghaus Brewery. They had a lot of taps, but only three poured Doghaus's own beer, and none of those were German-style. Of the remaining taps, two actually were German, but both of them— Schofferhofer Radler and Radeberger Pilsner—were readily available at every 7-11 in the Pacific Northwest.

That the Bavarian village's best food came from a wok or a pizza oven wasn't particularly surprising, as sauerkraut and gravy-stewed meats are simply bad ideas cloaked in tradition, but no German beer? No Paulaner? No Einbecker? No Ayinger?

#

Leavenworth was originally a hub of the Great Northern, but when Stevens Pass proved too costly to maintain between winter avalanches and summer rockslides, the railroad was rerouted. Like Everett, Leavenworth continued on as a lumbering town, being situated along the Wenatchee and still able to use the pass for road transport. But after World War I and the Depression, the timbering industry fell on hard times. Leavenworth was dying. Businesses closed. People moved away. Even the local high school was condemned. Things got so desperate that town officials contacted the University of Washington to conduct a study on how they might possibly save their community.

Then, in the 1960s, a couple of World War II vets from Seattle—one of whom had been stationed in mountainous southern Germany—dreamt a big and really weird dream: maybe the answer was to turn the mud-and-spittoon town into a Bavarian Disneyland?

Sure enough, it worked. The village now attracts a couple million visitors per year. Of course, a skeptic might say the frontier lumber and railroad town is actually long dead, the polka and lederhosen just a requiem and shroud. But you certainly can't blame the locals for doing whatever it takes to keep the furnaces warm. Home is where the herz is, after all.

A sad footnote to the Leavenworth tale: the guys responsible for the Bavarianization were not only friends and war veterans, but partners. Perhaps understandably, considering the era and rural locale, they never felt entirely comfortable coming out to their friends and neighbors. Although they lived in the community for nearly thirty years, they lived in secret and in their old age moved away to Palm Springs and lost all contact with the town they'd done so much to save. Still, wandering around Leavenworth today amidst all that oh-so-darling kitsch, their presence is felt.

Down at Waterfront Park, in the shadow of a resort under construction, I sat along the river and flipped through the *Anatomy*. Burton quotes the poet Crato on Bohemian beer: "Nothing comes in so thick / Nothing goes out so thin / It must needs follow then / The dregs are left within." Nevertheless, I felt obliged to drink at least *one* decent German beer while in Leavenworth, and so I marched back up to the tourist thoroughfare and soon came across The Loft, which promised "The Most European Beers in Town." But once in The Loft's loft, the most interesting German beer on tap was Franziskaner Hefeweizen, which is also available at 7-11. Der schwindled once again. Worse yet, the bartender stuck a lemon slice on my glass, and for a dedicated craft beer drinker, fruit on the rim is a rankling faux pas.

So I was a bit disappointed, yes. The prospect of having driven all the way to Leavenworth just to drink Franziskaner made me long to be someplace else, someplace that sucked on its own terms. But it was getting late in the day and I was tired, and so I sat and ordered a half-dozen more rounds of Franziskaner and put to bed my dreams of frothy fräuleins and fresh-brewed bräu-weisse.

A few hours later, pounding the pavement in search of a cheap motel, I noticed a man dressed as an Alpine hiking guide. Lederhosen and suspenders. The jaunty cap. Maybe he piloted a horse-drawn carriage along the strasse, or emceed the nightly yodeling contest? Whatever. But the getup didn't stop there. No, this man standing not a dozen feet away, gamely bending his knees in time with the blasting polka and snapping his suspenders with the balls of his thumbs—this man wore a *codpiece*. The contraption bulged grotesquely over the late afternoon pavement and cast an outrageous and sinister shadow. It was the year 2016 in the state of Washington in the United States of America. There were women and children about. I mean, the sheer audacity of this costumed pervert gallivanting around in broad daylight—have you no shame, Leavenworth?

#

After a pricey night's sleep at the Bavarian Howard Johnson, I set off again on the Cascade Loop. Heading east, I passed through Peshastin, a small town whose hillsides were ripe with softly flowing pear orchards and garish signs promising to MAKE AMERICA GREAT AGAIN.

In *Driving Home*, Jonathan Raban describes the Cascade Range as the topographical embodiment of Washington's political tensions, with coastal liberals and high desert conservatives split down the middle like a schizoid personality. This geographical rift has colored life in the Northwest since the inception of the territories, with a primarily urban and industrial coastal population oftentimes at odds with a sparser inland population engaged in land use. But if anything, today's political situation seems even more divisive than when Raban traveled through in the early '90s.

Consider migrant workers. Eastern Washington's booming agricultural industry employs an army of upwards of 100,000 Mexican migrants, the lion's share of whom work under questionable documentation. These people pick apples, cherries, pears, and (most importantly) hops, under conditions most Americans simply will not tolerate. This was made evident a few years back, when orchard owners couldn't secure enough pickers and the harvest died on the vine. Passing through, one notices the little towns surrounding these fields are full of taco trucks and burrito stands, whereas the hired help labors in the shadow of massive signs advertising Donald Trump and, by implication, his "big, fat, beautiful wall" along the southern border.

Demonizing working-class minorities has a long history in Washington State, unfortunately. The great railroads, for instance—the Northern Pacific and the Great Northern—were built with low-wage Chinese labor, but once the track was laid the Chinese became competitors for other jobs and calls rose to expel them. Anti-Chinese sentiment was across the board. Socialist labor organizers hated the Chinese. The Irish, themselves having recently immigrated to escape the Potato Famine, hated the Chinese. Even Ralph Waldo Emerson, that great advocate of self-reliance, deplored Chinese immigrants, calling them mere tools for other nations to use, while his literary associate Horace Greeley ("Go West, young man!") knowingly declared all Chinese women prostitutes.

As Murray Morgan writes in *Skid Road,* these were "the arguments of hate." Instead of being contributors to Manifest Destiny, the Chinese became unclean and uncivilized opium fiends and almond-eyed lepers and rat-eating yellow rascals, much as when Donald Trump announced his candidacy for president and undocumented Mexicans became criminals, drug dealers, and rapists. This stuff has predictable effects, such as in September of 1885 when a hop farm located east of Seattle saw a mob fire shots into the sleeping tents of Chinese workers. Three were killed, three others gravely wounded, and the camp razed in what came to be known as the Squak Valley Massacre. The following month, the murderers were found innocent by a local jury, despite one of the men having freely confessed. Around the same time in Seattle, Chinese immigrants were herded onto ships and expelled, while Tacoma's Chinatown was burned and a parade thrown for the arsonists—a group which included no less than the mayor, the president of the local YMCA, and the fire chief.

Down in the sage-covered Wenatchee River Valley, I found the town of Cashmere and Milepost 111 Brewing. A schooner of Pinnacle IPA poured dark and smelled like fruit cocktail in heavy syrup. This wasn't by any reasonable definition an India Pale Ale. In fact, the turbid liquid tasted so much like the surrounding pear orchards that I wondered about the influence of terroir. Being situated in Washington's fruit basket, Milepost 111 apparently couldn't help but make their bitterest style of beer sweet as cider. Out on the patio, sunburned river folk lazed, sipping pints and munching burgers. It was a pleasant enough little brewpub, and it got even pleasanter when my tab came. $1.75 for a glass of beer? By traveling east of the mountains, had I also traveled back in time?

The Washington writer David Guterson actually published a novel titled *East of the Mountains*. While Guterson is best-known for *Snow Falling on Cedars,* which depicts a murder trial in the shadow of the Japanese Internment, it's this other book that truly captures the melancholy spirit of the

Pacific Northwest. The story concerns a widowed doctor with colon cancer who plans one last bird-hunting trip into the eastern Washington of his boyhood. The novel opens on a rainy Seattle day with the doctor pondering "the meaningless trajectory his life would take into a meaningless grave" and fitting a shotgun into his mouth to make certain his arms are long enough to reach the trigger.

Maybe the poor guy just needed some vitamin D, because a stroll around Cashmere proved invigorating. A plaque claimed I stood near the exact geographical center of Washington, which seemed significant in the way only truly pointless things can, while another revealed Cashmere was named after a poem about India. Being desperate for tourist dollars to replace the dwindling resource economy, these dusty western towns all lay vague claims to historicity, and Cashmere's downtown was no exception. Logging and hardscrabble loggers. A railroad that once promised to come through before going elsewhere. Some gold in the nearby hills and an infamous brothel to relieve the lucky prospector of his bonanza. This is not to say Cashmere lacked all historical significance, though.

In Riverside Park, I found the 9/11 Spirit of America Memorial. This series of monuments included a twisted section of column from the 60th floor of one of the Twin Towers, a chunk of cornice from the Pentagon, and a ring of bronze statues looking heavenward with which the viewer is meant to close the circle by joining hands with a stewardess and fireman. Off to the side was the Survivor Tree, a slender pear tree grafted from the wreckage. But why this elaborate memorial in a little town a continent away from New York?

Broke and jobless, I'd graduated college just a few months before September 11th. I was contemplating law school back then—although I had little interest in actually practicing law—and wondering if adulthood really was as inane and meaningless as it had always seemed. Then the world flipped topsy-turvy courtesy of al-Qaeda and CNN. I was visiting family in rural Indiana at the time. In the wake of the attack, Hoosiers formed mile-long gas lines at the local Chevron stations, as if hijacked Boeing 757s somehow meant no more fuel for their Ford F-150s. I remember feeling an urge to rush to New York and help somehow, and yet that would've been just as useless as hoarding gasoline. What could a know-nothing kid like me have possibly done for traumatized Manhattanites? Still, here was *the* event of my lifetime, a searing horror unfolding on the TV while I drank coffee and nibbled a burnt cinnamon roll.

David Guterson was visiting Washington D. C. that day, and the tragedy sank him into a depression he chronicled in a memoir titled *Descent,* wherein he writes that any response to the world besides excruciating sadness is willful delusion, and that the sight of newly washed SUVs merely reminds him the universe will someday devolve into an eternity of frigid darkness. Lastly, he puzzles over the futility of his duties as a boys basketball coach, considering those boys will someday die and rot, only to make way for more boys who will die and rot.

Yes, other people's pathos can spiral into inadvertent hilarity, but it is writings like these which make David Guterson the quintessential Melancholy Northwest Writer. His crowning achievement was a 2013 commencement speech at his alma mater, Seattle's Roosevelt High School. Happiness and how to find it was the purported theme, but the meat and potatoes was fear and anxiety. Guterson recalled being a teenager who avoided thinking about the fact he would one day grow old and die. He wondered why God (if real) would create a universe where happiness was impossible due to our foreknowledge of death—"We find ourselves afraid of the universe," he said, "because it is either the work of a God who seems inexplicable at best and malicious at worst or a place completely indifferent to us . . ."

Just picture all those smiles begin to droop. This wasn't what commencement speakers were paid to say, was it?

Guterson then spoke of the avoidance strategies his audience likely used to avoid thinking about their inevitable death—cell phones, Facebook, video games, marijuana—before explaining how American society would only sink new graduates deeper into the existential mire. "The world might seem full of possibility," he said, near the end of his remarks, "and it is that way, but it's also a place where you can very quickly find yourself among the living dead—a being without the means for happiness."

Toss high the mortarboards! Cue *Pomp and Circumstance!*

While Guterson's speech went over like a Bee Gees album in a funeral parlor, I can sympathize with his desire to speak frankly for once about the big dying elephant in the auditorium, much as I sympathized with Cashmere, Washington's need to feel some connection to 9/11. But it was hardly a somber day. The park was full of people in swimwear prepping for an afternoon on the river, slathering their limbs in sunblock and inflating rafts, some just looking to float and drink a few beers, others prepared to brave the white water rapids.

A path beside the Wenatchee led back toward Milepost 111. As I neared the path's end, a pair of brown-skinned boys zoomed past on their bikes. They both carried fishing rods and wore floppy hats, SPF mom. They hurried down the bank and flung lures into the water, casting and reeling with the studiousness of very old men. I paused just long enough to eavesdrop on their chatter and, sure enough, those little boys spoke of fish and the river in perfect English.

THE CASCADE LOOP - PART TWO: DUMB BLONDE ALES, SIX-SHOOTERS, AND MASS SHOOTERS

Wenatchee is home to approximately 30,000 Wenatcheeans, making it the second largest city in central Washington after Yakima. It sits where the Wenatchee River meets the Columbia, edged by rugged mountains and washed in high desert sunshine. A sign shaped like a big red apple welcomes visitors to the official "Apple Capital of the World."

But the wholesome first impression soon gave way to a sunbaked eyesore. Driving along Wenatchee Avenue, the casual motorist finds himself buried in a mudslide of signage, of McDonald's and Taco Bell and competing cell phone carriers, a dizzying valley of logo and trademark, of UPS, Citgo, and Sherwin-Williams—a new growth forest of Les Schwab, Grocery Outlet, Denny's, and Godfather's Pizza, all struggling upward for air and light from a forest floor crowded with car lot signs and pawn shop signs and every other conceivable species of signage.

A skeptic might question the wisdom of piling signs atop each other so densely that the signs could never possibly help anyone locate anything. Why not ban such aesthetic pollution? After all, if everyone would simply agree to the obvious—that businesses shouldn't ruin their community's looks—then extraneous signage could be done away with and nobody would be worse off, as people would still need the same goods and services, and would use their own initiative to find them. Instead, Wenatchee's business district was like a kindergarten classroom with all the pupils yammering for attention at once.

Certain signs can be helpful, though, such as the one for Badger Mountain Brewing along Orondo Avenue. "Ales with Attitude," this sign promised. Unfortunately, however, once inside the brewery, that attitude proved one of sexism. The Padunkadunk Pale Ale logo featured a beer glass shaped like a curvaceous ass, and the chauvinism continued further down the taps, with the Bimbo Beach Honey Blonde, an easy and tasteless ale depicting a bikini-clad young woman in a hammock. Surprisingly enough, no females patronized Badger Mountain. Instead, the bar was lined with middle-aged dudes with child-bearing hips.

Headed north, I passed Rocky Reach Dam (informational tours and salmon ladder viewings available, but no beer served) and then the highway tunneled through the mountainside before spilling down to the sparkling blue of Lake Chelan. Pretty vineyards rowed the hills east of the lake, as the area boasts upwards of twenty wineries, and was recently declared an official American Viticultural Area by the wine police. But instead of wine, I visited Stormy Mountain Brewing on Woodin Avenue, where I ordered a schooner of 25 Mile Cascadian Dark Ale, a style that combines roasted malts with prominent hopping of the piney, citrusy, Cascade variety. These beers are frequently called Black IPA, although the "CDA" moniker fits better due to the nonsensicality of something being both black and pale at once. Certain more radical members of Cascadia Now!—a Northwest independence movement with secessionist fantasies—often drink Cascadian Dark Ale in honor of the region. I suspect California-bashing Karl from Bellingham might've enjoyed a pint of CDA, had he known it meant he got to have his very own country.

Beyond Pateros, ribbons of salmon-colored light faded into the dusk and a fingernail of crescent moon hung over the mountains. I entered the old mining town of Methow, blinked, and saw Methow shrinking in my rearview. The town of Winthrop was my destination, but feeling tired I stopped for the night in Twisp, population 900. I was also famished, as I'd eaten nothing but beer all day. While Burton notes that Crato adviseth the melancholy eat sparingly, my motives were more practical. First, skipping meals came in lieu of my habitual Cistercian Beer Fast.[3] But it was also simple necessity—how else can one travel on the salary of an adjunct English instructor?

Unfortunately, all of Twisp's finest eateries were closed. So I settled for a good night's sleep at the only motel with a vacancy. Nearing the office, I glanced through a window and saw the clerk snoring in a recliner, awash in the ghostly light of a muted television. I rattled open the sliding door to the foyer and waited while he carped and groaned his way up from the cushions. Once at the window—the inch-thick, bullet-proof window—he woozily looked me over, as if unsure why I'd disturbed his slumber. His hair stood up in greasy tufts.

"So, uh, howzacanIhepya?"

I requested a room, nonsmoking.

"Andahowzamanyareya?"

---

[3] See Chapter 8.

"Just me."

"Howlongyastayinfer?"

"Just tonight."

"Ummhmm," he said. Then, bell clear: "That'll be $65."

Considering the isolated locale and my not having made a reservation, sixty-five bucks seemed reasonable—until I toured the accommodations, that is. Room #6 may well have been designated nonsmoking, but some old tobacco funk would've actually been welcome, as the room smelled as if previously occupied by Sasquatch. More accurately, Room #6 smelled as if previously occupied by Sasquatch if Sasquatch had spent a week relaxing nude on the bed, drinking Canadian lager and eating canned chili. The odor was so potent it bordered on synesthesia: an ochre malaise. Worse yet, the pillowslips were adorned by troubling nests of dark, curly hairs.

"I'd like a different room," I told the clerk, again having roused him.

"Howzat?"

"There are hairs on the pillows."

"Hairshuh?"

"*Hairs,* yes. And the room smells awful."

"Smellshowyasay?"

"Not to put too fine a point on it, but it smells like flatulence."

The clerk rubbed his blue jaw, frowning as if I'd really winnowed down the problem. But then he explained I was shitouttaluck because there weren't any other rooms available. So I returned to a blinking gas station I'd passed on the edge of town for a large bottle of beer and a few sleeves of peanuts. Back in Room #6, I stripped the bedding, chugged the beer, forgot all about the peanuts, and soon fell asleep atop a mattress soft as a sheet of fresh-cut pinewood.

#

Like Leavenworth, Winthrop has a theme: the Old West.

Never mind that Winthrop was founded in 1891, by which time the cowboys and Indians stuff was pretty much dead in the stirrups. Owen Wister wrote *The Virginian* after honeymooning there, although Wister was hardly a cowboy, having been educated in Europe before attending Harvard (where he roomed with one of Winthrop's eventual founders). The town's sidewalks were wooden and the storefronts duded-up like a *Gunsmoke* rerun. After ambling past the inevitable souvenir shops—such as Miss Kittie's Old-Time Photo Parlor, where happy couples have the opportunity to commemorate a multi-century genocide by posing for sepia-toned photographs with the fella wearing an Indian headdress and his girl costumed up like a prostitute—I located Old Schoolhouse Brewery.

Although I'd heard good things about this particular brewery, my experience in Leavenworth had left me skeptical of themed towns. Nevertheless, Old Schoolhouse's motto was "We're All About the Beer" and being so far from civilization, I could only hope that proved true. Just before I headed in, a man walked over and steadied himself on a nearby hitching post. He frowned and scraped his shoe against the planks.

"Horse apple or cow flop, pardner?"

He studied the waffle of his sneaker. "Labrador, most likely."

"Look on the bright side—at least there's beer."

"If the wife drags me to one more place like this," he said, "I'm calling my attorney."

Inside, Old Schoolhouse was long and narrow, with a hallway leading to a deck over the river. I saddled up to the bar and asked the bartender for a schooner, his choice. He smiled and went to it. A moment later, he placed my beer on a deckle. "This is our Ruud Awakening IPA."

Then I noticed a tap called the Double D Blonde Ale. You can easily enough imagine the handle's design. Sensing a theme, I asked how long he'd been bartending at Old Schoolhouse and how he liked living in Winthrop, and whether there might perchance be a lack of single women in eastern Washington. There was historical precedent for this, actually, as the territory's early boy-girl ratio was somewhere around 10 to 1, which led to a booming turn-of-the-century brothel industry, as well as various schemes whereby entrepreneurs collected large sums from lonely loggers on the promise of delivering a virgin bride from the East Coast.

But the bartender merely frowned. "Why do you ask that?"

"Never mind. Just a pet theory I'm developing about blonde ales."

Then he glanced over his shoulder at the outrageously buxom tap handle, as if seeing it for the very first time. "I love it out here," he said, "but it's a long commute. I live in Kirkland."

This was certainly odd. "As in the Kirkland right next to Seattle—the one four hours away on the other side of the Cascades?"

"My brother and I just bought the place. It was too good of an opportunity to pass up."

Turned out he was a Microsoft employee looking to make a career change. Couldn't quit the day job quite yet, but driving out on the weekends was nice. Then I tried the Ruud Awakening and it was nice, too. A quintessentially sativa-like Northwest IPA. When I complimented the beer, he explained it was named after Old Schoolhouse's former owners, the Ruuds. Then I asked him why the Ruuds had thought to start a brewery clear out in Winthrop.

"That," he said, "is a whole other story."

But it was also too long a story for one afternoon beer. Later, a bit of web-snooping revealed that back in the eighties Casey Ruud was an inspector at the Hanford Nuclear Reservation in eastern Washington, up the Columbia from Wenatchee. Hanford was where the U.S. government processed and stored the plutonium used for all the nuclear bombs needed to destroy the U.S.S.R. over and over again. In fact, Hanford plutonium powered Fat Man, the bomb that leveled Nagasaki. Going about his job, Casey Ruud noticed a number of Chernobyl-like issues at the Hanford plant—poor construction leading to potential leaks, unsecure materials, and so on— which he dutifully filed audits on. These were swept under the greenly glowing rug by the private contractor who ran the site. So Ruud blew the whistle. *The Seattle Times* was happy to report on such terrifying irresponsibility, and Ruud soon found himself testifying before Congress and the Hanford facility

THE LAND OF ALE AND GLOOM

found its operations suspended. Doing his civic and humanitarian duty won Ruud no friends, of course, and he was soon (illegally) fired, and he and his family had to move to the Methow Valley where nobody knew them. Later, they bought Winthrop Brewing and turned it into Old Schoolhouse, and went from monitoring radioactive waste materials parcel to arming ICBMs to monitoring the ABVs and IBUs of craft beer.

A glance at the menu showed Old Schoolhouse billed the Ruud Awakening a "Destination beer worth the drive to taste on tap." Maybe all great beer is a destination of sorts—a quest for a certain brewery and a specific pour and the proper surroundings, all aimed at capturing an elusive state of mind?

Finished with Winthrop, I soon found myself deep in the North Cascades National Park, which features 700,000 federally-protected acres and one of the most spectacular stretches of road in all the Northwest. As I gained elevation, the air grew cold and mountains rose like a broken-toothed sawblade. Glaciers, glaciers, glaciers—the area contains hundreds—shone blue in the sun. I was busy admiring them, figuring I'd best get my fill before global warming melts them all like ice cubes in a tumbler of bourbon, when the Honda's odometer ticked past 190,000 miles, which is over three-quarters of the distance to the moon. This reminded me of the staff parking lot back at Everett Community College, which is full of the rusted-out Studebakers and Model-Ts the faculty have been driving on their twenty-year odyssey of student loan repayment. While it's been said that poverty is the whetstone of virtue, consider for a moment that Odysseus—despite ravenous giants, ruinous sirens, and his crew being transformed into swine—needed a mere decade to find his way home and kill-off his enemies, whereas repaying Uncle Sam takes twice as long.

And teachers don't even get to fire a single arrow at Sallie Mae, let alone hack a limb from those greasy congressmen who set the interest rates.

The Honda seemed to be running just fine, though, and after a series of evergreen-lined passes the road sidewindered down to Ross Lake, a dam-created reservoir on the Skagit. The lake was ringed by peaks with melancholy names: Damnation, Despair, Fury, Isolation, Terror. One of these peaks—Desolation—was well-known to Jack Kerouac, as he lived in a clapboard shack atop the mountain while working as a fire lookout in the summer of 1956. Jack had hoped to settle deeper into his newfound Buddhism and come to peace with life, but after taking a boat across Ross Lake and then climbing the six steep miles up to Desolation, he realized the peak's name was no mere poetic tag. In addition to its extreme remoteness, the shack was peppered with rat droppings and the bed made of rope, as metal springs would've called down lightning.

Kerouac's experiences living in the North Cascades ("unbelievable jags and twisted rock and snow-covered immensities," he writes, "enough to make you gulp") show up in a few of his books, notably *Desolation Angels*—where, driven batty by loneliness, Jack alternately meditates while standing on his head, misses his mother, writes bad poems, and indulges tawdry fantasies involving sex and Chinese cuisine—as well as *The Dharma Bums,* wherein he and his friends dabble with Buddhism, sipping tea and discussing the empty space inside rocks and the Impossibility of the Existence of Anything.

Farther down lay another reservoir, Diablo Lake. I pulled over into thrashing winds—winds that'd bent the pines into antigravity sculptures and now lashed the breath from my nose and throat—but I hardly noticed the cold, because Diablo Lake was turquoise. Not *just* turquoise, but the glowing aquamarine ideal of turquoise. The Platonic Form of turquoise. Put simply, it did not appear quite real, but instead like something from those old Bob Ross ("The Magic Painter") landscapes on PBS. The extraordinary color owes to glacial erosion, silt turning the lake into the sort of natural spectacle that obliges tourists to shiver in the wind while struggling to capture the perfect iPhone selfie with those gulp-worthy snow-covered immensities as backdrop.

Down the western slope of the Cascades waited the creepy little town of Newhalem, a series of identical featureless white buildings. Newhalem had all the charm of a company town, because it really was a company town—that of the hydroelectric company that operates those dams along the Skagit. It was also a setting for Tobias Wolff's memoir *This Boy's Life,* as the author lived there with his mother during his adolescence and later got the snot beaten out of him by Robert De Niro in the Hollywood adaptation. As for those creepy white buildings, Wolff claims they were actually converted barracks formerly used to house German prisoners of war.

Before escaping the North Cascades for good, Wolff attended high school in the town of Concrete, another company town (a cement company this time, described by Kerouac as "Kafkaean gray"). Wolff wasn't particularly fond of Concrete, though—he describes it as a place where the children of blue-collar parents already held jobs themselves, working not to save for college, but to soup-up their cars—and yet, back in 1938, Concrete briefly garnered the national spotlight courtesy of Orson Welles's famous CBS radio broadcast of *War of the Worlds.*

Apparently, just as the invading Martians incinerated New Jersey (Welles moved H. G. Wells's story to America), a random power outage dropped Concrete into absolute darkness. Terrified survivalists lit out for the mountains, while the more stalwart grabbed their double-barrels and took to the streets, ready to give those extraterrestrials a taste of red-hot American buckshot. The absurd story made the wires and everyone had a good laugh. Then again, a lot of people fell for Welles's Halloween Eve prank. According to my mother, this included my grandfather, who reportedly came home from work shouting about canned food and boiled water. Still, driving through Concrete today, it's difficult to fathom why anybody believed Martians would travel 225 million miles just to commandeer pine trees and gas stations.

On the far side of town was Birdsview Brewing and a poetic roadside sign: NO BUD / NO RAINIER / JUST 8 CRAFT BEERS / ALL BREWED HERE. I parked on a grassy lot crowded with muddy 4x4 pickups, most of which either carried or towed ATVs. Prepared as I was for an authentic experience with rural beer, it was disappointing to find a Ditsy Blonde Ale on tap. Aren't country folk supposed to have better manners than that? Amazingly enough, just below this offering was their 3-Way (as in three hops) IPA.

I asked the bartender—who didn't look quite old enough to shave—for tasters of both beers.

"So you want a Ditsy Blonde and a 3-Way?" he parroted back.

"Hope springs eternal," I said.

But hope was also what stopped this bartender from getting the joke. The young, taken as a whole, are seldom very funny, though. Whereas Burton points out (via Aristotle) that melancholy people tend to be witty, and the wiser someone is, the more melancholy they often will be. Wolff seconds this idea, but as a function of youth: "When we are green, still half-created, we believe that our dreams are rights, that the world is disposed to act in our best interests, and that falling and dying are for quitters."

Kids, in other words, are so busy feeling optimistic that they don't even notice all the disappointing crap that's right under their nose. And that's probably a blessing.

Tasters in hand, I headed for the beer garden to savor my bubbly and illicit little tryst among the good-natured and beer-loving descendants of those Concretians who'd long-ago taken up shotguns against the Martians.

#

Finally, the Cascade Loop carried me back to Puget Sound, through Sedro-Woolley and Burlington and over Swinomish Channel onto Fidalgo Island. Across the bay loomed a smoke-belching Texas-based oil refinery—which, along with another company, had recently settled with the EPA for $425 million in pollution cleanup—but past this eyesore was the pretty little harbor town of Anacortes, where a busy ferry terminal carries Washingtonians to the San Juan Islands for orca-watching tours and stays at expensive bed-and-breakfasts.

Anacortes was founded in 1879 by a railroad surveyor whose wife's maiden name was Anna Curtis. Like Everett and Bellingham, residents once dreamed Anacortes would be named terminus of the Great Northern Railroad and boom into a world-class city. But dreams collide with reality, and what fragments remain are left to coalesce into other things, such as cod fishing, logging, crude oil refinement, a bustling art fair along Commercial Avenue, and, finally, Anacortes Brewery. It shared space with a seafood restaurant, and business was brisk, all the tables and seats full, the oily scent of fish and chips wafting up from the plates.

It took me a while to catch the young blonde bartender's attention, but she finally got around to pouring a few tasters while bopping her ponytail around in a way which surely kept the tips rolling in. Her cuteness brought once again to mind all those lewdly-named blonde ales. Maybe beer and sex are part and parcel, and we shouldn't begrudge breweries who aim to capitalize on that to sell product? On the other hand, maybe we'll look back in a decade and feel embarrassed that we'd ever thought this all in good fun? Better yet, perhaps female-owned breweries will emerge, only to flood the market with Brad Pitt Pale Ales, the tap handles of which might be in the shape of an armless torso with rippling pecs and washboard abs?

Back on the road, I crossed Deception Pass on the 180-foot two-span bridge that links Fidalgo and Whidbey Islands. Whidbey was named after another of George Vancouver's men, Master James Whidbey, whose charting of Deception Pass proved Whidbey really was an island after all. Later, Master James suggested Puget Sound might make a nice halfway house for England's new prison colony in Australia, but the rest of Vancouver's men—including Peter Puget himself—thought he'd probably underestimated the value of the local real estate.

In the town of Oak Harbor was Flyers Brewing. Oak Harbor is home to a large naval air station, and so Flyers beers have aeronautical names. Afterburner IPA. Heat Seeker Hefeweizen. Syphilitic Laotian Streetwalker Blonde Ale. These offerings were all pretty good, but the Pacemaker Porter was surprisingly great. An ode to the dark chocolate and coffee-like possibilities of roasted malt, the Pacemaker wasn't too sweet, wasn't too bitter, but was that ever-elusive Goldilocks beer: the wholesome type of beer described by Burton on cures as not too thick but also not too strong, a beer fittest by virtue of being perfectly *middling.*

Making my way south down the island—it took a while, as Whidbey is the largest island on the Sound—pastorals of grazing cattle and rolling fields backlit by a golden sunset led into Coupeville, where journalistic integrity compelled me to stop at Penn Cove Brewing.

The brewery was near to Ebey's Landing, which memorializes the first official claim—made by Colonel Isaac Ebey—on the Oregon Donation Land Act of 1850, a piece of legislation that gave 640 acres to any couple (half as much for bachelors) who settled on the land. In the five years this law was in effect, all the best farmland of the Oregon Territory and much of the Washington Territory was laid claim to. As one might imagine, the Donation Land Act was very popular with white Americans, but less so with the tribes who'd been living on the freshly donated land for the previous 11,000 years. In fact, one local tribe was so unhappy that they paid a visit to Colonel Ebey's home whereupon they shot him and chopped off his head.

But Penn Cove Brewing was already closed for the night, so I kept on past Freeland (founded by a group of South Dakota socialists) and Useless Bay. Rain spattered my windshield and my stomach didn't so much growl as roar. Beer had sustained me over four-hundred miles through the Cascade Range, but now I was hollowed out in a way that no amount of gas station peanuts could assuage. As already discussed, the *Anatomy* has much to say on the subject of diet, although most of the advice is conflicting and—with the notable exception of Burton's admonishment to drink more beer—unhelpful. He does, however, mention one dish that all the ancient scholars seem to approve of: boiled ram's brains. The recipe is simple. You start by chopping off the head (a la Col. Ebey) and removing the horns, and then, with your crock pot set on low, simmer the whole works, "skin and wool together" with cinnamon, ginger, nutmeg, and cloves. Bread or an egg may be served on the side, but nothing else should be eaten for two weeks. Also, for some reason, it's important the unlucky ram "never have meddled with an ewe."

In Clinton, which overlooks Possession Sound, I loaded onto a ferry—The Kittitas. Rain and gulls. Blue people shrouded in yellow slickers inside the ticket booths. A line of cars, engines idling, cabs glowing with the toxic radiance of cell phones. The dusk faded to navy as the Kittitas sounded her cavernous horn and shuddered away from the dock. Washington State ferries actually do serve beer, but I was tired and spent the passage dozing in the Honda.

Upon reaching Mukilteo station, yet another brewery: Diamond Knot. It was named after a ship that sank in the nearby Strait of Juan de Fuca, which runs between the Olympic Peninsula and Vancouver Island. Sailing on a foggy night in 1947, the Diamond Knot—packed with seven million cans of Alaskan salmon—collided with another freighter and suffered a punctured hull. Soon, the ship rested at the bottom of the sea.

The salvage operation used a super-powered vacuum to suck up all that valuable fish, although what any of that had to do with craft beer in Mukilteo was hard to say. My apartment was nearby, so I already knew Diamond Knot's beer. As usual, it was fresh and good, but the tacos I ordered (the kitchen was out of ram's brain stew) were another story. They tasted like something a traveler might encounter in Tonga or Vanuatu, as if made with tinned pig. Maybe I should've ordered the salmon tacos, circa 1947?

I soon lost my appetite anyway, as everyone around the bar was discussing a recent local tragedy. Apparently, while I'd been off driving the Cascade Loop, a local teenager named Allen Christopher Ivanov, heartsick over a breakup, had attended a house party thrown by his former classmates. But instead of chips and dip, Ivanov brought along the AR-15 rifle he'd recently purchased online—a military-style weapon that's instruction manual he read while sitting in his vehicle outside the house—and murdered his ex-girlfriend and two others. A few days prior, Ivanov had posted his intentions to become a "future shooter" on Facebook. No one took him seriously, though. After all, when was the last time a teenage boy went nuts and shot everyone?

In the ever bloodier decades since Columbine, Pearl Jam's old radio hit "Jeremy" has come to seem less like a pop culture shock piece about a troubled kid who shoots himself at school, and more like the best possible outcome. I grabbed a copy of the *Mukilteo Beacon* from the stack beside the door. But I couldn't bring myself to read the heartfelt articles and prayerful editorials, because when I opened that week's edition an insert fell out for Cabela's. The sporting goods chain was advertising a sale on assault rifles. For just $599 a person could buy, more or less, the same weapon Ivanov used to murder his classmates. The specs were sexy. Cold-hammer-forged barrel. Ergonomic pistol grip and milled gas block. One 30-round magazine included. After he was apprehended, Ivanov called his AR-15 "a symbol of power." Apparently, he hadn't heard that the millions of these objects sold by Smith & Wesson and their ilk at places like Cabela's are meant only for family-friendly sport shooting.

Things weren't entirely grim, though. Because later I visited Diamond Knot's restroom, and so far as restrooms go, this one was pretty special. First, they'd cleverly fashioned a urinal from a keg of Budweiser. The sight reminded me of AB-InBev's "America is in Your Hands" campaign, of all those hundreds of millions of cans of characterless swill with the name of our great nation so callously emblazoned across the aluminum. Second, the door had a steel plate attached to its bottom edge, so after washing my hands I was able to open the door with my foot and thereby avoid touching the germy handle. That all bar bathrooms don't have foot-plate openers is almost as perplexing as why so many breweries insist upon insulting half their potential clientele with sexist branding, not to mention why America continues to allow disturbed teenagers to buy assault rifles on the internet, but not beer in grocery stores.

DE LIBERTAS QUIRKAS: THE ARTISTIC REPUBLIC OF FREMONT

I ended up living in the suburbs thanks to my teaching job. But while there's something to be said for peace and quiet, for taking long walks on lightly-trafficked streets, for waving at the neighbors as they tend their pristine lawns, for not having to sprint drunkenly away from late-night muggers while clutching one's backpack and swearing you're too broke to be worth robbing, I missed Seattle. And not just the urban beer scene, either. No, the ennui of life in the 'burbs can make a thirtysomething guy wonder about things a thirtysomething guy doesn't really want to wonder about—especially amidst a community-wide and weekend-long yard sale.

Now a yard sale may not necessarily sound like a bad thing, but this was the type of yard sale where the less affluent flooded in from miles around in order to sift through the castoffs of the better-offs, while the better-offs themselves relaxed on expensive patio furniture, sipped Arnold Palmers, and pondered how much they could charge for items they had no use for and had long-ago replaced. A sale on dignity, in other words. 50% off class consciousness.

The bargain-hunters arrived bright and early, only to battle like horny young goats for parking nearest the "best" sales. How they knew ahead of time which sales were most desirable is something a mystery. Maybe they scoured the *Mukilteo Beacon,* assuming they could find the classifieds amidst all the buy-one-get-one-free assault rifle coupons. Regardless, droves lurked down the block in their dusty beaters, just waiting for some unsuspecting local to leave his apartment and walk toward his Honda, at which time they raced straight for him while tossing covetous looks at the $5 toasters and $7 scum-crusted aquariums piled along the curb.

The spectacle was enough to sour a guy's coffee. Time to head to the city.

So I scooted down I-5 to Fremont, an artsy, greenie, truly *Seattle* neighborhood that in 1994 lobbied the King County Council to see itself declared "Center of the Universe." The council approved the petition, and the Artistic Republic of Fremont has been proclaiming its freedom to be quirky (*De Libertas Quirkas*) ever since. Regardless of whether this sort of thing strikes you as cute or cloying, Fremont is great. It's well-located, being close to the beer-friendly Ballard neighborhood, and just north of the Lake Washington ship canal along Highway 99, an artery that shoots south past Queen Anne into the high-rise hubbub of downtown.

Like all of Seattle, however, Fremont is weathering the population explosion. It's crowded and full of ridiculously overpriced apartment complexes, and thus packed with frustrated drivers who seethe at all the other frustrated drivers for being stuck—right alongside themselves—in the endless honking congestion. I remembered this feeling all too well. That crush of Seattleites collectively pondering through the haze of seasonal affective disorder just why, exactly, they worked so very hard to pay the outrageous fees to live in neighborhoods where they cannot even drive their brand-new Subaru Outbacks.

After circling around for thirty minutes looking for any available eight-by-ten rectangle of pavement where I might conceivably put my vehicle, I strolled down Fremont Avenue. Bustling with bearded hipsters and slinky women in yoga pants, the avenue had an espresso café every three steps. But it wasn't $5 shots of milky caffeine I was after. Fremont Brewing was the destination. The brewery's slogan—*Because Beer Matters*—touched my heart.

Fremont's beers are uniformly great, but especially the Cowiche Canyon line of fresh hops (named after a spot in the Yakima Valley where the hops are harvested) and their barrel releases, such as the Dark Star oatmeal stout. The founder was a homebrewing lawyer who'd specialized in beverage and hospitality law, a niche that could only exist in the Northwest. My own flirtation with lawyering ended when I drank myself blind on corn liquor and failed the bar exam, which is actually tougher to do than it sounds. But maybe I would've actually enjoyed the legal profession, had I known of the option to practice beer law on the West Coast.

Imagine twenty-four-year-old me walking into my law school's career services office back in Illinois and declaring my intention to practice beverage law. "Well, wouldn't that be nice!" the advisers, themselves no strangers to happy hour, would've said. Or might I have breached the subject with my classmates: "Hey, guys, instead of the whole rat race and billable hours thing, I'm gonna practice beer law." Hearing this, they would've raised their veiny faces from the tabletop—from which they'd been snorting crushed up lines of Adderall and Ritalin, as legitimate cocaine fell outside a student budget— only to laugh like demons until watery orange blood trickled from their nostrils. Then again, the intellectual property ramifications of Miller Lite trademarking that fruity spelling, not to mention the possibility of representing Old Milwaukie in a throwback ad campaign featuring the Swedish Bikini Team, might've provided a solid base for Midwest Beverage Law, LLC.

Somewhere amidst all this second-guessing, I'd drifted to the Highway 99 underpass. In the darkness below the bridge, crawling up from the shadowy earth, was a troll: the Fremont Troll. One hubcap-sized eye was covered by a wild shock of black hair, his nose was every bit as ugly as the nose of a nocturnal people-eater should rightly be, and a massive concrete hand clutched a very real Volkswagen Beetle, as if he'd reached up and snatched it from the stream pouring into downtown. I'd seen this weird piece of urban art before, but the memory was hazy. This was back when I'd poured craft beer at Toronado Seattle, a stepchild of the famous San Francisco Haight Street namesake. I'd been out somewhere in Fremont downing pints, and vaguely recall stumbling along with a crowd that finally converged upon the troll and commenced to dance around him and spark joints and make other assorted pagan offerings. It was that sort of night, I guess.

Once at Fremont Brewing, I ordered one my very favorite Seattle beers. The Summer Ale tasted and smelled powerfully of orange zest, and yet was made of only one malt (2-row pale) and one hop (amarillo), and yet this simple combination, on a sunny day in a lively beer garden, approached the sublime. But as the Brussels lace notched down the pint ring by lacy ring, people at the surrounding picnic tables gossiped and complained about the same boring stuff people gossip and complain about in the suburbs: work and money. With all their talk of staff meetings and salary comparisons, it seemed these

PHILLIP HURST

young people were simply revving up for an inevitable exodus to the very 'burbs they'd now surely bemoan.

"No way Thomas makes more than me," said the twentysomething at the next table over. "I mean, he's good at what he does—don't get me wrong, I like Thomas, I really do—but still, I don't see a guy like him out-earning *me*."

"Just telling you what I heard," said another guy.

"Sorry, but I'm not sure I believe it."

"Who asked you to believe anything?"

"In fact, who's to say Thomas didn't start the rumor in the first place?"

He repeated similar sentiments—"I mean, do *you* guys think Thomas should be making more than me?"—over and over again as I struggled to enjoy my Summer Ale. Each time he whined, I traded smirks with his obviously bored girlfriend. I can only hope our conspiratorial eye-rolling plays at least some small part when she finally dumps the greed-head, although she'll probably just move on to some real go-getter, like Thomas.

Later, things improved when I met Abbie and Tyler. A young married couple, they were beer enthusiasts and regular patrons of my old bar, Toronado. We reminisced about the place—I hadn't visited in months—and Tyler assured me the tap selection remained topnotch.

"I enjoyed working there," I said, "inasmuch as I'm able to enjoy any sort of work. The beer was great and so were my coworkers. Nice customers, too."

"Then why did you quit?" Tyler asked.

I explained that I hadn't quit; that I'd been laid off due to slow business.

"Sorry to hear that," he said. "Are you still in the industry?"

I admitted that, while I still did bartend occasionally, I'd largely switched from the provision of inebriation to higher education.

"That's great," Abbie said, but then trailed off into silence.

People often regard me strangely when I confess to having went from beer-tender to English teacher. Disparate professions, sure, but more so I suspect they can sense I'm not entirely happy with the swap. How, those who've never taught wonder, could service work beat getting to call yourself a *professor*?

One answer, as always, comes from the *Anatomy*. A scholar himself, Burton spills much ink contemplating the miseries of his fellow scholars, we "university men, like so many hide-bound calves in a pasture" who "tarry out our time" only to "wither away." Although Burton frequently lauds the subtle virtues of a melancholy life, as a healthy wearisomeness ensures we don't get too carried away with the vain and transitory pleasures of this world, he nonetheless argues those who spend their days languishing in obscurity for the public good would in any just society be fairly compensated. But despite the laborious tasks, irksome hours, and general tedium of academic life, after their long apprenticeship scholars graduate not to a sustainable career, but to poverty and beggary, receiving only labor for their pains until they grow old and die penniless and alone. In the chilling words of Petronius, "you shall likely know them by their clothes."

I looked down at my shorts. How old was this pair now—ten, eleven? It was entirely possible, I realized, that I was actually wearing *teenaged* shorts, if not even shorts that might've applied for a Washington State driver's license. The crotch had long ago split along the seam, which required I always remember to wear matching boxers.

"The problem with teaching," I said to Abbie, "is that it requires me to drink more beer than I can really afford. It's like being a long-haul trucker with an empty gas card."

She looked concerned, but Tyler just laughed. "We're planning to open our own bottle shop," he said. "We'll have a dozen taps to fill growlers and a big selection of Belgians. We've even got the spot all picked out. There's a thirty-block swath up in Shoreline with no good beer."

"And you two are going to change that?"

"If all goes according to plan."

"That's great."

"We hate our jobs, too," he said.

"I don't *hate* my job," Abbie said, and immediately raised her cider to her lips.

Tyler smirked and sipped from his own glass. He was drinking barleywine, despite it being eleven a.m. and warm outside.

"Screw working for The Man," I said. "Life's short. Open your bottle shop."

Tyler said that once they had her up and running, I should come pour for them, assuming I wasn't too busy being a college teacher.

"Don't tempt me," I said, "or I just might."

Abbie and Tyler were a pleasure to talk with, a pleasure simply to be around. They'd reminded me of something I'd learned in my various stints working at craft beer pubs: beer people are almost always good people, too.

#

After leaving Fremont Brewing, I finally recalled where I'd been drinking that night I first saw the troll—Brouwer's Café. The place is iconic in the Seattle beer scene and plays host to various festivals throughout the year, including Sourfest and the Hard Liver Barleywine fest. The owner of Toronado Seattle—before laying me off—told stories of the days back when he'd run Brouwer's, wheeling and dealing for rare kegs, balancing the books, and generally doing his best to avoid any prolonged interaction with the public.

A short walk ought to have brought me there, but I got sidetracked by still more odd statuary. This time, Vladimir Lenin. Twenty or so feet of solid bronze, Lenin was decked out in heavy jackets and a porkpie hat. Barrel-chested, his stride was conquering and his expression dour. But the connection of this communist revolutionary to a neighborhood street in Seattle was hardly apparent. A violent reading of Marx? The gulag? Millions dead? In Fremont?

The statue was apparently commissioned in Slovakia. Abandoned after the dissolution of the Soviet Union, the statue was purchased and shipped to Washington State by an American teaching abroad. He'd intended to use Lenin as decoration in a restaurant—again, educators prefer the food and beverage industry—but he died in a car wreck before his plans could get off the ground. Next of kin, unsure what to do with such an oddity, negotiated a deal with the Artistic Republic of Fremont to display the statue in a spot where it would best confuse the public at large.

At Brouwer's, a pissing cherub greeted me at the door. The space was cavernous and oval, with an urban gothic feel. A winged monster made of papier mache perched on the second floor balcony and heavy metal blared over the stereo. Normally, I can do without electric guitar, but 150 decibels of Megadeth seemed a small price to pay for sixty-four taps pouring some of the finest suds on the planet. The list was helpfully split into American craft beer, Belgians, and other imports. Brouwer's food was "Belgian-inspired" as well, which meant you had to call the fries "frites." I ordered some and washed them down with a few Belgian ales.

With 5,000 years of brewing tradition, Belgium enjoys a unique beer culture. Compared to German beers and their New World children in America, Belgian beers are defined by a certain looseness of style, as her brewers never worked under the constraints of the *Reinheitsgebot*, a taxation scheme disguised as a purity law which decreed beer could only be made with hops, barley, and water. Belgian brewers, for instance, might add coriander and curacao to an otherwise lightly flavored wheat ale, which works out nicely—but too much freedom isn't always a good thing, as was evidenced by the next establishment I visited.

To get a sense of the Outlander Brewery and Pub, imagine every house you ever got drunk and puked in back in college. Now replace the greasy, sexed-up couches and shoddy linoleum with pub tables and hardwood, put a little bar in one corner and pile it with books that are clearly just for decoration, and don't change the bathroom at all. There you have it.

While the Outlander played better music than Brouwer's, I really should've turned around and left. First of all, the beers had food in them. Peanut butter stout. Basil pale ale. Asparagus saison. I'm all for experimentation, but food-beer is often a bad sign. The Summer Ale back at Fremont Brewing may have tasted like an orange or a tangerine, but the brewers don't chuck oranges and tangerines into the kettle. The crux of beer's joy lies in simplicity, in doing more with less, not in getting your money's worth out of a food processor.

But I'd have likely been happy enough with the beer, if not for the guy pouring it. Anyone who's spent time in West Coast cities would recognize this bartender: the tattoo sleeves, the man bun, the deeply unbuttoned shirt, the rings on his thumbs, and—most of all—the attitude. He's not just a bartender, he'll have you know, he's a *bar star*. He's a musician, of course. Probably an actor, too. A poet in a past life. He's a renaissance man, an undiscovered James Franco. He probably attended some college back around Y2K, although he doesn't like to talk about it much, and his every move, his every word and gesture, is calculated to assure all in his orbit that he absolutely *slays* the millennial girls.

It took me a long time to get this character's attention, as I'd suspected it might.

"Hey," he finally said, followed by a chin nod.

Actually, thinking back on it, I'm not sure his lips moved at all. The entire communication might've been via chin.

"How's your day going?" I asked.

He glanced away. Clearly, he was thinking of ignoring me further but couldn't come up with a suitable excuse. Finally, he squared his shoulders, flexed his chin at me a few more times, and deigned to speak. "You, like, want a drink, man?"

He'd asked this question—absurd as it was, considering I was standing inside his place of employment with my wallet in my hand—in a tone which left no doubt he'd prefer I just went away. I was not his preferred demographic, after all, being male, un-tattooed, and comfortably within his same age bracket. Also, I have a theory that bartenders like this somehow just know that I, too, have worked the opposite side of the oak. It's like a confrontation between two grizzled magicians, where one has grown weary of fleecing the marks, while the other is still out there slinging the same old cheesy razzle-dazzle.

Okay, so maybe not *all* beer people are good people. I briefly considered reaching across the bar and rubbing my dirty thumb in his eye, but just ended up ordering a basil pale ale instead. Not sure why I didn't simply call it a day and leave. Maybe basil beer sounded marginally better than peanut butter beer, or maybe I was afraid that depressing yard sale was still going on back in the 'burbs and, if I were to drive home, I'd have to stomach the sight of my fellow proletarians nosing through the scraps of my bourgeoisie neighbors.

\#

That Outlander beer must've restored me to some extent, though, because after leaving Fremont I found myself not headed back north up I-5, but east along the shipping channel toward the University District. My destination was a proletarian relic on 45th Street known as the Blue Moon Tavern, an old hangout of Theodore Roethke's from back when he'd taught poetry at the University of Washington from the late '40s until his early death in 1963.

A drinker, fornicator, law school dropout, and occasional visitor to the sanitarium, Roethke's genius was to express in image and symbol that deeply personal brand of depression which Robert Burton might've labeled "inveterate" or innate melancholia—sadness to the manor born. Reading Roethke is a harrowing encounter with a voice at once in love with natural beauty and yet ill at ease with its own existence. Take "Night Crow", wherein the image of an ordinary crow alighting clumsily from a branch turns suddenly inward ("Over the gulfs of dream") to see the bird headed "Further and further away / Into a moonless black / Deep in the brain, far back." A blunt metaphor for depression and mortal anxiety, perhaps, but one which illustrates a knack for finding shades of the infinite in the finitudes of nature.

Once parked, I headed for the Moon. In the alley behind the bar, a green street sign read "Roethke Mews." A clever naming, as "mews" can refer to both a dwelling built up along an alleyway, a hiding place, as well as the punning of the word "muse." Strangely, though, the blue and orange mural painted on the wall—seabirds, VW bus, assorted primates, a panpipe-blowing satyr—was dedicated not to Roethke, but the novelist Tom Robbins. Then again, lots of writers gravitated to the Blue Moon over the years. Dylan Thomas, a friend of Roethke's, is rumored to have drank there, as did Jack Kerouac's friend and literary confidant Allen Ginsberg (and maybe even Kerouac himself), along with the influential Montana poet Richard Hugo.

Inside was a cave-like den with a cracked concrete floor and mismatched backless stools ringing a cramped bar. A few patrons milled about, older folks, not university kids, pounding cans of Rainier and gin-and-tonics. Although it wasn't quite dark yet, the only light seemed to emanate from a string of blue Christmas lights and the neon glowing in the streetside windows. I took a seat at the taps only to glance up and see a cobweb-festooned brazier stapled to the ceiling. The garment was seventy years old if it was a day. The walls were papered in leftist counterculture paraphernalia: Ralph Nader for President, 1996; Bernie Sanders, 2016; a Vietnam-era bumper sticker— War is the Real Enemy; and a large poster of a boxer (who bore a distinct resemblance to Ken Kesey, with that same halo of curly blond hair ringing his large head) and the following slogan: Union Busting isn't a Fair Fight. There was so much of this sort of thing that'd it take a dozen trips to soak it all up.

Next door was a newly-opened brewery—Floating Bridge, named after the bridge that spans Lake Washington between Seattle and Mercer Island—and the Moon served their pale ale. It poured warm, which wasn't particularly pleasant and yet somehow fit the workingman's vibe. Then a middle-aged black guy wearing a highway worker's reflective yellow vest sat down and ordered a double vodka. He sported a half-dozen bracelets on his wrists and when he removed his hardhat the hair beneath was conked, a style popular from back in Roethke's day. I was about to strike up a conversation with this time traveler, but then the Nitty Gritty Dirt Band finished up "Mr. Bojangles" and I happened to spot the man I'd come to see.

The poet manned the east wall just past a pool table watched over by the overblown likeness of a defiantly afroed Jimi Hendrix (born in Seattle just a few years before Roethke began teaching at the university). Portly and bejowled and haunted around the eyes, he was dressed in a rumpled brown jacket and tan vest. He held his spectacles in one hand, as if perhaps they'd come to worry the bridge of his bulbous nose, and his red tie was askew, as if he might've allowed himself a cocktail or two already. The cumulative effect was of a tenuous dignity. I carried my beer to his booth and sat. The scarred and wobbly pub table was varnished hard as a turtle's back. Fittingly, the booth was lined with books, including a compendium of *Esquire* stories which included "Neighbors" by another depressive Northwest writer, Raymond Carver. But I'd come to the Moon for rich verse, not minimalist prose, and so I opened an edition of Roethke's collected works which I'd been slowly digesting.

Taken as a whole, the poems spoke of the transience of life tense against the pleasures of the flesh, the aching beauty of rivers and seashores and forests, the mysteries of sex and bafflement with God. Melancholy beats like a heart through the lines, the author seemingly unable to view the natural world without turning it back upon himself, the ebb and flow of tides, blooming flowers in a greenhouse, the ugly death of a cat in a far field, all ultimately speaking to Roethke alone. He also writes of journeys—"the long journey out of the self"—both afoot and in automobiles. "A man goes far to find out what he is—" he writes, but sitting alone in the Blue Moon Tavern, it seemed Roethke had done his most important traveling right there, behind his own hangdog eyes, with a drink in one hand and a cigarette smoldering in the other.

THE CISTERCIAN BEER FAST

Considering all the grainy beer washing down his throat, the river of high-gravity ales and potent lagers, the torrents of porridge-thick stout and massive double IPA, one may be forgiven for wondering if your intrepid beer pilgrim isn't perchance a tad out of shape.

Quite to the contrary, however; as of the time of this writing, he's fit as a Celtic fiddle.

So does he run five miles each and every morning? Not even close. Was he blessed with the metabolism of a high-strung teenager? Hardly. Does he subsist on nothing but shoots and sprouts? Definitely not.

What, then, is the secret?

Well, once a week—preferably (although not necessarily) on Sunday—he partakes of an ancient and holy tradition: The Cistercian Beer Fast. This monastic ritual has been a well-kept secret for nearly a millennium now. Its roots trace back to Medieval France, where an order of Benedictine monks near the town of Citeaux split off to form their own abbey because they felt their fellows had gone soft. These old-school monks, the Cistercians, sought a life dedicated to prayer, work, and silence. In fact, they practiced such hardcore self-denial that their fasting schedule became nearly impossible to maintain. It's one thing to fast occasionally, for a day or two here or there, but in their ecclesiastical zeal some of these Cistercians were fasting almost as often as they were eating. The human body, however, is an engine that runs on calories, and no amount of faith can overcome that. So the Cistercians found a novel way around their strict interpretation of the Rule of St. Benedict: they declared drinking didn't count against their fasts.

While the Cistercians in France drank their native wine, those in regions where grapes didn't grow quite as well turned to beer. Their logic was that since bread and water were allowed during a fast, and because beer was made of the same ingredients, surely God wouldn't mind if they simply ingested their bread and water in the manner most pleasant. These monks were brewing their own beer, of course (more on this in a bit), but the modern day ascetic has a simpler option—namely, bottle shops. In fact, a successful Cistercian Beer Fast can be planned out days or even weeks ahead of time, so long as the bread and water are kept cool in the fridge.

First, one must choose a bottle shop of sufficient variety. Then come questions of taste and philosophy. What, for example, constitutes the perfect breakfast beer? What would make a nice afternoon pick-me-up? What's best for dinner and what for dessert?

I prepare for my own fasts at a place called Special Brews. Because Special Brews offers draft beer in addition to its bottle selection, I'm able to sip a pint while browsing, which helps generate zeal for the enterprise. Choosing the ideal bottles can be difficult, though, and this is one reason why I shop Special Brews: it's not too big. Certain other bottle shops run the risk of overwhelming a monk with too many choices—especially the rare and expensive choices—thus sending him into fits of doubt as he realizes the plethora of worldly pleasures he's forsaken by taking a vow of poverty in pursuit of literature.

Robert Burton approves of all this, by the way. While he never recommends a beer diet per se, in his section on cures for melancholy, he notes that the discreet physician should always exhaust all possible dietary remedies before meddling with medicinal herbs and tinctures. Moreover, on religious melancholy, he writes that to fast piously and well is excellent not only for the body, but as "a preparative for devotion, the physic of the soul," by which one may provoke chaste thoughts, restrain his concupiscence, and expel his lusts and humours.

Indeed, my scheduled fasting day called for beer in lieu of both solid food and women, so I was prepared in the Burtonian sense: having pledged myself to a higher calling, I filled my six-pack and thus saw my faith renewed.

#

It's now nine-o'clock on Sunday morning and I've just cracked a sixteen-ounce can of Evil Twin Brewing's Wet Dream. It's an absolutely terrible name for a beer—the sort of aggressively cheeky marketing that too many craft brewers wallow in, even outside the realm of blonde ales—but I've decided to try it anyway, mostly because it's breakfasty: a brown ale brewed with Kenya espresso beans via a "coffee collective" in Copenhagen.

Upon first sip, the espresso notes are subdued, but it's fairly tasty stuff—especially for a brown ale. A bitter coffee aroma cuts through the malt sweetness, similar to how a healthy dose of dry-hopping cuts the sweetness of a pale ale or IPA. Besides, knowing there's coffee involved helps assuage the vestigial guilt of drinking beer well before noon.

Interestingly enough, Evil Twin has no actual brewery. It's a so-called "gypsy" brewer, meaning the beers are produced on contract. Thus, Evil Twin writes the recipes and then partners with a physical brewery to make the beer, which sounds a lot like the future of craft beer in a world where creativity is plentiful but capital is scarce.

Evil Twin also has an interesting relationship to Mikkeller, a Danish brewery operated by the brother of Evil Twin's owner. The brothers—twins, of course—were originally business partners in Copenhagen. The younger had opened a bottle shop, and the older a brewery to supply the beer. A copacetic relationship, until the brewer brother opened his own bar down the street, which pissed off the bottle shop brother so much that he founded Evil Twin clear across the Atlantic.

While the Wet Dream was made somewhere in Connecticut and distributed out of Brooklyn, somewhere in the whereabouts of Death Valley I have an older brother whom I haven't spoken with in any meaningful way in years. One night when I was home visiting Illinois, we were road-tripping down a dark country lane at midnight, when a confrontation decades in the making finally boiled over. We'd been drinking too much (as usual), communicating badly or not at all (as always), and, long story short, I ended up getting so frustrated with my brother that I shoved him—shoved him harder than I'd meant to—and he fell to the ground, only for him to later pull a very sharp-looking knife on me, only for him to still later flash that same sharp knife in our father's face while demanding the old man get up from his recliner and finally acknowledge and accept his fair share of responsibility for the lump-headed and embarrassing violence of his drunken and deleteriously macho sons.

So an ugly scene, by any measure. And it only got worse, as the following day, after I'd managed to put five hundred miles between myself and my hometown, my brother fell unconscious. A neighbor discovered him and called an ambulance. The ER performed an emergency trepanning, drilling a needle through his skull to relieve the swelling on his brain. And that, as you can well imagine, was pretty much it for our brotherly beer-drinking sessions.

While that night marked the lowest point of an always troubled and melancholy relationship, I do hope my brother and I can move past it someday, much as I hope the brothers behind Evil Twin and Mikkeller can eventually reconcile. Because they should be making their good beer together. After all, sibling rivalries predate Cain and Abel, but unless you've actually *tried* to kill one another, there's got to be some way to get over that bitter taste.

#

Lunch is cheerier and far less heavy: a pint from Seattle Cider Company. Made exclusively from apples picked in eastern Washington, it's bone-dry and reminiscent of a nice sauvignon blanc.

Cider has a long history in America. Back in colonial days, all cider was hard cider, as the Pilgrims and other assorted religious mutineers couldn't figure out how to *stop* pressed apples from fermenting. A vexing problem, that one. The Founding Fathers must've all suffered from gluten allergies, too, considering how much cider they drank. Washington made the stuff at Mount Vernon, Jefferson did the same at Monticello, and John Adams supposedly drank a big tankard every morning for breakfast—all of which validates my doing the same now.

Why this cultural obsession with the Founding Fathers, though? Look in a bookstore or in the history section of Amazon.com and you'll find little besides biographies of these men. We're supposedly a secular democracy, but the way we revere the founders (and our presidents generally) reeks of prophets and scripture. Hagiography may land book contracts, but America's infatuation with kite-flying Ben Franklin and slave-romancing Thomas Jefferson borders on the pathological. It starts during elementary school, when all of American history is reduced to the exploits a few lordly white guys: General Washington gnashing his wooden teeth as he crossed the Potomac; Jefferson penning the Declaration of Independence (probably while sipping claret in a Philadelphia tavern, although Mrs. Bennett skipped that detail); and, later, Honest Abe's emancipation of Jefferson's great grandkids.

Yes, it's unfair in certain critical ways to judge people apart from the historical context in which they lived, and these men certainly accomplished many great things. They thumbed their nose at the world's most powerful empire; they embraced a revolutionary concept of liberty and brought Enlightenment principles to fruition in a republic for the first time in history; and that real estate deal Jefferson struck with Napoleon for the Louisiana Territory looks pretty good in hindsight. So, yes, the Founding Fathers were smart, idealistic, well-read, and farsighted individuals. Still, our modern toadyism is a bit much. To be totally honest, had I been alive in the eighteenth century, I doubt I'd have even liked those high-striding and grandiloquent snobs. Just look at their signatures, all calligraphy and curlicues. How long must they have sat around practicing their cursive like starry-eyed sixth grade girls?

Should I ever have children, I plan to tell them the truth: that the exploits of the Founding Fathers, while indispensable for understanding America, are presented in America's schools as a whitewashed myth meant to appeal to our basest instincts for hero-worship, and that the real founders were complex and flawed individuals, periwigged and knee-sock-wearing malcontents who drank hard cider throughout the workday, made property of other human beings, wrote the Second Amendment without having considered the possibility of their toothless and illiterate neighbors owning AR-15s, and killed a bunch of Englishmen mostly to avoid paying taxes.

#

After a brisk walk along the coast and some pushups to get the blood flowing, it's time for a mid-afternoon snack: the Vaporizer from Double Mountain Brewing out of Hood River, Oregon.

It's a dry-hopped pale ale made from a British Columbian pilsner malt. At first sip, the Double Mountain could be mistaken for an IPA, but after acclimating to the hoppy nose, the lighter body shows through. Still, the malt backbone retains enough chewiness to satisfy my hollow stomach and satiate the brain's demand for carbohydrate fuel. It feels like a daytime beer, a workingman's beer, but—just like breakfast and lunch—the Vaporizer clocks in at a healthy 6% ABV and comes not in a wimpy twelve-ounce can, but a pint.

Luckily, beer is also food. In the distant past, beer helped spur the agricultural revolution by providing a use for surplus crops. Beer fortified and nourished our ancestors and remains the most enjoyable way yet discovered to consume grains. After all, would you rather have pumpernickel, or pumpkin ale? A slice of rye, or rogenbier? Sourdough, or lambic?

Eat the bread if you insist, but it's better fermented in water.

Beer fasting would make for a wildly popular diet, if only Oprah and Jillian Michaels would recommend it on TV. After all, would a person who needs to lose weight rather run on the treadmill and suffer vinaigrette salads and broiled cod month after dispiriting month, or just drink some beer? Would that new mother rather shed her baby pounds by jogging behind that stroller, or might she prefer to drink some beer? Would the morbidly obese rather have their abdomens filleted open and surgical rubber bands fixed around their stomach organs, or might they be happier simply drinking a few beers?

#

Dinner is served: Chimay Grande Réserve, a Trappist ale with roots tracing back to the very heart of the Cistercian Beer Fast.

The Trappists came about in the seventeenth century, when monks at France's La Trappe monastery decided the old Cistercian code—which you'll recall was stricter than the earlier Benedictine code—still wasn't quite strict enough. God wanted His helpers to work and pray a lot more, but to skimp on solid food almost entirely. Hence, a densely caloric style of ale was needed to nourish the order during this near-constant fasting.

Today, bottles of Chimay are labeled with a little brown hexagon and the words, "Authentic Trappist Product." This lets you know you're drinking bona fide monk's brew, not just some secular abbey ale. The label doesn't indicate any certain style, as Trappist ales vary widely. Instead, it's more like a designation of origin protection, as with the AOC in wine. It also assures the drinker his quaff was brewed in an actual monastery (although most of the brewing isn't really done by monks these days) and that the aim wasn't solely for profit, as after the needs of the order are met, much of the proceeds go to charity.

Knowing all of this makes me feel considerably better about eating nothing but beer for dinner. The Grande Réserve weighs in at 9% and is so fruity that after it warms up and the champagne-like bubbles of the secondary fermentation melt away, it could almost be a funny-tasting red wine. It's spicy and herbal, bready and thick. It's truly wonderful stuff, and a worthy main course for this week's Cistercian Beer Fast.

The bottle was pretty expensive, though. Nearly sixty cents an ounce. But then, what are a few extra bucks to get right with God?

#

It's currently a little past nine p.m., a full twelve hours since my beer fast began, and I have to admit that I'm feeling headachy and suboptimal. Robert Burton warns of this pitfall and elucidates the ways in which fasting can turn dangerous if overdone. First and foremost, one runs the risk of being seduced by devils, not to mention becoming vertiginous, hearing things, conferring with hobgoblins, and shriveling away to skin and bones. So, in the interest of health, I'm medicating with a gose from Reuben's Brewing out of Seattle, which makes for a nice change of pace after the viscous Chimay.

Gose (*goze-uh*) is an old and—until the recent explosion of craft breweries—nearly extinct style of light-bodied and tart German ale (originating near the town of Goslar) made from a blend of barley malt and wheat fermented in concert with a healthy dose of lactobacillus. Gose is traditionally spiced with coriander and sea salt, with hops playing only a bit part. These ingredients add a richness and zing to the sourness, not unlike how people in the Southwest doctor their cans of Tecate with salt and lime. Reuben's gose is light and lemony and refreshing—and gone in just a few swallows, just like my headache.

#

It's coming on midnight now, and this week's Cistercian Beer Fast draws to a close. My nightcap is a bottle of Old Rasputin Russian Imperial Stout from North Coast Brewing.

Grigori Rasputin, the wild spiritual healer and self-proclaimed holy man, glares out from the label with a mystical glint in his animal eyes, as if contemplating a lusty murder or a vicious fuck. Rasputin's ale is rich as chocolate mousse. Underneath its leathery sweetness are layers of roasted coffee, dark chocolate, and licorice. The stuff rests on the tongue like cognac, boozy and warming. It's a magnificent beer, and one that owes to the court of Catherine the Great. In the late eighteenth century, the empress commissioned shipments of English stout and the kegs arrived marked "Imperial" in reference to the Russian nobility. But the moniker outlived the monarchy and now belongs solely to the beer.

Of course, I don't live in Russia and therefore need no additional warmth, and I certainly never seduced the wives of any tsars or kick-started any revolutions—let alone would my assassination require poisoning, stabbing, shooting, *and* drowning—as Grigori Rasputin's legend holds. But still I sip with the confidence that this week's fast has been a success, and that my jawline grows more defined with each malty swallow.

But how effective was it really?

Well, besides gaining a wealth of spiritual insights, my fitness tracker claims I burned 3,214 calories throughout the day, whereas I consumed only 1,288 beer calories, leaving a calorie deficit of 1,926. Multiplying this sum by fifty weeks (factoring in holiday breaks) results in a yearly net loss of 96,300 calories, and dividing *that* sum by 3,500 (the calories constituting a pound of bodyweight), reveals my monkish discipline has saved me from gaining an unwanted twenty-seven pounds!

Cheers, friends, to healthy living.

WHERE'S WALDO?

Of the two peninsulas west of Seattle, the Olympic is by far the largest and certainly the most glamorous. Teddy Roosevelt, having witnessed the elk herds slaughtered and the ancient forests clear-cut, declared large tracts of the peninsula a National Monument in 1909, and his cousin Franklin finished the job in 1938 by declaring the Olympics a federally-protected National Park. Today, herds of Roosevelt Elk tromp about in tribute to these farsighted presidents, and the Hoh Rainforest, now off limits to loggers, is strung in tensile webs of moss so improbably delicate it's as if troupes of Irish spiders decorated for St. Paddy's Day. The coastline is a rocky boom of crashing waves and sea spray, the shoreline entrenched with spines of driftwood. Glacial peaks puncture the rain-swollen clouds, and deep inside the dark, damp, eerie forests, hemlocks and cedars grow so freakishly huge that, like skyscrapers, they defy photography.

But what good is all that natural beauty without beer?

No, the craft beer scene west of Puget Sound lies on the other, smaller, less biodiverse, and not federally-protected peninsula—the Kitsap. The drive there was long with traffic, though, and after grinding past downtown I noticed the old Rainier Beer Building with its iconic red "R." Taking this sign for a *sign*, I exited onto the West Seattle Bridge.

Rainier has long been famous throughout the Northwest. A character from *The Dharma Bums* (1958) actually sticks his head into a cold mountain stream and then compares the experience to a commercial for Rainier Ale. While the beer is nothing special, today's skinny jeans-wearing Seattleites chug Rainier the way Portland hipsters slam Pabst Blue Ribbon. But their precious irony misses the nonconformist mark, as beers like Rainier and PBR are far more "corporate" than local craft beers. In fact, Rainier's signature lager hasn't been brewed in Washington State in well over a decade, and the Rainier Beer Building currently produces no beer whatsoever.

Still, thinking I could surely find a real beer somewhere, I headed for West Seattle's Alki Beach. On the thirteenth of November in 1851, this spot saw the arrival of the schooner *Exact,* which had sailed up from Portland carrying a group of settlers now known as the Denny Party. Upon canoeing ashore, the women stepped onto the vacant beach and smelled the brine and felt the cold drizzle and immediately began to weep. The Alki locals, clad in buckskin breechclouts and cedar bark skirts, didn't make those good Christian ladies feel any better. They dug clams out of the muck, let their children run around naked, and showed little sign of ever having read the Good Book. Worse, the party had been assured a pleasantly rustic log cabin awaited them at Alki—but the builder had neglected to add a roof.

Not long afterward, a hard-drinking physician known as Doc Maynard, who'd followed the Oregon Trail to Olympia, made the acquaintance of a Duwamish chief named Sealth—"a big, ugly man with steel-gray hair hanging to his shoulders," according to Murray Morgan. Chief Sealth convinced Doc to head up north and talk sense to the Denny Party, who'd obviously chosen the wrong spot. Upon arrival, Doc was in agreement: they'd have been better off across Elliott Bay, where the waters ran deeper, and the shores were protected from the wind. And so the newcomers left Alki, and after divvying up the land that today constitutes downtown Seattle, Doc suggested they name their new town after his big, ugly Indian chief friend.

A few settlers remained at Alki, though, and West Seattle grew until it was finally annexed in 1907. Still, it feels pleasantly remote from the city. I parked along Harbor Avenue. Across the bay, the downtown skyline was bookended by the charcoal dark Columbia Tower and the looming tumescence of the Space Needle—a civic eyesore Jonathan Raban compares to having hung a velvet Jesus on the living room wall. Ferries crossed to Bainbridge Island and sailboats dotted the water. An ideal afternoon for a stroll, although the signage was ominous: WARNING, it read, PARALYTIC SHELLFISH TOXIN. NO FISHING! TOXIC SHELLFISH!

Admiring the apparently toxic bay, I recalled Chief Sealth's famous (but probably phony) letter to President Franklin Pierce. Frequently anthologized, the letter warns of how the white man abuses mother earth, kills the animals, dirties the rivers, and shows up at the party without any snacks. "Continue to contaminate your bed," Chief Sealth probably never really said, "and you will one night suffocate in your own waste." Because the prose is stirring, everyone wants to believe this letter authentic, despite the fact that nobody has ever actually seen it and there's no record of its delivery to President Pierce—and even though it reeks of the Indian as Super Environmentalist stereotype.

Then I noticed another sign, this one complete with a skull-and-crossbones: DANGER, it read, TOXIC BUTTER AND VARNISH CLAMS! DO NOT EAT!

Past this sign, down at dock's end, was a man—not an Indian chief lamenting the poisoning of the sea, but a shirtless white guy standing on his head. He slowly bicycled his legs and then split them into a V before bicycling some more. Somehow, his sunglasses remained in place all the while. Watching him, I again thought of Jack Kerouac, who performed similar headstands while camped atop Desolation Peak. A hobo he'd met riding the rails suggested headstands might ease his painful phlebitis, but Jack found in the practice something more meaningful. "I could indeed see that the earth was upsidedown," he writes, "and man a weird vain beetle full of strange ideas."

Weird and strange is right. But maybe this guy on the dock was like old Jack—a spiritual seeker—and not just the attention-seeker he appeared at first glance?

A group of West African boys, siblings by the looks of them, hustled up beside me and searched the rocks at water's edge for starfish, pointing and shouting and jostling each other, as boys that age will do.

"Starfish are cool," I said to the tallest of them. He was about ten. "But do you see that man over there?"

"Yes, sir."

"The headstanding man?"

"Yes, de headstand man."

"That man," I told the boy, "ignored the warning signs"—now I pointed out those, as well—"and ate a bunch of toxic butter clams."

The boy's eyes widened. "He did this bad thing?"

"He did. And now he's crazy."

"He's a crazy man?"

"Well, he doesn't seem to know he's standing on his head, and that sounds pretty crazy to me. And see how his legs are still trying to walk? He thinks up is down and down is up."

"The man down the dock is crazy!" the boy informed his little brothers. "He ate the bad clams. Now he believe he can walk wid his head!" And with that, the boys ran back to their parents, with what I can only hope is a lifelong phobia of shellfish.

Walking north, condos of smoked glass alternated with sea-scoured bungalows decorated with old wooden surfboards and buoy-netting. Many of these bungalows had decks built atop the garages, the perfect place to drink a few beers and catch the sunset—and what a sunset it would be. Alki commanded a superb view. Across the sound, Bainbridge Island and the Kitsap lay forested in spruce and cedar, while beyond, through a feathering of clouds, rose the snow-capped Olympics. The foreground was a little less majestic, though. Geezers with sun-leathered chests zoomed past on rollerblades, seemingly unconcerned with hip fractures, and a young woman stooped to pick up her dog's feces, seemingly unconcerned with her manicure, and a pair of bicycle cops pedaled by, seemingly unconcerned with the lack of authority implied by short-shorts, while teenage girls in bikinis were honked at and revved up by dudes in low-riders, seemingly unconcerned with court-mandated ankle bracelets and life in a nylon tent under the I-5 overpass.

Eventually I came to Duwamish Head, a promontory with a memorial for the 1906 collision of the *Dix* and the *Jeanie,* in which "forty-two persons were carried to an early watery grave"—as opposed to a timely watery grave, that is—and then the trail met a beautiful crescent of beach. Sun-bleached logs littered the sand and a quartet of tan young women played volleyball, high-fiving and slapping each other on their glorious butts. Despite signs saying they weren't allowed on the beach, dogs were everywhere, as were children, although I must've somehow missed the signs banning them.

There were plenty of other signs, though, including this one: WARNING! POSSIBLE SEWAGE OVERFLOWS DURING AND FOLLOWING HEAVY RAIN. Beneath the words, unlucky circle-headed figures swam and fished near a drainage pipe gushing sludge. Then, after dodging a careening surrey piloted by a howling and terrified-looking Asian grandmother, I found a still scarier sign: City Ordinance 18.12.257 - BEER AND INTOXICATING LIQUOR PROHIBITED.

But not five steps away, just across Alki Avenue, was West Seattle Brewing Company. The bartender seemed to know little about the beers—or maybe he just didn't feel like conversing with a sweaty guy wearing a backpack—so I ordered a pilsner. After plopping into a lawn chair, I read for a while, basking in the gentle sun, and the pilsner really began to shine. That's the thing about beer: it's a reliable mood-enhancer, a substance of consistent uplift.

Later, I came upon a pair of monuments. First, the Birthplace of Seattle, which was made of stone quarried and shipped from Plymouth Rock (a la the *Mayflower*) to commemorate the landing of the Schooner *Exact*. Then came Alki's kitschiest sight: The Little Sister of Liberty. She's just like the one welcoming the huddled masses to Ellis Island, but only one eighteenth the size. Between 1948 and 1952, the Boy Scouts placed a couple hundred of these replicas around the country. The Alki statue faces the Pacific, as if welcoming the Hawaiians, who flock to Seattle in droves. This makes sense considering the only mainland city Hawaiians seem to love more than Seattle is Las Vegas, which has its very own Lady Liberty right there on the Strip, a beacon of hope shining down upon the casinos and nudie bars.

Hours later, on still another beachfront patio, I drained the last drops from the day's last pint just as the sun eased behind the Olympic Range and enameled the sea in gold. The mountains were named by Captain John Meares who, unlike his fellow British explorers, wasn't quite vain enough to simply name landmarks after himself or his shipmates. Unsurprisingly and disappointingly, American legislators later pushed to rename the Olympics in honor of our presidents. While the native names of these peaks would be preferable to the antique Mediterranean names bestowed by Capt. Meares, had less fatted heads not prevailed, Mount Olympus would now be known as Mount Van Buren.

#

Speaking of native names, before Tacoma was a mid-sized working-class city on Commencement Bay, it was the indigenous name for Mount Rainier (later christened by George Vancouver to honor some rear admiral who fought against America during the Revolution). The morning was a cloudy one, though, and thus the volcano—by whatever name—wasn't "out," as Washingtonians so quaintly put it.

But after passing through Tacoma and just before Route 16 would've brought me to the Narrows Bridge, which leads to the Kitsap Peninsula, I veered south toward the marina and Narrows Brewing Company. There was one particular beer I'd been meaning to drink at this brewery, and after ordering it I stepped out onto a little deck with a view of the mile-long twin suspension bridge that soars over Puget Sound. While this bridge was the site of one of Nirvana's very first photo sessions in 1988, it wasn't the original Narrows Bridge, and the beer I'd ordered—Galloping Gertie Golden Ale—reflected this strange fact.

Back in 1940, another suspension bridge was constructed, the third-longest in the world at the time and a true marvel of engineering. But the workers who built this marvel gave it that curious nickname which now graced my beer. The "gallop" referred to the bridge's tendency to buck like a horse come high winds. Authorities, as you might imagine, were perturbed. And sure enough, just four months after the toll bridge opened, a gust of strong lateral winds had Gertie galloping like mad. An engineering professor named F. B. Farquharson hurried down from Seattle with a movie camera. By the time he arrived, the Narrows Bridge was rippling end to end as rhythmically as a double-dutch rope. A lone car was abandoned in the middle of the expanse, and trapped inside was a cocker spaniel named Tubby. Professor Farquharson—a dog person if ever there was one—ventured onto the undulating bridge heroically, or perhaps a bit rashly, if not even foolishly, in hopes of saving the poor mutt. Unfortunately, however, Tubby got scared and nipped his would-be rescuer's hand.

The professor barely made it back to safety before the bridge collapsed. And what a collapse it was. A slab of concrete the size of two football fields broke loose and crashed into the sound, punching an immense geyser into the sky. Girders bent like putty, massive bolts sheared through beams, steel cables snapped and flew about ("like fishing lines" according to the professor), and Tubby enjoyed what must surely be the single most remarkable death in all the annals of cocker spaniel history.

Based on the nose, I'd have sworn Gertie's namesake golden ale was actually a lager—would've sworn this as surely as that engineer would've sworn he'd built a sturdy bridge—as it was dry and crisp with German pilsner malt. But whatever it was, it went down smooth, and when it comes to the day's first beer, especially if it's still early enough for coffee, you don't necessarily want anything too exciting. The senses aren't ready for all that wow and pizazz quite yet. This is much the same way I feel about crossing suspension bridges, and thankfully my eventual trip across the rebuilt Narrows Bridge proved equally unremarkable.

The fishing village of Gig Harbor was home to 7 Seas Brewing. The Judson Street taproom was quiet. Behind a pane of glass stood a mash tun and kettle, three 8.5 barrel fermentation tanks, along with a few conditioning tanks. There were no TVs—a good sign—and the men's room featured a tasteful strawberry blonde nude. While I disapprove of sexist names for blonde ales, blondes in the men's room are another matter. Everything has its place.

I asked the smiling young woman working the taps to pour me a schooner of something light. "I've got a long day of beer travel ahead of me," I informed her, jauntily pulling out my notebook. Between her snug t-shirt and ponytail, she warranted a good impressing.

"Beer travel?"

"Traveling and writing," I explained. "I'm on trip—a pilgrimage you might even say—from one small-town brewery to another. Today I'm touring the Kitsap."

"Who do you write for? *Imbibe*? *Northwest Brewing News*?"

Caught off guard, I was forced to admit I was doing it on spec.

She cocked an eyebrow. "On spec?"

"The journey of a thousand steps," I said, "begins with a single sip."

She laughed just enough to make it clear the laughter was for my benefit alone. "That's clever," she said, "I'm sure whatever you write will be great."

"Hey, even if it stinks I still get to drink beer, right?"

"That's exactly how I felt about college," she said, and then poured me a gose, explaining that the tartness would open up my palate and get me ready for my long day of beer travel.

This sounded all well and good, but then I got my nose down into the glass and sniffed. Perhaps it was some byproduct of the lactic fermentation process, but my prospective book wasn't the only thing that smelled a little fishy. Much as how that IPA back at Milepost 111 in the middle of orchard country had tasted of pears, fishing villages on Puget Sound apparently couldn't help but reflect the local catch in their sour ales.

A stroll through historic downtown—there's a putatively historic downtown in every coastal village in the Northwest, as well—revealed a bunch of boats in the harbor and a used book store called No Dearth of Books. I was just about to head inside for a browse when I was bowled over on the sidewalk by teenagers with their faces buried in their iPhones. "Head's up," I said to the first kid who bounced off me, but he barely seemed to notice. When the crown of the next kid's head struck my shoulder, I suggested he might want to watch where he was going. But this too was ignored. Hive-like, they scurried off.

Was this just typical adolescent rudeness, or had something happened—some national tragedy?

A few miles north lay Bremerton and Silver City Brewery. Inside, the biscuity odor of malt washed over me, that olfactory ready-set-go of any good brewery stop. Left of the bar, serving as dividers for the seating area, were a number of 59-gallon Heaven Hill bourbon casks.

"Absolutely," the young woman tending bar said, "those really are full of aging beer."

"Then I think I'd better do a taster board."

She asked how many I'd like to try.

"*All* of them," I said, and soon had a dozen little tasters at my greedy fingertips.

First up: Have a Nice Day session IPA. Even though session IPA is arguably little different than regular pale ale, considering IPA evolved as a bigger version of pale ale—which means that to lighten IPA is to return it to the state from which it came—I'm an unabashed fan of this style. Session IPAs are as light or lighter than Budweiser, but packed with hop character. They often show a curious soapy flavor, though, a residue of hops with the malt backbone stripped away. But compromise is parcel to growing up, as is the move to subtler beers. To continuously and stubbornly drink nothing but full-octane

IPA—which a lot of dudes do—is evidence of a failure to grasp the more nuanced implications of the craft beer revolution.

Curious about what filled all those bourbon barrels, I next sampled an aged version of the Giant Made of Shadows Belgian-style quadruple. This style of beer—the quad, as it's known—is the logical next step in the dubbel (or double) and triple tradition of abbey-style ales. The Giant's oak flavors showed through the dense bread and a distinct booziness warmed my tongue. It tasted fine in a two-ounce glass, but like a gregarious friend, might a long pour quickly lose its charm? Thinking of this reminded me of the infamous New Coke debacle—well described in Malcolm Gladwell's *Blink*—which has ramifications for both soft drinks and not-so-soft drinks.

Around the time Michael Jordan was a rookie, Coca-Cola was losing market share to Pepsi. A panicked batch of taste-test research pitted a more acidic and raisiny sample (Coke) against a sweeter one (Pepsi). Soft drink consumers tended to prefer the latter. Hence, New Coke, which was essentially just Coca-Cola made to taste more like Pepsi. Everyone hated it, of course, and Coca-Cola had to start making Coke Classic, which was the same old Coke they'd been making before they spent a fortune researching, developing, and branding New Coke.

The problem? People don't consume cola by the sip, but by the twelve-ounce can. The sweeter beverage may taste good at first, but it quickly grows tiresome. One might think sweet, rich beers would suffer the same problem, but beer has a distinct advantage over cola: alcohol. Where the dense malt of a big quad like the Giant Made of Shadows could grow overwhelming, alcohol has a lightening effect that balances out the sugar. That, and—unlike either Coke or Pepsi—a full glass of the stuff would reward the drinker with a nice little buzz.

But it was a workday for me (of sorts), and buzzes would have to wait.

I headed toward Silverdale along Dyes Inlet, named after the aptly-named taxidermist of the United States Exploring Expedition, led by Captain Charles Wilkes. The captain was a tall and aloof man with a disciplinarian's reputation, largely due to his penchant for beating his crew bloody with a cat-of-nine-tails. While the Navy said a dozen lashes was the most any errant sailor could rightly endure, Capt. Wilkes often tripled that figure to make sure his point was taken. In fact, the man was such a tyrant that some say he was Melville's inspiration for Ahab.

Parked near the waterfront, I didn't encounter those portents of doom which haunted the *Pequod*, but I did run across more ominous signs. First, another caution as to the local shellfish (BACTERIA! VIRUSES! CHEMICALS!), and beside that a shamefaced cartoon dog and a steaming pile of mess. YOUR DOG, read this sign, YOUR DOODIE. NO EXCUSES! An arrow pointed to a box of yellow plastic gloves labeled "Mutt Mitts."

I grabbed a pair in preparation for my walk around Silverdale, figuring that way I'd be safe to dig for shellfish. But soon I came across Cash Brewing, where I found a cache of TVs. Quite literally, there were more televisions in Cash Brewing than there are in stores that sell televisions. They hung side by side and back to back in the center of the room, approximately one every three inches, with still more circling the walls, a blinking, glowing, chattering menagerie of Samsung and Sony, as if a customer might miss a crucial pitch or touchdown if he so much as turned his head one degree to the left or right. My initial count of thirty-one TVs gave way to thirty-two after encountering one in the men's room, at eye-level with the urinal. This necessitated a reconnaissance into the ladies, where two more TVs were discovered, for the nearly unbelievable total of thirty-four in all.

Sports bars are yet another thing that everybody except for me seems to like. This is odd, really, considering I love bars and played basketball for years. But putting bars and sports together somehow spoils the best elements of both—what should be a quiet refuge against the workaday world, under the pernicious influence of ESPN, becomes a place where sad-eyed men pine for their glory days on the field and court.

Fearing the worst, I ordered a taster tray. Sure enough, the brown ale was yellow. It must've been a kölsch—a mistaken pour. Next up were the pale ale and IPA. Pales are a brewery's traditional workhorse. Sierra Nevada set the bar back in the '80s with their classic Northwest pale ale, which showed the world the potential of Cascade hops. In gauging a brewery, the pale ale should rightly be tasted first, because if a brewery can't get that right, chances are they can't get much else right. And IPA, while often overdone, remains the standard-bearer for most American craft breweries—a style by which brewers aim to leave their signature. But whether Cash's examples were any good I cannot honestly say, because the golf, NASCAR, and tennis highlights blasting from all those TVs had already put such a bad taste in my mouth.

Fortunately, just down the block was The Old Town Alehouse and Eatery. A dilapidated building with peeling paint, the Old Town seemed sketchy at first glance. And second glance. The carpet was a stapled together patchwork of putting green turf, while the ceiling and walls were covered in dollar bills doodled with raunchy drawings. The air smelled like deep-fried pickles and the juke was playing Willie's "You're Always on My Mind."

The Old Town also featured a 2-for-$1 taco special. Down the rail sat a three-hundred pound man who'd ordered approximately two dozen such tacos. This bounty lay spread before him on a platter, and I watched as he mechanically dressed each one with tomato, onion, sour cream, and a liberal shot of cayenne pepper sauce.

But instead of discount snacks, I ordered an oddly named beer.

"Valhöll Brewing?" I asked the bartender.

Flo was her name. She was in her fifties and very friendly, although she moved with the forethought of one whose joints ached. "Oh, you know how those Vikings are," she said.

"Actually, I don't."

"Up in Poulsbo, don't you know?"

The huge man chomped into a taco and orange grease squirted all over the bar top. Flo shook her head and tossed a handful of napkins at him.

"Poulsbo has beer-brewing Vikings?"

"Of course," Flo said. "She's little Norway on the fjord."

Unsure what to make of this, I asked about the Old Town's history. "It's got a lot of character," I added.

"*Characters,* is more like it," Flo said. "Look at Fat John down there, hogging his tacos."

I glanced his way and Fat John stared back, eyes and cheeks bulging. When he sucked grease from his thumb, his splayed hand resembled a Mutt Mitt blown up like a gag reel balloon.

"I swear these guys don't eat all week, just so they can come clean me out," Flo said. "This keeps up, I'll have to put a limit on tacos."

"Only a dozen per customer?"

"Can you believe I spent a full hour browning ground beef this morning?"

Indeed, Fat John had been joined by some buddies—Stout Steve and Hungry Hank, perhaps—who were soon enough dressing equally massive taco platters of their own.

"This place was a livery back at the turn of the century," Flo told me. "Then it was a brothel and later on a roller-skating rink. It's only been a bar since the forties."

With so many tempting rejoinders available, I froze and said nothing at all. Flo continued. "The upstairs has apartments now, but I don't see how folks can stand to live up there."

"Because of the noise?"

"No, we keep pretty quiet around here. But if you choose to live above a bar, it just says a certain something about your— how to put it?—about your trajectory in life."

"I guess so," I said, thinking that I might truly enjoy living above a bar.

Then she dug out a dusty old album and showed me approximately eight decades' worth of photos. In one, a bartender with a towering bouffant and wine-dark lipstick stood beside a glitzy cash register. The barman wore a crisp white shirt, bowtie, and suspenders. They could've been pouring drinks at the Drake.

I looked at the guys down the rail. "Time's change."

"Hold that thought," Flo said, "I gotta go refill their Diet Cokes."

Only then did I detect a genuine flaw with the Old Town Alehouse—my beer was served in a cheater pint. But I guess Flo had to subsidize all those fifty-cent tacos somehow.

Just before I left, a scrawny old coot ambled in wearing loud blue basketball shorts. Without a word, Flo mixed him a slopping martini in a smoked purple glass. "If the president calls," the old man said, and slurped off the top inch, "I'll be out in the beer garden."

"Thought you and Obama was on the outs these days?" Flo said.

"We are," the man replied. "But he's starting to grow on me, considering the alternatives."

#

Like Flo said, Leavenworth wasn't the only town in Washington with a northern European theme. Poulsbo (pop. 9,500), evoked a Scandinavian fishing village from the days of yore. Resting on the scenic edge of Liberty Bay, the town was founded in the 1880s by Jürgen Jorgenjorgenson of Fjordefjordland, Norway (or something like that). More settlers followed, and soon a fishing industry gave birth to a logging industry which gave birth to a shipping industry, churches and schools were built, and so arose Little Norway on the Fjord.

Along Viking Avenue stood a twelve-foot concrete warrior complete with horned helmet, broadsword, and cape— VELKOMMEN TIL POULSBO!

After stashing the Honda in King Olaf Free Public Parking, I visited the Poulsbo Maritime Museum. It was full of interesting stuff, such as intricate scale models of boats— tugboats, cod fishing vessels, Viking warships with dragons for bowsprits—and a hodgepodge of nautical gadgets: chronometers and calipers, sextants and an assortment of old telescopes, taffrail logs and even a turn-of-the-century Evinrude engine. While I was admiring these watery artifacts, the museum's proprietor—a tall and gloaming older man— approached.

"I believe he's hidden too well this time," he said.

"Excuse me?"

"Waldo."

"Pardon?"

"You know Waldo. The famous traveler who wears spectacles and a striped shirt. He hides and they search; they search and he hides."

At first I thought dementia, but his eyes were clear and bright. Then the man told me that, despite the massive resources deployed, he doubted they'd ever find Waldo this time. On the wall over his left shoulder hung a King Salmon the size of a gluttonous collie. Museums are odd places. Especially the little, quixotic ones like the Poulsbo Maritime Museum. It really might drive a person nuts to spend day after day surrounded by stuffed and dusty objects from a world gone by, watching strangers wander in, furrow their brows, and then wander back out.

"I'll keep a lookout for Waldo," I said, easing past the proprietor.

"Oh, they've been looking all day." He followed a smidge too closely and his voice tailed me onto Front Street. "But I suspect this time he's gone for good!"

A block from the museum, I was admiring a mural of a Viking warship painted on the Boehms Chocolates building when another teenager crashed into me, again without a word of apology. But before I could snatch his precious phone and dash it pieces, he was long gone, his legs carrying him down the sidewalk and his head lost, apparently, in cyberspace.

Not far from the Viking mural (after a quick stop Slippery Pig Brewery, where a dandelion bitter evoked memories of sticking a dandelion in my mouth at age five, the intervening years having seen little improvement in the flavor of dandelions), was the aforementioned Valhöll Brewing. A sign above the bar read "VELKOMMEN TIL VALHÖLL" and the warrior of the logo wore a braided beard that dangled clear down to the gleaming taps. The interior was finished in darkly stained wood and matte steel—a beautiful taproom. All of Valhöll's beers proved strong, as well, about 2% higher than usual for the style, which seemed appropriate for a warrior culture. But instead of seagoing marauders, the clientele were local firefighters. They were all huge people, tall and thick and bearded—even the lady firefighters—and it seemed these really could've been the descendants of Vikings. I struck up a conversation or two with them, but soon found myself content to just listen, as I didn't know enough about car wrecks or strokes or heart attacks to contribute very much. Hearing them talk shop was humbling, though. These folks risked life and limb to save the lives and limbs of total strangers, which suggests first response work must carry with it some element of a calling.

Having reached the bottom of my schooner, I headed down to the less Scandinavian end of Viking Avenue and Sound Brewing, where I sampled a couple of delightful Belgian-inspired ales—the fruity-funky Monk's Indiscretion, and the Ursus Spelaeus Imperial Stout, a high-gravity soup of coffee and spice—before making my way south again. Then I realized I'd neglected to perform a single *beer near me*, craft beer being so prevalent along the Kitsap that it hadn't been necessary. But the magic words didn't let me down.

LoveCraft Brewing was a block off the waterfront in downtown Bremerton. Considering the octopus-headed and pint-wielding Cthulhu logo—not to mention the dubbel entendre of the brewery's name—I suspected LoveCraft might prove interesting. Still, had I taken a moment to stand on 5th Street and gather all the clichés I could possibly muster for what sort of people might congregate at a brewery named after the horror and fantasy writer Howard Phillips Lovecraft, I couldn't have conjured a more nerdy vision. Every table was filled with narrow-shouldered guys wearing wire-rim glasses and mousy-looking girls with thick-framed glasses, all immersed in role-playing games of the Dungeons & Dragons and MERP variety.

While waiting for the beertender, I thumbed through a pile of comics, tossing aside *Thor* and *X-Men* in favor of *Alf: The Swimsuit Issue*. But there was more serious literature afoot, notably a tome of Lovecraft's collected works thick enough to rival Burton's *Anatomy*.

"I'd like a couple tasters," I told the bespectacled beertender, when he finally found a minute, "of the Eldergod bière de garde and the Moon Beast rye IPA."

When he returned with these, I quizzed him about the brewery and he said they'd only been open since November, although they'd been so busy that it was hard to brew enough to keep up with demand.

"Looks like you're doing something right," I said, and then sampled the tasters. Both were surprisingly good, especially the bière de garde (a French-style pale ale meant for aging), which is tough to get right.

"Excuse me," said the guy one stool over, "but have you read any of Lovecraft's writing?"

He must've seen me browsing the collected works. His wire-rimmed glasses were smudged, his ponytail unkempt. His arms as thin as the skeletons haunting Lovecraft's stories.

"A little."

"Yeah? How is it?"

I admitted that I found Lovecraft pretty darn weird, but not necessarily due to the monsters and ghosts, but because the writing style felt older than it actually was, like a period homage to Edgar Allan Poe.

"Well, I was thinking about giving it a shot."

"The beer's that good?"

He sipped his pint. "I like it."

I slid the book toward him. "There's a story called 'The Outsider' that's worth a look."

I'd actually taught this story in a course on Gothicism the year before. It's about a ghoul who doesn't realize he's dead, even as he crawls from his crypt back up to the surface world. Eventually he gets lonesome and crashes a party, but the party is a bust because everyone is inexplicably frightened of something. Then the ghoul gets scared, too—especially after he catches a glimpse of his own rotting face in a mirror. The point isn't the horror trope switcheroo, though. Instead, "The Outsider" has a bizarrely happy ending, as the ghoul finds his way to Egypt (somehow) and makes some new monster friends to ride the night-winds with. But before we could speak further about the weirdness of Lovecraft, a group of teenagers sprinted past the window down 5th Street. Again, they all stared maniacally at their phones, as if possessed.

"What in the world is going on today?"

"Pokémon Go," the guy explained. "Haven't you heard of it?"

I admitted I hadn't and he filled me in. Pokémon, it turns out, were virtual cartoon characters that players angled to capture and enslave, for whatever reason. In the "augmented reality" of the game, players ran around looking at GPS replicas of the world that just so happened to have fantastical creatures dropped in. Thus, a real-life, real-time street, but full of Japanese anime.

"So there's a Pokémon outside right now?"

"There's a bunch down by the water," he said. "It's a hot spot."

"What's the point, though?"

"It's fun. Like a virtual reality scavenger hunt. Sort of like—"

"Like Where's Waldo," I said, with a shudder of Lovecraftian horror.

Along the waterfront, I passed a 3,400-pound torpedo and the battleship Jay Turner, her turrets aimed at the clouds, and I thought of Zbigniew Brzezinski waking to that three a.m. phone call and wondering whether to rouse President Carter with the news that everybody was about to get burnt to cinders. Still, I resisted the curmudgeonly urge to see apocalypse writ in Pokémon—even as more teenagers plowed into me while herding cartoon dinosaurs.

I stopped a random kid and asked how the game worked. He held up his phone so we could both see the screen. Down the block, a purplish monster bobbed on dainty wings. It looked mischievous. I wagged my finger like the kid showed me and a thingamajig flew out onto the virtual dock and wrangled the little monster. I must admit, the experience was oddly thrilling.

But being old enough to recall grade school nuclear fallout drills during the dying days of the Cold war, not to mention being an aspiring writer, made *me* feel like an outsider—"I know always that I am an outsider," declares Lovecraft's newly self-aware ghoul, "a stranger in this century." Sure enough, it was me who'd lost touch. The kids were capturing e-dinosaurs, but I was the real dinosaur: the one with his head stuck in a book. And while Seneca teaches that reading is to the soul as meat is to the body, kids in ancient Rome didn't have iPhones.

While the fate of the book remains imperiled, craft beer is thriving. The movement arose in response to the corporatization of an age-old artisanal product. Prohibition hammered America's small breweries and coagulated wealth in the hands of those brewers big enough to survive the lean years by making other products—soft drinks, malt extract, vinegars, industrial alcohol—and so our immigrant beer traditions nearly died out, leaving little but indistinguishable corporate lagers, a substance with echoes of the oily gin supplied by Big Brother in *1984.*

The beer revival of the last thirty years has changed all that, though, and a healthy percentage of Americans are once again able to recognize real beer from a crude facsimile. This, of course, is a good thing—a great thing—and yet other aspects of our culture, like books, remain in flux. A twenty-first-century conundrum: after the dark decades post-Prohibition, we find ourselves awash in wonderful beer, but with less and less of substance to talk about over a pint. Those teenagers goofing off in augmented reality weren't the problem, though. The problem was how technology and the e-mindset—useful as it so often is (*beer near me . . .*)—muddles the attention span. We find our lives at once sped up and dumbed down. Plugged in, synced up, and wired, we can now perform inanities faster and more efficiently than previous generations could've ever dreamed. Maybe what's called for is a craft beer revolution writ large: a counterculture movement like the Acid Generation of the 1960s, trading LSD and flower power for lovingly made beers of great depth and a way of life that reflects that taste?

Just then, a kid zipped past on a skateboard, his phone aimed dead-ahead.

"Pokémon Go!" I shouted, and he looked back and wagged a hang-ten.

"Pokémon Go?" I quietly asked the Korean girl picking her way along the steps. She glanced at me, startled eyes goggling behind her thick glasses.

"Pokémon Go?" I asked an older gentleman, but he merely stared. Upon closer inspection, the object in his hand wasn't a phone at all, but a shiny pack of cigarettes.

After stopping for coffee, I passed back through Gig Harbor and came again to the Narrows Bridge—only this time, heading east, I had to pay a toll. "That'll be six dollars," said the lady in the booth. While she broke change, I opened the recently downloaded app on my iPhone. I held the device above the dash and aimed along the bridge. The screen looked eerily similar to Professor Farquharson's footage from 1940. This time, however, instead of galloping slabs of concrete, a creature waited on the bridge, like a troll from a fairy tale.

"Are you playing that new Poke-ee-man game?" the toll collector asked.

"There's one out there right now."

"People keep saying that. I had to have a kid show me what all the fuss was about."

"Me too."

"This probably makes me sound old, but I think the whole thing's kinda spooky."

Tubby the cocker spaniel came to mind, and I wondered if I might be seeing not a Pokémon, but a ghost. I hit the gas, still holding the phone above the dash. In the lighted screen, the creature grew larger and better defined. A blob of fire glowed at the tip of its tail. No cocker spaniel here, unless it was one from the realms of Lovecraft. Then I hit fifty and bore the thing under the Honda's wheels, and so ended my exploration of the Kitsap Peninsula.

A CAPITAL TOUR: PART ONE — OLYMPIA

Growing up in rural Illinois, nearly every school year saw my classmates and I herded onto a big yellow bus for the sweaty and jostling ride to the capital at Springfield. Inevitably, these field trips were Abraham Lincoln-themed. We toured Lincoln's home, his library, his law office, his church, his tomb, and so on. We listened to period actors in top hats recite the Gettysburg Address, and suffered in the unrelenting heat while our teachers insisted we pay attention to the spot where The Great Emancipator had once split a cord of wood or maybe just eaten a hotdog.

Though these field trips were brutally dull, and while Olympia has no historical personage on par with Honest Abe, I still felt a Washington State transplant like myself owed the capital a visit, if only to do my civic duty and investigate the beer scene.

Situated on the southernmost point of Puget Sound, Olympia came to prominence as the terminus of the Cowlitz Trail, the northern extension of the Oregon Trail. With the best plots in the Willamette Valley claimed within just a few years of the great migrations of the early 1840s, settlers began to look north of the Columbia. For a time, it was thought England and the Hudson Bay Company would control this area, but land-hungry settlers quickly established a permanent American claim to the Puget Sound basin by clearing land, building homesteads, and—most of all—by making lots more little Americans.

Today, Olympia presents an unassuming face of modest single-family homes, low-end restaurants, and anonymous state buildings. It reminded me of a college town without the college, although there actually is a college—The Evergreen State College—which not only believes in the value of throwaway articles of grammar, but does *not* believe in assigning grades. Instead of As, Bs, and Cs, the college asks students to write self-assessments upon largely self-created curriculums. Indeed, my liver shudders to imagine the abuse it'd have suffered had I chosen to matriculate at The Evergreen State College.

I fed a downtown parking meter and walked to Fish Tale Brewing. A banner declared Fish Tale the 2015 Washington Beer Awards Brewery of the Year, which was promising stuff, although the beer garden was full of dogs. A hydrophobic French Poodle snarled and lunged at the end of its leash, a Pomeranian grinned idiotically while attempting to put the moves on my ankle, and a boxer rammed her cannon ball skull into my table, sloshing and spilling my tasters. I shook loose the amorous Pomeranian, floated a ten-dollar bill atop the spilled beer, and hopped the fence.

Feeling hungry, I stopped at a little taquería that shared space with Fish Tale. After ordering a plate of tacos (not two for a dollar, but a steal nonetheless at $.99 apiece) and a cold Pacifico—the best of the readily available Mexican imports—I found a table out on Legion Avenue and began doctoring my lunch with lime and cilantro. All was well, until I felt a gentle spatter upon my left wrist. Was it drizzling? I looked up, only to realize my table was beneath a power grid that doubled as a stoop for a family of crows.

A mortaring struck my right leg, wetting my shorts clear through to the skin. I lurched backward, disgusted, only for a second barrage to foul my arm from biceps to wrist. Standing now, my plastic chair toppled over, I wished for the first and only time in my life that I owned a BB gun. The final volley exploded directly atop my taco plate, coating everything— tacos, Pacifico, even my phone—in a runny gray salsa.

Call me superstitious, but while soaping up at the sink of the taquería's little bathroom, it seemed those crows were trying to tell me something.

Then again, Three Magnets Brewing was just around the corner. It proved a colorful place, with stained glass windows depicting Mount Rainier and a sunset over Puget Sound, along with a bartender with bright green hair. But the music spoiled the ambiance. Although Kurt Cobain wrote most of Nirvana's best songs while living in Olympia, the stereo blasted Aerosmith. Never one for noise, I ordered a sample tray and headed outside to sip in peace, only to find a construction project across the alley even louder than Steven Tyler's screeching ode to transvestitism. Every three or four seconds the power saws were interspersed with a percussion of nail guns and a bass of falling cinder blocks.

Back in the bar, Aerosmith soon gave way to Bon Jovi's "Living on a Prayer."

"Could you please turn down the music a little?" I asked the green-haired bartender.

She shook her head. "Say again."

"The stereo—it's awfully loud."

"*What?*"—now she pointed at her ears—"*Huh?*"

Desperate, I looked for anywhere else I might conceivably drink my little cups of beer, but I was trapped. Noise-polluted and shat-upon and trapped. Why had I driven all the way to Olympia? Even as I'd brewed my morning coffee, hadn't I known it'd be lame? The angst of "Smells Like Teen Spirit" really should've been a clue. What was I planning to do here— tour the Capitol Building and listen to state representatives debate what color to paint the curbs? Why was I wasting my summer driving around to all these cruddy little places—what was the point? I wasn't going to learn anything or find anything interesting in these backwaters. May as well have just stayed home and drank on the couch while counting down the hours until death.

But then, having resigned myself to the racket outside, I calmed down enough to finally try a beer: a saison blended with barrel-aged ale. Saison has origins in Belgium and France, and is often used synonymously with farmhouse ale. Think a mix of grains and wild yeast character, beer's expression of rustic charm. Three Magnets had made an excellent one. It was dry and mildly sour, with a whiff of brettanomyces funk to keep things interesting. Feeling a little better, I happened to look up just as a seagull floated between the buildings, its angelic form glowing in outline. Ivory wings levered against the updraft and it seemed I could almost hear the mechanical click of well-tailored cartilage. The gull was graceful and beautiful (and it didn't try to shit on me), and as I sipped more of the wonderful beer I was heartened to realize that I'd lost all desire to ring the bird's delicate neck and thereby doom my capital tour.

\#

Capitol Campus stands on a knoll overlooking Capitol Lake, and beyond that the waterfront serving Budd Inlet, which like the waterways around the Kitsap, was named by Captain Wilkes in honor of some crew member whom he'd grown tired of whipping with his cat-of-nine tails. I walked along the eastern edge of Capitol Lake and admired the nearly three-hundred-foot tall classical dome of the Legislative Building. It's the tallest masonry dome in North America, an elegant tower of sandstone and marble, and looks better suited to the other Washington. But the lake itself was another story. Formerly an estuary where the Deschutes River entered the inlet, a dam was built and the lake formed in 1951. Due to accreting sediment, the lake requires frequent dredging at enormous cost. The water was scummed with brown algae and littered with trash. Bottle-green dragonflies helicoptered around the mess, as if reconnoitering the scene of a disaster, while battalions of ducks paddled through the cattails, bobbing their slick heads into water so unaccountably frothy it resembled a kettle of fermenting wort.

Then I rounded a bend and encountered a few dozen people huddled together with their faces buried in their phones. Nobody so much as glanced at me, not even after I began to dance and snap my fingers.

"Pokémon Go?" I asked a girl of about twenty. She had blue hair, not green.

"Oh yeah," she said, without even a cautious peek at this large male stranger who'd unaccountably approached. "People are here past two a.m. most nights. It's pretty rad."

Past the blue-haired girl, a man about my age was bent over his phone. At least—and I'm estimating conservatively here—at *least* six inches of hirsute and gloaming derriere showed above his sagging pants. Oblivious, he continued to imprison Japanese dinosaur-creatures.

"Ever toured the Capitol Campus?"

The girl swiped her phone with her index finger. "The what?"

I pointed up at the gleaming dome with the ornate cupola and house-sized American flag. I kept pointing for a full ten seconds, until she finally looked.

"Sure, back in grade school they dragged us up there once or twice."

"Pretty boring, huh?"

"Totally boring."

"When I was in school, they dragged us to Springfield to learn about Abraham Lincoln."

"Springfield?"

I explained that Springfield was the state capital of Illinois.

"You grew up in Illi-*noise*?"

"No, I grew up in Ill-*annoy*."

"Got one!" the girl said, gasping with excitement and aiming her phone at an empty spot on the sidewalk.

A trail led from the lakeshore up to Capitol Campus. Inside the north vestibule of the Legislative Building stood a ten-foot statue of Marcus Whitman, a frontiersman and physician who helped bring early settlers to Washington. In the mid-1830s, along with another missionary couple, Marcus and his wife Narcissa made the first crossing of the Rockies in a covered wagon. This statue really should've been of Narcissa, though, not Marcus. They were both pioneers, but she doubly so, as the first woman to prove women could travel the American West. Narcissa Whitman had a flair for riding sidesaddle. She was a schoolteacher. And she also managed to give Marcus a good canoodling somewhere west of Missouri but east of the Columbia, and therefore owns the distinction of having conceived the first child on the Oregon Trail.

Later, in the fall of 1847, at the mission they established near present-day Walla Walla, the entire Whitman clan was murdered by Cayuses who'd grown tired of both Christian proselytizing and the sad fact that white children usually recovered from the measles while their own children most often died. Considering no one present at the mission, Christians nor Indians, possessed a workable understanding of the germ theory of disease or immunology, it's perhaps understandable why the Cayuses came to believe Dr. Whitman either wasn't trying as hard to save sick Indian children, or was outright poisoning them with his so-called medicines.

The Whitman Massacre drove frightened settlers west across the Cascades and was the catalyst which led to the Oregon Territory finally coming under the protection of the United States government. But, politics being a predictable evil, the event was also used as an excuse to eradicate tribes and steal their land throughout the decades bookending the Civil War.

Nevertheless, Marcus Whitman's motto, engraved on his statue, was a good one: "My plans require time and distance." Add "beer" to this and it could double as my own motto.

While I stood scribbling notes, a tour guide approached. "The marble throughout this rotunda was quarried in Alaska," he said.

"No kidding?"

"Yes, sir. And if you'll notice that chandelier there"—he meant the five-ton bronze one hanging by a hundred-foot chain from the dome's opulent ceiling—"it was made special by the Tiffany Company of New York, as were the firepots in the room's four corners. In fact, this building features the largest collection of Tiffany lighting in the world." When I raised an eyebrow, he kept on. "Are you just visiting, sir? Where's home for you? And what, if you don't mind my asking, are you writing in that little yellow notebook?"

While fending off this onslaught, I wondered why he was so intent on telling me about the stonework and lighting. I was just another tourist, after all. But a quick look around provided the answer: of the three-dozen people milling about the steps and rotunda, I was the only one who'd both passed puberty and wasn't being paid to chaperone.

"Why do the legislators need all this Tiffany lighting?" I asked. "Wouldn't regular old General Electrics do just fine?" But the guide was already moving away, pasting on a smile for a group of towheads being dragged through the door by their harried-looking adult guardian.

On the fourth floor, I peeked into the House and Senate galleries, which were both out of session. Washington legislators are "citizen-legislators." This means they're part-timers—people with actual jobs, in other words—which is probably how it should be in the other Washington, too. After glancing inside a third floor reception room full of heavy red velvet and teakwood and more marble (Italian this time) and still more ostentatious Tiffany chandeliers, I passed a huge bust of George Washington, his nose rubbed brassy by schoolkids.

Capitol Campus was designed by the same guys who designed Central Park. Back outside, I found the grass honed, the rhododendrons in bloom, the war memorials elaborate, and the gardens sunken. There was even a slab of rock from Wake Island commemorating Pearl Harbor. While initially skeptical, I ended up enjoying the Capitol. The experience wasn't lame at all. If there hadn't still been beer in need of drinking, I could've spent all day there, just lazing around the grounds and people-watching.

Headed back downtown along Capitol Way, it seemed Olympia had validated Burton's advice on avoiding idleness ("wit without employment is a disease," he writes, "the rust of the soul, a plague"), because after having my tacos bombed I'd been ready to give in to melancholy, whereas busying myself exploring Capitol Campus had left me feeling spry and cheerful. Burton understood the mind cannot help but constantly do its work, which is to ponder and gauge, to ruminate and predict, and so when things are going poorly one's only relief is to somehow distract the mind from being quite so mindful. He also writes that cousin-german to idleness is solitariness, a condition (especially if voluntary, as was mine) that causes us to run headlong into labyrinths of anxious thought. All of this seemed to suggest it was high time to chat with a few Olympians over a beer, although the gentle scholar does warn against fending off solitude "with lewd fellows in taverns and alehouses."

Nevertheless, I typed the magic words . . . *beer near me . . . .* and was directed to a bar with the irresistible name of Cryptotropa.

The route passed through Sylvester Park. Like many parks, it was full of homeless people. They lay on blankets beside overstuffed shopping carts, squinting and sipping from bottles tucked into paper bags. Midway across, I paused beside a group sharing a makeshift lunch. They had a dog with them, and the animal gave me a funny look. What'd stopped me was a statue of John Rankin Rodgers, a political radical twice voted governor of Washington and the author of the Barefoot Schoolboy Law, which codified the bleeding-heart promise of a basic education for poor kids. But what would Governor Rodgers have made of the barefoot forty-year-old men sparking joints in the shadow of his memorial?

The dog lunged at me and barked.

"Quiet, Doobie!" one of the men shouted.

#

Sidetracked by the well-lit and tidy Orca Books, I discovered a collection of stories by Lucia Perillo, a local author. The title, *Happiness is a Chemical in the Brain,* was so flabbergastingly depressing that it might've doubled as title for David Guterson's commencement speech at The Evergreen State College. Reading, I could almost feel the gloom of small-town life in the Pacific Northwest. "Inside every dissolute romantic," Perillo writes, "there's a brooding Schopenhauer, with a chronic melancholy that he nurses like a sourball in his cheek."

Lovely words, and ones which suggest the book's title might be truer than we'd like to believe. What if happiness is merely an illusion born of dopamine with a biological purpose not so different from our constant anxiety? What if Jack Kerouac and his Buddhist friends were right, and life's essence is to desire things we probably can't have, or at least can't have for very long, and thus to suffer in equivalence to how stubbornly we chase after wrongheaded notions of bliss?

Back on the street, I passed another park called Artesian Commons. It too was full of homeless people, one of whom had left a quote from Bukowski in chalk on a brick wall:

We are all going to die

All of us

What a circus!

That alone should make us

Love each other

But it doesn't

Verse that might've inspired both Robert Burton and the humanitarian spirit of John Rankin Rodgers, and words that inspired me to drink a pint at Cryptatropa. It proved quite the place. Much like the Mirkwood & Shire Café was a Middle-earth bar, Cryptatropa was a satanic bar. After admiring the ghostly nativity scene in the streetside window, I entered and ran my fingers along the cool porcelain of an old-fashioned embalming table. Then, atop a different table far back in the eerie red-lit gloom, I noticed a small man crouched as if in genuflection. Once my eyes adjusted, I realized this man was actually a bat-winged, cloven-hooved, curly-horned and cavalierly handsome Prince of Darkness.

I considered taking a seat at the Devil's table and perusing Burton, but reading the *Anatomy* there would've probably been overkill. Instead, I bellied up to the rail. With his stringy hair, pasty skin, sleeveless black shirt, purple tights, and leather wrist cuffs, the heavyset bartender looked a lot like the rock star Meat Loaf, whose 1977 album *Bat Out of Hell* was a favorite of my knife-wielding older brother. The beer he poured me, though—Cavatica Stout from Fort George Brewing in Astoria, Oregon—was dark, dense, and perfectly in tune with the underworld theme. The Latinate origins of *cavatica* refers to something born in caves and darkness. Cavatica is also a species of large and scary-looking barn spider, as well as the last name of E. B. White's famous literary arachnid, Charlotte. Best of all, it was only $2.50 during happy hour.

Cryptatropa was a true feast of oddities. A Rock-ola groaned and droned German pipe organ, and a series of confessional pews were jammed into vampy little grottos. The walls were painted black and there was a plethora of heavy red velvet, much as in the reception room back at the Legislative Building, while a few *Blair Witch* stick sculptures dangled from the ceiling. The patio was empty (creatures of the night sleep through happy hour), and the bar had just one other customer besides myself, a man whose conversation soon had me wishing something wicked might come along and bite his neck.

"It ain't like a carb's an engine," he said. "It ain't no tranny, either."

"Carb's just a carb," Meat Loaf said.

"A goddamn *carb*," the man said. "A carburetor. Little fucking thing that mixes air and gas. I mean, that's all it really is."

Meat Loaf shrugged. "But what can you do?"

"Everyone's aiming to screw you these days," the man said. "You show me an honest mechanic and I'll show you Santa Claus."

"I hear you, brother," Meat Loaf said.

"I mean, I *work* for a living. I drag my tired ass outta bed every damn morning and if that truck won't run, there ain't nobody gonna pick up the slack for me."

"No doubt," Meat Loaf said.

"And those crooks want five-hundred freaking bucks just to pop the hood."

"It's highway robbery," Meat Loaf said.

"You're damn right it is."

"You're right."

"I *know* I'm right," the carb man said.

"Well, I hear you."

"I'm sure as shit glad somebody does."

"No doubt, brother," Meat Loaf said.

And so on and so on. If it turns out that Christians like Robert Burton are correct and Hell really does exist, I can only hope it won't be quite as purgatorial as listening to half-buzzed guys bitch about auto maintenance. Still, the Cavatica was a tasty brew and the hour perfect for drinking it. I wanted to bask in Olympia's netherworld. I craved iniquity and vice, maybe even a little black magic. Was it too much to ask for some ashen-faced baddie to emerge from the restrooms in a twirl of smoke, sporting a velvet cape and a van dyke goatee?

Then I noticed the backbar—a wall of precisely-fitted blond wood and sleek mirrors. Atop it were posed a series of eyeless dolls and animal skulls, as well as a pair of taxidermied cougars with yellowed cobwebs draped between their ears. The cougars pawed and growled at the ghosts which surely hovered all around us.

"That bar almost looks like it could be Prohibition Era," I said.

"Actually," Meat Loaf said, "it was designed by Frank Lloyd Wright."

Sure it was, bub, I thought.

"You ever try Midas?" asked the guy down the rail.

"Not sure they do carb work," Meat Loaf said.

"Well, fuck me running . . ."

Then I asked what was up with all the occult paraphernalia, somehow stopping myself from also asking what old Frank Lloyd Wright would've made of that. Judging from Meat Loaf's expression, however, I gathered he may have answered this particular question a time or two before. Still, he was patient with me. "The owner was a goth collector," he said. "Guess he just needed somewhere to put his stuff."

"The wife didn't appreciate Lucifer over there squatting on the kitchen table?"

"I grew up around here. For the longest time this place was just a filling station."

The Rock-ola switched songs. This time it played the soundtrack to a nightmare: all lonely echoes and groans, howling wolves, moaning winds, and the laughter of evil children. For a moment, I could've sworn it was the opening of "Thriller."

"Looks like progress to me," I said. "I grew up in Illinois and our state capital—Springfield—really could've used a little craft beer and Satanism."

"No doubt, brother," Meat Loaf said, and then resumed hypothesizing as to the best spots around Olympia for affordable carburetor repair.

LOST IN THE BEERMUDA TRIANGLE

I meant to continue my tour of Northwest capitals the following morning, but on the way to Salem, Oregon lay the Beaver State's *real* capital: Beervana, aka the Beermuda Triangle.

While silly, the nickname is also accurate, as there's so much great beer in this particular swath of Southeast Portland that an ale-loving guy could simply vanish amidst the bubbling waves of wort. In fact, it's the beeriest neighborhood in what is quite possibly the most beer-centric city in America. I'd worked there a few years back, pouring pints for the hopheads at the Green Dragon (named after the famous Boston tavern where the Sons of Liberty conspired to dress up like Mohawks and steep British tea in saltwater) which lay square in the Triangle's sudsy heart. Put bluntly, a true beer lover cannot honorably drive past Beervana without stopping. It'd be like a bibliophile skipping Hemingway's house in Key West, or a fan of rock music passing through Memphis without touring Graceland.

But I had to get to Portland before I could commence drinking all that beer, and as soon as I left Olympia an Old Testament-style deluge pounded Interstate 5. Caught by surprise, I squeezed the wheel in both hands and drove straight into the eye of this white squall, hunched and sweating and muttering obscenities as walls of gray water crashed over the Honda. I couldn't see jack-shit, as the kids say, although I felt the all-wheel drive kick in to avoid a hydroplane spin that would've almost certainly ended with the vehicle flipping a half-dozen times and my freshly-ejected body landing in a roadside ditch like an old tube sock stuffed with tomatoes.

Why not just slow down and pull over? Because I was far from alone on the roadway and when Northwest drivers see a blinding typhoon of wind and rain, it's their curious instinct to accelerate. Speeding vehicles menaced my bumper, honking with impatience, only to swap lanes and whip right past me, tossing even more water onto an already opaque windshield. Long beleaguered by the rain, my fellow drivers seemed to want to show Mother Nature who was boss, to take a measure of insane revenge against the soggy bitch by daring her to do her absolute worst. Keep in mind, these are the same drivers who on dry roads with perfect visibility will plod along five miles per hour under the posted limit.

Then, as if I'd punched through an invisible wall, it was clear skies the rest of the way.

Washington was separated from the Oregon Territory along the Columbia in 1853, by order of Millard Fillmore (whom a recent polling determined was never actually a president), and I crossed over that river on the Vancouver-Portland bridge. Twenty minutes later, I walked into one of the finest breweries in the Triangle: Hair of the Dog on southeast Yamhill.

It was started by a chef and homebrewer named Alan Sprints whose beers were at the initial forefront of bottle fermentation, barrel-aging, and Belgian-inspired experiments—all standard markers of today's craft beer. The tasting room was Portland Chic: repurposed industrial with exposed piping and duct work and a garage door open to the street. The picnic tables were full of people sipping tasters, not drinking pints, which was a good sign. Taster boards cost a little more by the ounce, which meant these folks hadn't come simply to get buzzed on IPA, but to experience the width and breadth of Hair of the Dog's lineup.

Speaking of tasters, mine arrived in elegant little snifters. It's important glassware do justice to a beverage, especially when that beverage is named after the well-known Portland beer writer Fred Eckhardt. The Fred was a big golden ale brewed with rye and Belgian candy sugar (which results in a beer of paradoxical dryness, as yeasts digest simple sugars more readily than malted grains). Fred Eckhardt was Hair of the Dog's very first customer back in 1993, and he chronicled the craft beer revolution from its inception. One of his more eccentric ideas is that we should *listen* to our beer and enjoy that faint crackling as the head dissipates. I put my ear to the glass, but if Fred was talking, I couldn't make out the words. He also published books, such as *The Essentials of Beer Style*, which is dedicated to his mother, who was run down and killed in a crosswalk in where else but Everett, Washington. Sadly enough, she'd been headed out to buy her son a sixer of Rainier as thanks for helping around the house.

Then I tried Cherry Michael, a Flanders-style red. The Michael was named after Michael Jackson—the bearded and beer-loving one from England, not the Moonwalking and chimpanzee-owning one from Gary, Indiana—whose advocacy of Flanders ales, particularly in his widely influential *Beer Companion,* helped keep this endangered style alive. Modeled on Rodenbach, the Cherry Michael left an already four-year-old sour ale on cherries in French oak for another four years. Balsamic notes combined with lush pinot noir and vanilla, all girded up with a tannic undercurrent. Tasting the Cherry Michael raised a question relatively new to America's beer scene: was this beer really still a beer? Because that acidic-yet-sweet flavor was unmistakably vinous, the ABV potent, and the overall feel one which encouraged wannabe beer writers to wax poetic much like a wine critic.

"You really should try the Cherry Michael," I said to the guy on the next stool over. "It's interesting."

"I think I will," he said, and upon sipping the concoction I saw the true beer connoisseur's light, a gently rising glow, suffuse his being.

We got to talking. His name was Colin. He'd been living in Los Angeles, where the craft beer scene wasn't so hot. He'd just moved back to Portland and Hair of the Dog had called to him like a siren. "I missed this place so much when I was down there," he said. "My girlfriend was finishing grad school, but once she was done I begged her to let us come back."

Then I told him about my beer travels, that I was ultimately headed south to Eugene. "I went to college at the U of O," Colin said. "You should start at Oakshire. It's a great first beer sort of place. Ninkasi is walking distance from there, too. Ninkasi was the mothership."

"It got the ball rolling beer-wise?"

"Eugene's special," he said. "If Portland didn't exist, that's where I'd want to spend the rest of my life."

"The beer's that good?"

"Everything about it is good. It's enlightened. You'll see."

Enlightened? I liked the sound of that. When I also mentioned my plans to visit the coast, Colin brightened even more. "You can't miss de Garde out in Tillamook," he said. "They're top three in the world for revolutionary wild ales."

I couldn't help but frown. *Tillamook?* I'd been in Tillamook once, years before, and there was nothing in Tillamook except cows and a factory that turned what cows leaked into cheese.

Colin glanced at me aslant. "Wait, you know about wild ales, don't you?"

I said of course, absolutely, and rattled off enough factoids about spontaneous fermentation and the impact of local yeast terroir to assure Colin he wasn't revealing secrets to the uninitiated. Seeming relieved, he promised I'd love the place.

After he tabbed out, I thanked him for the recommendations.

"No problem," he said. "We're all beer people, right?"

"Right!"

Sure enough, Colin proved once again that beer people are most often good people, too.

#

At Cascade Brewing on Belmont Street, I entered through another lifted garage door. Even after the industrial quadrant's recent gentrification, these doors remain such a symbol of the Portland beer scene that a brewery without a garage door—or any need of a garage door—might have to install one just to fit in. Redevelopment will only intensify, of course, and soon enough Southeast will be just another high-rent Pearl District full of soulless moneylenders who'd cut their auntie's throat for the latest Apple gadget. Considering how hip Portland has become and how many people are pouring in from elsewhere, this transformation is probably inevitable, and it may well bring certain benefits—but what will become of the beer and the beer culture?

Cascade seemed to be doing just fine on both accounts, though. In fact, it took quite a bit of waiting and lurking to finally swoop a seat at the bar. The taps emerged from wine casks built into the wall, a hint of what was in store, as Cascade is known for its lactobacillus soured ales (they call their Southeast location the "House of Sour"), most of which are barrel-aged. From bourbon barrels to French oak to American wine casks, Cascade has beer maturing and blending in over 1,400 barrels. For a guy like me, a place like this is dangerous. It's a compulsive gambler entering the Mirage, or a sex addict hitting the Red Light District. The House of Sour tempts a man to go overboard. To blow his roll. To sniff and sip and fawn until he's made an utter parody of himself.

The barman approached—and I say *barman* instead of "bartender" or "beertender" (let alone the dismally neutered "server") because the guy was living the role. His manner was salted with superciliousness, suggesting a tourist like me had best not treat him like just another tap monkey, because he knew his beer and took pride in his expertise. Notably, his handlebar mustache was waxed to points, like Stalin or maybe the Pringles guy—or, better yet, like Fred Eckhardt, who'd sported the same jaunty facial hair. Best of all, while welcoming me to his establishment, the barman called me "comrade."

Comrade!

Here was what I'd come to Portland for. A little of the old Wobblie red solidarity and a dose of recognition that we (meaning me and the Pringles guy) were fighting the good fight and would continue fighting even if rents were going through the roof and Chipotle burrito restaurants were popping up every ten feet and the working class were being less-than-delicately scooted farther and farther away from the city center. Nevertheless, I was so flattered this fellow had recognized me as one of his own—or at least pretended to—that I almost could've kissed him, had he not been a man and had it not been for that ridiculous mustache.

Then we got down to business. First up, Sang Rouge. It was plummy and acidic, aged partly in foudres up to three years—not quite Cherry Michael territory, but definitely interesting. The follow up, Sang Royale, was a boozy sour aged alongside cabernet sauvignon grapes in wine and port barrels. Complex and delightful beers, both.

Later, I was reading and enjoying still more tasters when someone grabbed my shoulder, hauled me halfway off my stool, and shouted, "Hey, you douchebag!"

"Max?"

"What the fuck are you doing here, man?"

"Tasting sour beers. What are *you* doing here?"

"Getting wasted," he said.

We'd worked together a few years back at the Green Dragon, which stood just across Belmont. The Dragon had briefly been an independently-owned star of Portland's craft beer scene, until financing ran short and ownership fell into bitter disagreement and the pub was swooped up by Rogue Ales, a large craft brewer headquartered out of coastal Newport that many in the local beer community were skeptical of, based on Rogue's corny marketing schemes, higher than average prices, and subpar food. The Dragon had been special, though. Besides a world-class rotating tap list, it'd been one of the first pubs to regularly hold meet-the-brewer events, a practice which has since become commonplace, and it featured interesting little touches such as a "secret tap" meant only for the rarest of kegs and in-the-know clientele.

As for Max, he was as I remembered, still pale and skinny, his hair dyed black and waist length (although now graying at the roots), his arms covered in a lively tattooing of 666s and demons. The hair and tattoos were part of his look, as he drummed in a Norwegian-inspired black metal band which, at least at one time, had performed under the name Sexecutioner. But Max wasn't as scary as he looked. In fact, he'd once shown me a love song he'd written. The lyrics were inscribed on a tea paper scroll tied with ribbon, the edges charred with a cigarette lighter to a suitably ancient look. The song's title, however, was pure black metal—"Satan Raped My Soul Raw" or something along those lines.

I asked Max how life was treating him these days.

"I'm excellent," he said, but then he launched into the tale of how he'd lost his job at the Dragon. He'd gotten a DUI in the wee hours and an investigator from Oregon Liquor Control had found this rather strange, considering Max was at work until well past the state-mandated last call. The higher-ups at Rogue Ales soon caught wind.

"Five years I worked for those fucksticks," Max said. "Five years of bending over backwards and cleaning puke out of the urinals and mopping the floor, and those pussy-ass backstabbing Republicans *fired* me. Just like that—boom! Like I was some stinky fucking shit they needed to scrape off their shiny fucking shoes."

I glanced out the garage door and across the street. "So I take it you don't visit the Dragon these days?"

This launched Max into a spittle-flying torrent which made his previous display sound like lines from Emily Dickinson. And never in this diatribe did he show the least recognition that he might've *deserved* to be fired, considering he'd apparently been drinking his employer's beer after hours, on the clock. Not that we all hadn't enjoyed drinking Rogue's beer after hours—we most certainly had—but while doing so we'd known and recognized that rules were indeed being broken and fireable offenses committed, which was the standard cost of having a little fun. In Max's defense, though, he'd clearly been drinking all day—all summer, perhaps. Slurring and woozy, glazed eyes and fermented breath.

Something briefly caught my attention across the room, but when I turned back Max had walked away without even saying goodbye. This hurt my feelings a little, but was also a bit of a relief. I felt bad for his harboring such resentment against Rogue, though. After all, we'd had some good times at the Dragon, even after the change in ownership. It was my first job working exclusively with craft beer, and I'd learned a ton. Most importantly, the Dragon was where I first experienced the emotional depth, the love, of Portland's unique pub culture. The community unites around beer. In a very real sense, craft beer *is* Southeast Portland.

Leaving the House of Sour, I hoped Max was wrong about Rogue, and that the Dragon would remain a part of Beervana we could all be proud of, even if the spirit wasn't quite the same as before. After all, Rogue had promised during the buyout that they'd leave the pub largely unchanged, that they were merely providing the capital necessary to keep a much-loved taproom afloat through the recession. Just a few months later, though, I was to find out that the Dragon had been slain and rebranded as the Rogue East Side Pub. Talk about a revolution.

#

But beer isn't the only thing Portlanders unite around. They also like a bit of smut—although even a windowless venue like Sassy's, just around the corner from the House of Sour, serves reliably terrific beer.

The place was dead at that time of day, though. Just a lot of great taps, myself and my little notebook, and a few regulars who hardly seemed to notice the nude young women romping around onstage. Not being a regular myself, however, these nude young women struck me as quite novel, and so I ordered a stout—a rich, decadent, chocolatey stout—and took a seat at the rail. The latest dancer was short, gymnastic, and pale as spilt milk. I sipped the stout (Chaos, it was called, from Barley Brown's out in eastern Oregon) while she spritzed the pole with Windex and gave it a good wiping down. How *Portland* was this?—sipping a wonderful Northwest ale in the early afternoon haze of a low-rent strip club.

Not that Sassy's was necessarily unique, mind you. Per capita, the City of Roses has more exotic dancing establishments than Las Vegas. What? Why? How? Because a refreshingly libertine interpretation of Article 1, Section 8 of the state constitution protects free expression, and therefore municipal ordinances (namely zoning restrictions) that might otherwise impede artistic freedoms, such as nude dance—which the honorable justices of the Oregon Supreme Court have adjudicated falls squarely under the umbrella of free expression—are not allowed.

The dancer's music came on and she banged around the stage, rolling her muscular hips and snapping her hair. Then she shimmied loose of her bra and immediately launched into a series of handstands, her legs cantilevered and her abdominals trembling from the strain of it all.

Beguiled by her talents, I sipped the Chaos, draped a few bills over the rail, and reminisced on my time in Portland. A city of animal rights activists who spend lavishly to support feral cat colonies, a place where to litter would be punishable by flogging, and a city where, despite the odds, progressivism actually seems to be winning. Teddy Roosevelt would've been proud of Sassy's, I think. Robert Burton, too, although he does cite the experiences of a Burgundian traveler in Brazil named John Lerius—as well as the essays of Lerius's countryman, Michel de Montaigne—as evidence that unclothed women are paradoxically less a spur to lasciviousness than the clothed variety. Nor should we overlook Burton's analysis of Portland's distinct lack of pasties. "It is as if," the gentle scholar writes, "by dint of custom and practice, the denizens of the Rose City had not even *heard* of the pasty. As if, by some devilishly provocative oversight, they'd nary the notion that a teasing coverage of certain sectors of the female form is, was, and always will be quite customary . . ."

The Brussels lace was notched low by the dancer's third and final song, whereas her lacy bottoms had disappeared entirely. She was naked as the truth, and the truth was, despite my appreciation of Portland's enlightened attitude as to exotic dance, I still felt a smidge guilty hanging around Sassy's. Maybe once a Midwesterner, always a Midwesterner?

While I needed to get moving if I was going to make Salem by dinnertime, it's not easy to leave the goodness that is Beervana. So, standing outside of Sassy's and squinting against the abrasive daylight, I struck a reasonable compromise.

. . . beer near me . . .

Baerlic Brewing was tucked away on a leafy side street. The Old English name means "of barley" and that was the scent I caught upon stepping inside. Above the taps hung a sign: THE BEER HERE IS NEAR & DEAR. I liked that very much, much as I liked my tasters of a 13% dry-hopped barleywine called the Old Blood and Guts, and a pale ale that proclaimed itself "Brettanomyces-like." Here was a true distillation of Portland beer culture: a tiny brewpub in a residential neighborhood may safely assume its patrons are sophisticated enough to approach a syrup-thick and licorice-like beverage that's potency is on par with a glass of Bordeaux, as well as decipher hyphenated multisyllabic descriptions straight out of a chemistry textbook.

Again, I really needed to get on with my comparison of state capitals, but they don't call it the Beermuda Triangle for nothing, and a few blocks south on 11th Avenue—while searching for a place with the intriguing name of The Beermongers—I ended up at Apex, which had enough taps to wet the whistles of half the city. I took a session ale out to the beer garden and sat under a big Weihenstephaner umbrella. All was decidedly well. Later, while sipping and admiring a sign specifying where tricyclists should park (as opposed to the more traditional bicyclists), I noticed another little sign in a window catty-corner across Division Street.

The Beermongers.

There, in a space that might've reasonably been confused for a homebrewer's walk-in closet, I chatted with some locals who were rooting for the Hillsboro Hops minor league baseball team to beat the Aquasox—a team from where else but Everett, Washington, the same ragtag mill town which shot the Wobblies on Port Gardner Bay, ran down Fred Eckhardt's mother in a crosswalk, and entrusted yours truly with ensuring its youth understand the importance of always rightly employing the Oxford comma.

A CAPITAL TOUR: PART TWO — SALEM

Besides those involuntarily committed at Oregon State Hospital (formerly the Oregon State Insane Asylum), it seems no Oregonian has ever actually been to Salem. Rumor has it, the governor hasn't even been to Salem. Furthermore, after winning election, numerous state legislators reportedly had to ask their constituents where Salem was located, and if it was *truly* incumbent upon them to go live there. While a majority of Portlanders are theoretically aware of their state capital's existence, and understand if they took the wrong exit off I-5 they might conceivably stumble into Salem, and therefore have to figure out some way of escaping Salem, there remains genuine skepticism as to whether it's a legitimately real place.

I wasn't quite sure what to expect, either. To make matters murkier, thanks to my tarrying in Beervana, darkness had fallen by the time I reached Vagabond Brewing, which sat in an industrial park on Salem's northern edge. On a dimly lit stage, yet another young woman with blue hair strummed an acoustic guitar, working her way through some Dylan tunes while I settled in beside the taps with a timely glass of the On the Road red ale—timely both because Bob Dylan was influenced by the Beat Generation, and also because I was thinking of putting Jack Kerouac on the syllabus for my upcoming travel writing class. I'd always loved his books, though. In fact, somewhere amidst the legalese and appellate briefs and endless cups of ramen noodles that constituted my law school experience, I reread *On the Road* for the third or fifth time and Dean and Sal really started whispering to me. *Hit the road, pal,* they said. *You don't know where you're going, but you gotta go. . .*

And so, on the day after graduation, I tossed my diploma in the trunk and lit out for the West Coast. I recall taking a last glance around Illinois, shrugging, and then aiming an even older and higher-mileage Honda west down the interstate, with no intention of stopping until the beer improved. My old cat traveled with me, too. He was a most excellent cat—agreeable, dapper, loyal (insofar as feline loyalty goes), and reliably comical with people—but he hadn't been a particularly good traveler. In fact, despite enough tranquilizers to fell a gorilla, he howled and hissed for all 2,200 miles of our journey. But the West is where lost Americans have always gone to reinvent themselves, and Portland was the only West Coast city my cat and I had any hope of affording, so that's where we washed up.

While Kerouac was a cat guy himself—as a boy, Jack was considered an oddball by the neighbor kids because he wouldn't allow them to torture kittens—my journey west was hardly Kerouacian. Still, it was the best journey I could manage at the time, and Kerouac's work is possessed of a peculiarly American variety of rootless and drifting wisdom. That, and exposing impressionable students to the Beats just might screw up a few otherwise promising careers, and life in contemporary America could only be enriched by a few more screw-ups like that.

Above the taps hung a banner—HOME IS THE JOURNEY WE MAKE. Some truth in that one, or so it seemed. I'd bounced around so much in the years since I'd taken old Jack's advice that I couldn't rightly say where home was anymore, or if home was anywhere at all. Because what does that word even mean if you never plan to go back—or if you can't?

In this melancholy state of mind, I approached the stage and asked the girl if she wouldn't mind covering Dylan's "Subterranean Homesick Blues."

"Sorry, honey," she said, "but I don't know that one. Is it a favorite of yours?"

"Not necessarily," I said, and put a couple bucks in her tip jar. "I'm just familiar with it."

#

As it turned out, it was a heavy travel weekend and all the local motels were either booked solid or asking exorbitant rates, and so—because I read too much Kerouac and became an English teacher instead of a lawyer—I found myself checking into one of the dirtiest motels in a life full of dirty motels. In fact, the hovel was so disheartening that I dropped my bags and immediately headed downtown where, at Kraftworks Taphouse, I met John and Alex.

The three of us had a long talk about higher education, as John was a Ph.D. candidate and Alex was helping him start up an educational consulting business. John's enthusiasm was infectious, and midway through my beer I found myself in agreement that teaching was a noble calling and that we educators had a duty to hold ourselves to a higher standard than caste and salary might otherwise indicate.

"Teaching," John said, clasping my shoulder, "is all about connecting people with their dreams."

The Tony Robbins-ishness of this got me wondering how he and Alex had come to work together. "Well, it's funny you should ask," John said, and then admitted that Alex had been dating his daughter for a while there. And only then did I realize Alex couldn't have been more than twenty-two or so, and that John was a somewhat older Ph.D. student, his beard having likely seen a dose of Just For Men. But I was in Salem, Oregon for the night, and so I passed a few hours sipping and talking with these guys about the purported joys of teaching. I told them about Vagabond and *On the Road.* I even admitted I'd been thinking of quitting the profession entirely. Of just standing behind a bar five nights a week and collecting tips.

"I'd earn twice as much money," I said.

"That's not the way," John said. "You can't let the world dictate your worth."

"And I'd probably still have more time to write."

"What you have is a chance to help people, to share what you've learned and been taught. To throw that away would be a shame."

While I wasn't sure John was entirely right, by the time I tabbed out his enthusiasm for all things education had rubbed off and I felt a little more optimistic. This lasted until I got back to the motel and realized my room was adjacent a dance club called the Flamenco. There'd been nobody there earlier, and so I'd hardly noticed it. But the Flamenco was apparently an after-hours club. Now the parking lot was jammed with lifted trucks and low-riders with big booming subwoofers in their trunks. Mexican pop screamed through the night—and right through my room's cracker-thin walls.

Come one a.m., I gave up on sleep and walked over to the Flamenco. I ordered a Pacifico and jammed a wedge of lime down the sweating neck. The place was curious, basically just a big hot shed filled with fake smoke. As for the clientele, the women all dressed alike in tight white pants and towering heels, with big hoop earrings and lots of makeup, but the men were another story. Half wore cowboy boots and Stetsons and two-stepped with their dates, whereas the other half dressed in baggy hip-hop gear and danced in a manner suggestive of anonymous coitus—all to the same music, remarkably enough. Whatever the case, everyone seemed to be having fun.

Outside was a little taco stand meant to catch the hungry after last call. While heating my order, the grillerman looked me over. "You just in there, amigo?"

I said "Si," and he laughed, shook his head, and handed me a paper plate loaded with tacos dressed with cilantro and fresh salsa. "You dance with any señoritas?"

When I confessed I'd never learned the two-step, he howled with still more laughter.

Back in the last-chance motel, I searched the *Anatomy* for suggestions on how I might finally catch some sleep. After absorbing the ancient wisdom, I snapped off the lamp and curled onto my right side so that my liver (the kitchen of my humours), could rest comfortably under my stomach (now happily full of tacos), and concentrated on telling myself the linens were "clean and sweet" as Burton would have them, and not—as they actually appeared—fouled and yellow.

An hour later, because it's well established those unaccustomed to strange noises cannot properly sleep amongst them, I imagined the gangsta rap blasting from the parking lot was the sweet music commended by Ficinus, or as Jobertus recommends, the pleasant murmur of *lene sonantis aquæ,* or gently trickling water. An hour after *that,* when the cacophony of car alarms and blatting engines had yet to abate, I began to consider the more drastic advice of Piso and Borde, who recommend a draught of strong drink.

#

Burton's causes of melancholy are telling. Spirits, demons, witches, and astronomy—all get run down in exhausting detail, as do seemingly all of the temperaments and foibles of mankind: our greed and passions and jealousy, our failing marriages and soured friendships, our want of honor and fear of death. Some philosophers, according to Burton, "lay the greatest fault upon the soul, excusing the body; others again, accusing the body, excuse the soul."

The upshot is that four centuries ago nobody knew what caused depression, just like nobody really knows today. We merely substitute talk of synapses and serotonin for the supernatural. The mechanisms are understood, at least in part, but not the root. Medical science would have us believe it's a biological malfunction, or that perhaps there's some evolutionary benefit to anxiety, but none of that addresses melancholy's real mystery: the manner in which a consciousness viewing itself is bent over time by its own lens. This, or something like it, lay at the heart of Burton's obsession. The soul, he notes, is both a miserable captive and an alien to the body, and as he aged and his thinking matured, so did his views on what he'd written of himself, which necessitated the numerous reeditions of his *Anatomy*.

With the old scholar in mind, I determined to visit the Museum of Mental Health at Oregon State Hospital. While it's since been renovated, the old asylum was the setting for the adaptation of the Oregonian novelist Ken Kesey's *One Flew Over the Cuckoo's Nest*—a book inspired by the author's own experiences working nights in a psychiatric ward while attending graduate school at Stanford in the early 1960s. But the history of Oregon State Hospital is darker and stranger than anything Kesey ever dreamt up. Mass poisoning, eugenics, impromptu psychosurgery—the 20th century medievalism which took place inside OSH would've made Robert Burton gulp.

I parked on a loop of manicured grounds. OSH remains a working hospital today, a handsome redbrick building with white trim, and the museum sits below some five-hundred actual patients.[4] Originally, the state asylum was in Portland, near today's Beermuda Triangle. The monomaniacs, the demented, and the howl-at-the-mooners were all housed there, along with those suffering melancholia. These people were moved down to Salem in the 1880s, and the modern OSH developed, adding buildings, a working farm, and even a crematorium that would later become a symbol of how the mentally ill are forgotten.

---

[4] Compare this to 1895, when according to the historian Diane Goeres-Gardner, the population of the asylum was double what it is today, while Oregon's total population was only about 30,000, meaning one in thirty Oregonians was institutionalized. Maybe the rain really does drive people nuts?

After paying the modest admission, I visited a sleeping room in Ward C, where an iron cot sat beneath a window with elaborate woodwork. But upon closer inspection, this woodwork was actually a grid of metal bars disguised with a clever paint-job.

Down the hall was an exhibit of the hospital's food service. In the fall of 1942, a busy cook asked a brain-damaged psychiatric patient named George Nosen to fetch some powdered milk for the scrambled eggs. Nosen helpfully did as told, grabbing a large canister from downstairs. The distracted cook then poured six pounds of sodium fluoride—a common roach poison—into the egg mixture. Come dinner, patients collapsed writhing upon the floor. They screamed in agony and vomited blood. Hundreds were sickened. Forty-seven died. The morgue at OSH being small, bodies were stacked in the hallways.

Next, a *Cuckoo's Nest* exhibit which included quotes from Kesey's novel as well as screenshots and memorabilia from the Oscar-sweeping 1975 film—most notably (and eerily), a black and white television which played a continuous loop of Jack Nicholson and friends watching a baseball game on that very same TV. Below was a replica of the marble hydrotherapy machine that Chief Bromden heaves through the window in making his climactic escape. Television arose as a common and effective treatment tool for the mentally ill in the late 1950's, or at least a common and effective sedative, and largely replaced hydrotherapy treatment which had been common practice for decades. Meditating upon his own experiences with hydrotherapy, Theodore Roethke, who was institutionalized for manic-depression numerous times, wrote, "Six hours a day I lay me down / Within this tub but cannot drown." The poem describes the frightening sensation for a few stanzas, and finishes with this: "I do not laugh; I do not cry; / I'm sweating out the will to die. / My past is sliding down the drain; / I soon will be myself again."

Then I noticed an old-fashioned black phone. I'd seen a few such phones placed throughout the museum. Curious, I lifted the conical earpiece and listened as a calm voice told of a man's suicide inside the hospital. The narrator had been the dead man's friend, and noted that "he must've wanted to die very badly," considering he'd done the act in a closet with a leather belt and therefore had to hold his own feet off the ground while strangulating.

I carefully replaced the earpiece.

Across the room sat another old-fashioned phone. A doctor read the case history of a patient named Melinda Applegate. For three solid minutes, I listened to a rundown of Melinda's dementia and biting, examinations of her flattened affect, fleshy abdomen, regular bowel movements and menstruations, and uncontrollable howling come nightfall. After fifty years in the asylum, Melinda died, and the doctor's voice clicked off like a ballpoint pen.

In the next room was a stainless steel table with metal restraints. It had a letter taped to its footplate. Dated from 1947, this letter was a request for funds by an OSH Superintendent named Dr. Evans. "Some of the relatives of our patients are clammering [sic] for the operation known as lobotomy," Dr. Evans writes, before extolling the virtues of trephining the skull with "a thin, sharp, knife like blade." The doctor explained this miracle procedure was especially effective on the depressed, and finished his appeal by requesting an allocation of $200 per lobotomy.

But at least Oregon performed its pseudo-scientific psycho-surgeries in a hospital with pseudo-scientific technique. Throughout the 1940s and '50s, by contrast, a doctor named Walter Freeman drove around the country to asylums dispensing miracles by the dozen. His treatment involved sedating patients and then hammering ice pick-like tools (or sometimes actual ice picks) through the flimsiest part of the eye sockets. Dr. Freeman performed about 3,500 of these procedures, relieving his patients of the burden of consciousness—and often of the ability to chew their food and use the toilet. Consider that Robert Burton wrote the *Anatomy* in the shadow of the Dark Ages, and yet the harshest cures he recommends—this from a man who debates the existence of witches and succubae—are bloodletting, cauterizing with hot irons, and applying leeches to the melancholic patient's hemorrhoids, none of which can hold a candle to drive-thru lobotomy. In fact, Burton's lone reference to trepanning suggests holes merely be drilled in the skull to let out the fuliginous vapours. Nowhere in all his pages does he suggest we dare *carve* the brain.

Around the same time that lobotomy came into use, many depressed Americans received electroshock therapy. Hemingway, a notoriously depressed alcoholic, tried it numerous times. The treatment was easy, cheap, and while inducing seizures via shooting electrical currents through the brain didn't actually cure the ailment, it did seem to do *something*. It also wasn't nearly as frightful as psychosurgery. In fact, if not for the dials and meters, the object could've been mistaken for a green tackle box. But instead of hooks and fishing lures, it held a car battery. A handwritten note reminded the clinician to turn the battery off after each use.

Amazingly enough, Ken Kesey reportedly arranged for a clandestine shock treatment of his own, so he could more authentically describe the experiences of Chief Bromden in his novel. Whereas another Northwest writer and an eventual friend of Kesey, Richard Brautigan (*Trout Fishing in America*), was institutionalized at age twenty for chucking a rock through a police station window in Eugene, only to tell his doctors that he was a poetic genius, upon which time they tried to burn the poetry from his brain with a dozen shock treatments in a month's time.

Around the corner hung a straitjacket. The thick white cloth was abraded around the lapel area, worn on both sides: chewed. Beside it, a cloth bag overflowed with handcuffs.

Ignoring more of those creepy old-fashioned phones, I finally came to the former office of Superintendent Dean Brooks, who played John Spivey in the film adaptation of *Cuckoo's Nest*. But a different film was playing in the office that day, one which concerned the 2004 discovery of thousands of canisters containing the cremated remains of a century's worth of mental patients. Some uncanny chemistry between copper and human ash had caused the canisters to grow an aquamarine fuzz like mother of pearl. While the weepy video insisted on the dignity of all those people socked away like so many tins of Folgers, the facelessness of such an end fit the dark history preserved throughout the Museum of Mental Health—a museum, suffice to say, which truly *belongs* in the Pacific Northwest.

#

Feeling about ready for my own coffee can, I decided to lighten the mood by comparing Salem's capitol grounds to those up in Olympia. While Seattle is the de facto capital of the Northwest, there's a longstanding tension between Seattle and Portland as to which city is truly the most livable, most eclectic, most progressive, and so on—and I wondered if this same spirit of competition imbued the state capitals.

Driving along Center Street on the far side of downtown, one first sees a huge golden Batman looming over Salem, much as the Dark Knight broods over Gotham City. Even though the lavish dome of Olympia's Legislative Building had seemed a bit gratuitous, Golden Batman seemed just plain silly. Following a quick but necessary detour to Santiam Brewing—where I sampled the notable Govna's Reserve, a rum barrel-aged coconut stout—I parked beside a World War II memorial and slung my backpack over my shoulders.

Across the park, a man with a leaf blower stood as if frozen, deaf in his protective headphones, the blower flattening a patch of grass. His utter stillness was spooky, like the Tin Man in need of oil, or maybe like a lobotomy patient escaped from OSH. Closer to the capitol building was a family of beavers, Oregon's official state rodent, sculpted out of bronze. They seemed to be hiding from the prospect of skinning in the shade of a giant sequoia. As for the building itself, it made quite a contrast to the marble and Tiffany opulence of Olympia's government buildings. Besides relief sculptures depicting the Oregon Trail and that gaudy statue atop the rotunda's bucket-like roof (up close, Golden Batman was actually a pioneer) the building could've been mistaken for an Art Deco prison. And a locked prison at that.

How had I forgotten it was the weekend?

Disappointed, I was about to leave when a state trooper pulled up, followed by another vehicle. An Asian family piled out and the trooper led them to the locked entrance. Sensing my chance, I hurried back to the door.

"Officer, will you be giving that family a tour?"

He looked me over and replied in the affirmative.

But when I asked if it'd be okay if I tagged along, the officer didn't respond.

"I wanted to check out the capitol building," I explained, "but forgot it was closed today."

In the face of his continued silence, I added that I'd driven all the way from Seattle. Then I watched this civil servant really look me over, gauging me, judging whether I was a threat or just some haggard-looking guy who for whatever reason actually wanted to tour the capitol building all by himself. The officer was about to relent and let me in. I saw it in his loosening body language. But then he spied my backpack—he looked right at it, at the straps, the dark bulk of nylon—and he set his jaw and shook his buzz-cut head.

"You'll have to come back on Monday during normal hours."

"But I'll be gone by then."

"Monday," the officer repeated, and then shut and locked the door in my face.

His prejudice got me thinking (yet again) of old Jack Kerouac, who had backpack issues of his own. Not only does a cop with a gun eye his pack suspiciously in *The Dharma Bums*, but people comment on it ungenerously and a malicious cowboy even tries to run it over with his truck. Kerouac senses why. There's talk of a rucksack revolution full of wanderers who refuse to work all day just for the privilege of buying superfluous consumer goods, of people living in a less materialistic and more nomadic, freer way. "I saw that my life was a vast glowing empty page," Kerouac writes, "and I could do anything I wanted."

This, of course, is hardly the sort of attitude police officers like to see from strangers come to their otherwise orderly and backpack-free little towns.

Hoping to give Salem another chance, I visited The Book Bin. Olympia's bookstore had been terrific, so The Book Bin had a lot to live up to. Things got off to a fair enough start. The aisles were wide and clean, the shelves well-stocked, the locals semi-recently showered. I even found an intriguing travelogue: *The Oregon Trail: A New American Journey* by an author with the pioneering name of Rinker Buck. Incredibly enough, he'd apparently retraced the Oregon Trail the old-fashioned way, in a covered wagon drawn by mules. I was thumbing through the chapters when I sensed eyes on me.

"Excuse me . . ."

A female clerk, very short, maybe nineteen or twenty. I raised a brow.

"Would it be okay," she said, "if we held your bag."

"My bag?"

"Your backpack."

Just like the state trooper, she looked right at it.

I mulled this over a moment and then responded in the negative.

"No? Well, um . . . the reason I'm asking is because . . ."

Then I patiently explained that my laptop was in the bag, along with my spare keys and the notes I was taking and the books I was reading, and that these things were important to me and therefore I felt uneasy about letting the backpack out of sight.

"I'm sorry, sir, but in that case we'll have to . . ."

Her habit of trailing off midsentence was annoying, mostly because it left me to draw unflattering conclusions about myself. "Are you saying if I don't surrender my backpack to you—you who are a total stranger, by the way—then I have to leave the store?"

She scrunched her nose and said she was sorry, but . . .

"So you're suggesting I'm a thief?"

She put up her hands. "It's store policy."

"No, you're suggesting I'll take this book"—I held out the $16.99 travelogue—"and put it in my backpack and walk out the door without paying."

"It's store policy," she repeated.

"I was just about to buy the book, actually," I said, knowing damn well I'd buy the book anyway, "but now I'll have to go buy it somewhere else, because you think I'm a thief, and that's insulting."

"Sarah!" the clerk called over her shoulder, "I need a manager . . ."

"Is my backpack really *that* bad?"

"It's just, I mean, are you a student or something? Because to be totally honest, you look a little old for that . . ."

Leaving Salem, pride wounded and wallet lightened by $16.99, I stopped at Gilgamesh Brewing. Considering the epic poem is both literature's oldest surviving travel narrative and one that's heroes enjoy drinking beer, I was cautiously optimistic. But literary inspiration doesn't always translate. TVs blared and the staff ignored me until I stared at them while clearing my throat. Finally, I managed to procure a glass of Cascadian Dark Ale made with coffee from the Governor's Cup, the café where I'd read about Burton's causes of melancholy before visiting OSH. The beer was decent, but they'd named it the Vader, as in Darth. Worse, their Irish Red was named after one of those early Adam Sandler films where Sandler portrays an infantile vulgarian who everyone comes to adore for no discernible reason. For a brewery to appropriate the name of a cornerstone of world literature only to wallow in the slops of Hollywood felt deeply misguided. Like the rest of humble Salem, Gilgamesh Brewing was a step behind the competition up in Olympia, and the contest for finest Pacific Northwest state capital ultimately proved no contest at all.

BREW U

In the 1840s, the first great migration of covered wagons lit out for the Oregon Territory, heading west from Independence, Missouri in a history-making chain of jettisoned cargo and mule poop. These pioneers had heard tell of an Edenic valley south of the Columbia: a wondrously green landscape rich with game and ideal for farming, a place of fertile soil and mild climate, of easily navigable rivers teeming with salmon, of fir and pine ready for the mill, all situated near the shores of the Pacific. The pioneers were willing to risk everything to homestead such a place, even to the point of traversing the breadth of North America at fifteen hot and bumpy miles a day, so just imagine how eager they'd have been had they known how well hops grew there.

In fact, today's Willamette Valley is the second largest hop-growing region in the country (after the Yakima Valley in Washington), and so it should come as no surprise that Eugene, the state's second largest city and home to the University of Oregon, brews a ton of great beer.

I took Colin's advice and headed for Oakshire Brewing in the neighborhood known as Whiteaker, passing a hotchpotch of industrial garages, coffee shops, single-family homes, and apartment buildings. This mixed-use feel—many of the restaurants and cafes could've easily been mistaken for private residences—imparted a palpable sense of community. Whiteaker had avoided those common zoning ordinances that, in some misguided effort to recreate Mayberry, discourage small businesses (such as breweries) from humanizing themselves and blending with the communities they serve.

Whiteaker was forward-thinking politically, as well, and has long been a home for radicals. Anarchists and militant vegans. A branch of the Occupy Wall Street movement. And the Cascadia Forest Defenders, who resist exploitative logging practices by planting themselves high up in old-growth trees. Whiteaker is the bluest slice of a city often acerbically called "Blue Jean"—a neighborhood of idealists dressed in thrift store castoffs and interested in cooperative living, who sip organic coffee from chipped cups while dropping quotes from the likes of Noam Chomsky and Howard Zinn.

But much like Southeast Portland, Whiteaker was also halfway down the yellow brick road to gentrification, and no amount of patchouli oil could hide the pervasive funk of capitalism. Still, the good folks at Oakshire were doing their best to keep it real. All the beers on my taster tray were well-executed and interesting. The Frog's Wort pale, for example, was almost chewy with hops. As the bartender loaded glassware into the dishwasher, I told her about having met Colin at Hair of the Dog, how he'd recommended I visit Oakshire first thing.

"I know him," she said. "He's sweet."

"He knows his beer, too."

"Everyone around here knows their beer. It's sort of a requirement." Then she gave me a few brewery recommendations of her own, which I dutifully jotted down.

Later, I was thumbing through the *Anatomy* when a pair of guys took the stools beside me. Before I could put the book away—it engenders odd questions—one of them spoke. "Dude, are you reading something with *Latin* in it?"

I allowed that I mostly skimmed those parts.

"Pretty ambitious," the guy said. "Especially in a town with so much good beer."

They were Casey and Joe, friends up from southern Oregon on a brewery tour. Joe was the one who'd spoken. He taught fourth grade (we fist-bumped), while Casey was in construction and had the ragged beard and beaten up hands to prove it. They both liked the stuff all Oregonians seemed to like—rafting, mountaineering, hiking, and craft beer.

"Check this out," Joe said, and pulled a crumpled map from his pocket. The Eugene Ale Trail, with over a dozen beer destinations marked by number. Joe explained they'd borrowed bicycles and visited half the stops already, drinking a pint at each before pedaling onward. "But I'm not sure our livers are strong enough to hit them all," he said.

"Drink tasters instead of pints. That way you can try everything."

"Nah, we're into pints," Joe said. "We like our pints."

A pint or two later, Casey rose without a word—he was apparently content for Joe to do all the talking—and crossed the room, seeming to carefully consider each of his steps. A twelve-foot ladder stood against one wall. Casey admired this ladder, looking it up and down, and then began to climb. Having reached the very top, with everyone in the brewery now watching, he simply stayed there, clinging to the rungs and surveying the scene below.

"Please get down from there," the bartender said. "Before you fall."

Casey cupped a hand to his brow, as if the ladder were actually a tree-sitting perch and he was scanning the forest for loggers. He held the pose for an uncomfortably long time. The brewery's descent into quiet reflected a communal certainty that the ladder was sure to slip.

"You gotta understand how his mind works," Joe told the bartender. "You guys left a ladder there, and so Casey's gonna climb it. He sees a ladder, he's going up. What's a ladder for otherwise? What's a ladder's purpose besides to be climbed? And why would you guys leave it there if he wasn't supposed to use it for its sole and intended purpose?"

"You guys must be on the Ale Trail," the bartender said.

Casey eventually came safely down and finished his pint. Then he and Joe tabbed out. "Here man," Joe said, and handed me his Ale Trail map. "You need this more than us."

"Thanks, Joe."

"You should meet us out later," he said, "after you're done reading your Latin book. We've got tickets to an EDM show. It's gonna be off the hook."

For those who may not know, EDM means electronic dance music, and electronic dance music typically means drugs. There was a little temptation here, actually, considering Robert Burton neglected to include a subsect on Ecstasy in the *Anatomy*—thus making this an opportunity to add a brick to the wall of human knowledge—but the only drug on my menu these days was beer, and I told the guys I'd have to take a raincheck.

"Have a peaceful trip, man," Casey said, before he and Joe wobbled outside and mounted their borrowed bicycles and continued on their quixotic journey.

#

According to my handy new map, Hop Valley Brewing was just down the block.

On the way there, I passed some U of O students enjoying a midafternoon beer bash. Kegs were iced and bad music boomed from deep in the house. Guys tossed a football while struggling to balance plastic cups in their free hands. As a whole, the students wore that collective smirk of the well-fed undergrad, an attitude secretly born of the suspicion that adulthood—morose parents with their soul-crushing jobs, ashen teachers reeking of despair—would soon enough come knocking. All unremarkable phenomena, I suppose, except that the keg on the porch was from Oakshire. Not Anheuser-Busch, not MillerCoors: Oakshire.

College students in Eugene apparently did not chug light lager to get cheaply drunk, as do college students everywhere else in this great nation. No, Eugene's student body was, to borrow Colin's term, enlightened. But with all this fantastic beer available, might the urge to blow off class grow well-nigh irresistible? My own college town, square in the heart of America's Beechwood Beer Desert, had lacked so much as a drop of craft beer—and yet I *still* didn't get much studying done, having been seduced time and again by the vomitus allure of the keg-stand. Had I spent my college days in Whiteaker, surrounded by endless kegs of wonderful beer, would I have even managed to graduate at all?

Then again, early exposure to craft beer might've paved the way for an earlier appreciation of beer culture, and thereby mollified my baser instincts. Because getting as plastered as seemed necessary at nineteen was a chore with only corporate lager for ammunition. How many thousands of Bud Lights did my friends and I drain with only faint dizziness, aching bladders, and sour taste buds to show for our efforts? It's not unthinkable that real beer would have elevated us. Under the wholesome influence of handmade ales and lagers, of bitters and milds, of kölsch and pils, might I have attended class with a more open mind and better embodied that freethinking ideal which underlies the liberal arts curriculum? A wild fermentation sour, for example, a beer far outside the boundaries of my known world, would've shaken my preconceptions to the core. In short, might early exposure to thoughtful beers crafted by actual human hands have rewired my very consciousness?

Questions, questions. I ducked into Hop Valley to mull them over.

It seemed like a nice enough brewery at first glance. Wyclef mused on the stereo, the bartender was friendly, and the taster tray was shaped like a great big hop leaf. Worrisomely, though, the first of these tasters was yet another Double D blonde. Hop Valley also had merchandise stacked everywhere, including small logoed Frisbees for a seemingly exorbitant $17 apiece. As suggested by the name, nearly all the beers were hop bombs. Even the Fruit Man, an apricot ale, was hopped to the nth degree. The beer was fresh and drinkable—some styles were really good—but the overzealous hopping was like a sophomore writer who's just discovered the elations and exultations of alliteration. By the time I'd finished the taster leaf, my tongue felt burned by alpha acids.

While I hadn't realized it at the time, Hop Valley had just been acquired by MillerCoors for an undisclosed sum. In retrospect, it makes sense. The overly aggressive beer. The overpriced merch. The aspirations to empire. Not that there's necessarily anything wrong with trying to get rich—I'm required to say that as a working-class American, else I'll be accused of envy—but compared to Oakshire, Hop Valley was a letdown.

Afterward, Whiteaker struck an off-key note. Trees cast a pall over the sidewalks, strangers stared a beat too long, and the voices of crows seemed a communal dirge. As our guide would have it, the day had left me like a lute out of tune. I might've just chalked this up to a string of nights with too little sleep and too much beer, except Burton notes this particular strain of melancholy—*lucida intervalla*—is often deceptively pleasing at first, largely because it feels so much like the truth. "A most incomparable delight it is so to melancholize," he writes, "and build castles in the air." Such feelings turn our otherwise trivial and distractible thoughts inward to where it seems our true selves, assuming we actually *have* true selves, must surely lie. But while the brooding Schopenhauer may enjoy this solitary musing, such indulgence is not without danger. In *One Flew Over the Cuckoo's Nest,* the despotic Nurse Ratched claims men are institutionalized because they won't conform to the rules of the Outside World, the most important of which is to avoid being alone, as time spent with others is therapeutic, whereas time alone only increases one's troubles. So what would Nurse Ratched make of a self-prescribed treatment for melancholy which involved traveling around and drinking beer all by oneself?

Around the corner was a food truck. Thinking a little sustenance might help, I ordered a burger and sat down to wait at a nearby picnic table. Then an old man pushed a baby stroller up beside me. In the stroller was an ancient and emaciated Chihuahua dressed in a purple cape. A matching crown sat atop its skull, an elastic strap looped under its tiny jaws. The dog's head drooped, as if the crown were too heavy for its neck.

"What's her Highness's name?"

"Chica," the man said. He was skinny, dirty, his clothes threadbare. Chica wasn't doing much better. She lay in the stroller, sickly and glass-eyed. The cape covered her like a shawl.

"She's cute."

"She was dressed like a princess earlier, but now she's the queen."

An employee delivered my food. The man looked at me, at the burger, then began fussing with Chica, who watched from the folds of the stroller with rheumy eyes. There's a useful thought experiment attributed to Socrates, whereby everyone in the world has the chance to pile their woes and grievances in a heap that will then be equally divided. The question: would you take your fair share, or stand pat?

"Would you and Chica like this sandwich?"

The man pursed his lips and looked away.

"Go ahead. I'm not all that hungry, after all."

As I stood and hoisted my backpack, he pinched off a nibble of meat and placed it near Chica's mouth. She opened her jaws and the skin pulled back from her gums. She tried to chew, but coughed and spat out the food. He encouraged her, cajoling in a singsong voice, but it was as if the dog attempted to eat only because she understood doing so would please her master.

Next, I headed over to Ninkasi, the brewery Colin had referred to as the "mothership." Despite a looming metal silo and a gaudy teal color scheme, like Oakshire, Ninkasi felt sewn into the cloth of Whiteaker. The odd name derives from a Sumerian goddess with a hymn written in her honor, a fragment of which has survived on a clay pot circa 1800 B.C. This hymn contains a rudimentary beer recipe. It talks of soaking the malt and spreading it on reeds, and compares the finished beer to the rushing Tigris and Euphrates.

I took a taster board out to the beer garden. The first sample, Tricerahops double IPA, was as resinous and boozy as pine cone schnapps. The double IPA style—let alone the triple IPA strong ale—is one that hopheads chase passionately for a while, but ultimately grow weary of. Back when I was making my acquaintance with craft beer, hop bombs like Tricerahops saturated the West Coast. Such beers were a logical step in the craft beer revolution, as supremely bitter ales with high ABVs are just about as far from corporate light lager as beer can get.

To their credit, Ninkasi chased big hops and big booze as well as any brewer in America, but this wave seems to have finally crested and broken with the rise of sours and session ales. The next phase in America's beer renaissance lies not in spectacle and size, but an exploration of gentler and nearly forgotten styles. The past, in other words. Roots. Tradition.

Maybe the culture at large could benefit from much the same?

#

Sam Bond's Garage wasn't marked on the Ale Trail map.

The woman at the door checked my I.D., stamped my wrist with what was either a purple skull or a sad clown, and then asked for three bucks. While this wasn't a lot of money, cover charges strike me as double-dealing. If your bar isn't good enough to make due selling drinks and food, why should people bother going there at all?

She noted my hesitation. "Actually, the three bucks is just a donation."

When I frowned, she asked if I could at least spare two bucks.

"What's this donation for, exactly?"

"Even one dollar would be appreciated," she said, not even bothering to hide her disdain, as my short hair and (relatively) clean clothes had marked me as just another yuppie intent upon draining the radicalism from the Whit. "It's just a suggestion," she added. "Don't not come in because of it."

"Are you sure you actually *want* me to come in?"

"I'll need to check your backpack first," she said.

"Fine by me, but that'll cost you three bucks."

She stared at me and I smiled. She kept right on staring.

"Two bucks?" I said.

Inside, a bluegrass duo performed "House of the Rising Sun." Figuring the suggested cover charge was for their slush fund, I stuck a few bills in the tip jar and settled in at the rail.

The duo was composed of a man with long gray hair and a redhead in a tight green dress. Aquamarine tattooing covered her arms and shoulders, the sort that in time will fade to resemble an old seafaring map. When her partner took five, the redhead slipped behind the piano for a solo and asked the crowd if anyone liked Leonard Cohen. A few people hollered and whistled.

"Well, my dad hates him," she said, before launching into one of Cohen's mournful tunes about oral sex in a sleazy motel.

The bartender bore an uncanny resemblance to Garth from *Wayne's World*. The same heavy spectacles and scrawny shoulders, the receding chin and spiked mullet. Behind him was a row of tap handles. Sure enough, Sam Bond's Garage doubled as a brewery, although they didn't even bother to advertise the fact. I asked Garth for a pale ale and a slice of pizza, and these items arrived in a mason jar and on a paper plate, which felt just right.

I was eating in the glow of a neon marijuana leaf advertising the dispensary beyond the streetside window, when a middle-aged guy ambled past. He looked distracted, preoccupied with his thoughts, and he was bent under the weight of a large backpack. Signs and wonders. I set aside the pizza and pictured myself a few years down the road, spine bowed under the weight of the frustrated ambitions I totted around like Sisyphus on his way to the big hill. Just then, as I worried over my fate, a car pulled up with a decal on the door that read: Green Health Pot Delivery. A sign on the roof promised $4.20 Pre-Rolls All-Day Every-Day. The bluegrass duo launched into another tune, while outside the delivery driver sparked a pre-roll and filled the cab with silvery velvet smoke.

Thus distracted, I hadn't noticed the older gentleman who'd taken the next stool over. Bozo tufts of white hair crowned his head, and he wore a dainty pair of cowboy boots. I watched him settle his jaunty little potbelly over an elaborate western-style belt buckle. Moments later, a young woman joined him. She was twenty-three at most and pretty, her eyes as green as the neon in the window, her hair soft and long in the sultry bar lights.

Eavesdropping, I deduced the man was a professor in the humanities at the U of O, while she was a student—although not *his* student—and that he had every intention of bedding her, and perhaps her him, as well. The professor was married, but he and the missus "had an understanding." The girl was new to town and "digging the vibe." Within minutes, the professor's small wrinkly hand was squeezing the girl's long supple thigh.

There's nothing ultimately wrong with any of that, I don't suppose, although Burton feels differently. On love melancholy, he argues there's little in this world more absurd than an aged lecher: those, "decrepit, hoary, harsh, writhen, bursten-bellied, crooked, toothless, bald, bleary-eyed, impotent, rotten old men." But take this with a grain of salt, considering Burton's own love affairs weren't with women, but with forgotten, stale, boring, creaky-spined, dusty, bloodless, orotund, squint-inducing old books. Still, it was an odd courtship. After all, how many $4.20 pre-rolls would a girl have to smoke before grandpa came to seem sexy? And how many ales did grandpa need to drink before commencing pillow-talk with a girl born nearly three decades after he'd filed his educational deferment to dodge the war in Vietnam?

A blurry amount of time later, I left Sam Bond's Garage lonely in my fading youth. Under the influence of numerous mason jars of ale, I weaved and dipped my way down the street to a crummy-enough-looking motel, where I nimbly sidestepped the inevitable passel of addicts gathered around the door picking at their facial scabs, and then commenced a haggling session with the polite Indian woman behind the counter.

"AAA discount?"

"No sir, sorry sir."

"How about an educator's discount? I'm a teacher, after all."

"No sir, sorry sir."

"A *professor*, actually."

"Sir?"

"AARP?"

A faint wrinkle creased her forehead. "I am very sorry sir."

Her stubbornness was admirable, but it was time to play hardball. I turned and pointed through the glass doors at the competing dump across the alley. "Betcha that place will offer me a discount."

Once checked into my room, I cracked open a forty of Pabst Blue Ribbon impulsively purchased on the walk. The first icy swallow seemed to anesthetize not just my tongue, but my brain stem. No use denying it; I was snoggered, totally mooneyed. I'd willfully and decisively taken off my considering cap. But sound advice underwrote this behavior, because after

Burton finally finishes discussing the many well-established benefits of blood-letting for melancholy, of applying horse-leeches to hemorrhoids (on the recommendation of the noted hemorrhoid experts, Faventinus and Hercules de Saxonia) and drilling holes in the patient's skull, he mentions a considerably more pleasant solution: getting drunk.

While Solomon doth saith in Proverbs that nothing but sorrow and woe comes to he who loves drink, we should remember that Solomon was talking about *wine,* not beer. No, taken as a whole, the weight of ancient evidence suggests drinking "whetteth the wit" and helps banish fear and sorrow. Avicenna and Seneca believe drunkenness a good physic, while Magninus prescribes tying one on at least once a month. Being a water-drinker, however, Burton feels compelled to add that such Epicureanism leads ultimately to loose living, indulgence, and atheism—tenants that, as I collapsed upon the stale bed, seemed like good physic for us all.

#

The open sign at Vero Espresso clicked on just as I climbed the front steps.

Coffee in hand, I spent the morning with the *Anatomy.* Reading Burton had its rewards, but it was also the very definition of leaving no stone unturned. To make use of the scholar's own style, his life's work is oftentimes wearying, slogging, trudging, sluggish, turtling, dense, impenetrable, murky, opaque, redundant, repetitive, repetitious, tedious, tiresome, irksome, exasperating, toilsome, brooding, dour, dreary, monotonous, wearisome, droning, and dull.

The only way to tackle such a monster was to digest a little each day, to take it slow and easy. In *The Oregon Trail,* another book I was easing into and taking my time with, Rinker Buck's covered wagon has the phrase "SEE AMERICA SLOWLY" posted on the bumper. A family slogan of sorts, and one with ramifications for reading as well as travel. Seen in this way, approached with patience and indulgence, Burton's exhaustive book teaches the reader via its very form a means of coping with its exhausting subject.

Later, I saw downtown Eugene slowly, as well, mostly because homeless people were camped out everywhere, cadging cigarettes and panhandling and begging for food. The sight of so very many struggling individuals made for a stark contrast with the easy libertinism of Eugene's pub culture—not that this is a uniquely American or even modern problem. Burton quotes Plato as comparing homeless people to ulcers and boils that should be purged from our cities as bad humours from the body. With a philosophical inheritance like that, it's no surprise thousands of years have done so little to remedy the issue. And sure, some of these people were almost certainly trustafarians—privileged kids only playing at hardship to rebel or make some misguided statement—but the majority looked authentically castoff.

One kid in particular caught my attention. A white boy with filthy dreadlocks, he ambled barefoot down the sidewalk on a pair of dainty feet black as pencil lead. His manner was hyperactive and boisterous, although his clothes were what really singled him out. He wore a stained and tattered onesie pajama suit. A Tigger patch, a baseball patch, as if he'd sewn his childhood blankets into a makeshift suit of clothes. The kid's appearance had quite the effect on an older couple who'd just

THE LAND OF ALE AND GLOOM

emerged from a nearby restaurant. They saw him, stopped, and simply stared. The old man's jacket was printed with the American flag. His blue jeans looked freshly ironed. He and his wife frowned deeply, not even bothering to hide their thickening disgust. What in Jesus' name was wrong with young people these days? How had America become the Land of Free and the Home of the Lazy, Good-For-Nothing Welfare Scum?

After picking up a butt off the pavement, splitting the paper, and siphoning the remaining tobacco into a little pouch, the kid approached a vegan food truck and begged something to eat in a reedy voice. I briefly considered buying him a plate, much as I'd given my hamburger to the man with the dying Chihuahua, but I was distracted by the old man's unabashed staring. Then he left his wife's side and marched up to the food truck. At first, I thought I'd misread him, that he was about to practice charity and buy the onesie kid some lunch. But instead he delivered a stern (and loud) lecture on how to walk the correct spiritual path. Credit to the kid for listening politely, only rolling his eyes a little here and there, even though the message delivered—what I could hear of it, at any rate—was hardly blessed are the merciful.

While I suppose it's possible a judgmental deity like that really is out in the cosmos somewhere tallying demerits, what of all those schizophrenic and substance-addicted homeless people? Free will meets poor choices, or something darker? On its face, at least, this world could be mistaken for a gnostic hell where some must suffer publicly so the rest get to feel a little better about themselves. As for the Burtonian take on such irreligious and "brain-sick" questions, the scholar hems and haws for a page or two, recounts some Old Testament sinners struck down with leprosy or blindness, and then simply admits that if God decides to punish you with a melancholy life, you're just up the purgatorial creek. This is followed, however, by a 10,000-word digression on melancholy caused by devils and other assorted malicious spirits. Examples include fiery and aerial spirits, watery spirits and terrestrial spirits, and carnally copulating spirits (which Burton slyly promises to expound upon in due time), along with a few well-documented instances of demonic possession—including a cooper's daughter named Katherine Gaulter, who in 1571 was compelled by dark forces to vomit for two straight weeks, in which time she purged great quantities of hair balls, wood and paper, coal, pigeon and goose shit, glass, brass, inscribed stones, and an eighteen-inch live eel.

But while it seemed unlikely that either heavenly or demonic spirits were to blame for Eugene's homelessness rate, seeing it up close was undeniably sad. So I followed a series of signs around the corner and down an alley to the fittingly-named Falling Sky Brewing House.

After perusing the offerings, I inquired about the Make America Wheat Again Ale.

"Sorry," the bartender said, "but we're all out of that one."

Was this a good thing, I asked, or a bad thing?

"Guess that depends on your point of view," he said.

"From what I've seen so far, Eugene isn't Trump country."

"You might be surprised. We get all kinds around here."

Then I said it was just as well, because I didn't normally care for wheat ales anyway, having found them tasteless and lacking in character. Hearing this, the bartender pulled off his beanie, gave his scalp a good scratching, and said I was preaching to the choir. "But just because a beer is simple," he added, "doesn't necessarily mean people won't drink it."

I felt a dark premonition. "So simple sells?"

"For every adventurous beer-drinker out there, there are two others who just want to get buzzed and forget about the workday. That's just how it goes."

Fearful words if ever I've heard them. But with no Trumpian beer available I had to settle for a few other Falling Sky pours, all of which were pretty good, although the Bare Hands Northwest Bitter was a bit confusing. The recipe apparently added Northwest hops to an English-style bitter, which is a terrific idea, but is also pretty much exactly how the classic Northwest-style pale ale (such as Sierra Nevada's flagship) came about back in the '80s. Maybe with so many people scurrying around trying to cash in on the same old schemes, all innovations, even those having to do with craft beer, are doomed to end in tail-chasing?

And perhaps it was my regret over not having attended college at the U of O back when I had the chance, or the sad reality of so much homelessness in such an otherwise enlightened city—or maybe I was still suffering the effects of that late-night forty of PBR—but I'd had enough of Eugene. A certain *tædium vitæ* had set in. The Pacific called. Before I could head out to the coast, however, there was a man in the nearby town of Springfield who I needed to see.

#

I found him downtown at the corner of 4th and Main, leaning against a wooden bookcase with one arm akimbo. Outfitted in a tan western jacket, baggy brown corduroys, and boots, he looked strong and robust, his forehead broad and smooth above a pair of eyes squinting into the distance. It'd been easy enough to locate him, as Springfield was small, really just a suburb of Eugene—that, and the man stood twenty feet tall.

There he was: The Chief himself, Ken Kesey.

His bookcase had a Springfield High School pennant atop it—he was voted "most likely to succeed"—and right next to that a golden wrestling trophy, as he'd also been a standout athlete back in his day. In fact, he became a star wrestler at the University of Oregon and might've even made the Olympic team, if not for a shoulder injury. Traveling south down that bookcase, however, the interests grew progressively more esoteric. A few volumes by Wendell Barry and *Leaves of Grass* were mainstream enough, but then came *On the Road* and then, one shelf down, *The Dharma Bums*, a slim volume of poetry by Kerouac's friend Gary Snyder (who appears in *The Dharma Bums* under the awkward sobriquet Japhy Ryder), *Naked Lunch* by the counterculture godfather and noted heroin addict William Burroughs, a few books on eastern religion, and then a few of the author's own works: *Sometimes a Great Notion, One Flew Over the Cuckoo's Nest,* and *Sailor Song.*

Also featured prominently on that same shelf was a book on MK ULTRA, a shadowy Cold War-era CIA project aimed at using psychedelic drugs to develop mind control and torture techniques for use on Soviet spies. Such a book was added to the mural because, in addition to those nightly shifts in the psychiatric ward that inspired *Cuckoo's Nest*, Kesey also signed up as a guinea pig in paid studies ($75 a day; not bad money back then) conducted at the Veterans Hospital in Menlo Park near Stanford. These studies involved the ingestion of mysterious capsules which sometimes contained a placebo, but other times contained lysergic acid diethylamide, better known as LSD. And yes, Kesey did go to his night job under the influence. He would later say the drug allowed him to see *into* the patients. He even wrote some of Chief Bromden's most memorable passages while tripping.

Besides drugging students, the CIA project also involved a scheme whereby unsuspecting men visiting a San Francisco brothel (Operation Midnight Climax, no less) were caught up in a sting and given the choice of ingesting a certain unmarked capsule or facing public exposure. After dosing these clandestine paramours, the government spooks sipped cocktails behind a two-way mirror while observing the results. Consciousness-altering drugs were also given, without knowledge or consent, to marginalized people such as addicts, prisoners, and the mentally ill.

While this may sound like an episode of the *X-Files* inspired by *The Manchurian Candidate,* it's all true, and on the bottom shelf—past *Moby Dick, Fear and Loathing in Las Vegas,* and a fat copy of Ginsberg's *Howl and Other Poems*—was a curious fallout of those experiments: a replica bus painted in fluorescent ultramarine Day-Glo swirls, as well as a big yellow license plate which read, FURTHR.

Basking in the success of *Cuckoo's Nest* and newly committed to evangelizing the world via the prophecy of psychedelics, Kesey and a group of friends who called themselves the Merry Pranksters outfitted a 1939 International

Harvester school bus with bunks and benches, movie cameras and audio equipment, as well as a ton of acid, and set out east from California, headed for the New York World's Fair. This bus—Furthur [sic]—was piloted by a forty-year-old and amphetamine-popping Neal Cassady (aka, Dean Moriarty, that friend and muse Kerouac immortalized in *On the Road*), and the debauched grooviness which took place inside of it, that spontaneous and intersubjective experiment in tuning in and going with the cosmic flow, remains one of the most recognizable symbols the 1960s counterculture, and one which acted as a bridge between the Beat Generation and the hippie movement. The Beatles actually went so far as to copy the Pranksters with their *Magical Mystery Tour*, and the whole bizarre thing, or nearly the whole thing, was Kesey's brainchild.

Such activities didn't set well with conservative America, of course, and Kesey was hounded by the FBI all the way to Mexico and back. LSD wasn't illegal at the time, but smoking weed was, and smoke weed Kesey did. Hence, he found himself a wanted writer, chased down and jailed, the authorities demanding he renounce his ways and tell the Flower Children to stop dropping the very same acid the government had turned him on to in the first place. The absurdity is famously chronicled in a surreal rush of loopy and lingo-laden prose in Tom Wolfe's *The Electric Kool-Aid Acid Test*. But what stands out most now, at least to me, isn't the salacious bits about Furthur's "love bunk" (a communal sleeping bag Wolfe claims would immaculately impregnate "any certified virgin" who crawled inside it), or how the Pranksters out-partied the Hell's Angels (whom Kesey met through Hunter S. Thompson, who was writing a book about them), or even the notorious Acid Test parties in Haight-Ashbury, but how much taxpayer money

THE LAND OF ALE AND GLOOM

was wasted fretting over a handful of bohemians getting weird in a crusty old bus.

But Springfield, Oregon, had chosen to honor their controversial native son, and that was a good thing, because underneath the Day-Glo and outlandish costumes, Kesey was a brilliant writer. While his literary output fizzled as his involvement with the counterculture deepened, over half a century after its publication, *Sometimes a Great Notion* remains our most vividly idiosyncratic depiction of the Northwest, and that alone seems mural-worthy. Best of all, Kesey was painted on the side of the building that housed Plank Town Brewing Company.

The brewery was themed after Springfield's mill town heritage, and had a woodsy cabin vibe, all thick beams and redwood tables. On the walls hung black and white photos of the old-time millworkers, as well as a couple of giant saw blades. Smaller versions of these same blades adorned the tap handles behind the horseshoe bar. I took a seat and ordered a schooner of the obvious choice: FURTHR AMBR. Here was a cleanly made beer with a pleasant bite of noble hops, but while it was a nice gesture to name a beer after Furthur, amber ale really isn't the best style to honor a provocateur and visionary like Ken Kesey. Ambers are as conventional and mainstream as a craft beer gets. Almost anyone can appreciate them, as they're inoffensive and safe, not too bitter and not too strong, nothing funky or surprising about them. In fact, when trying to convert a lifetime Bud Light drinker to craft beer, amber ales are often the ideal vehicle.

Then Lou Reed's "Walk on the Wild Side" came on the stereo, a story of the cultural outsiders Reed got to know while hanging around The Factory with Andy Warhol and his cohorts in the early 1970s. Candy Darling and the Sugar Plum Fairy feel like characters who might've easily been "on the bus" with Kesey and the Pranksters, and if they drank beer it's a safe bet they would've preferred a spontaneously-fermented wild ale, something funky and sour, full of barnyard notes and unpredictable yeast cultures, maybe even a beer infused with fruit zest, a hint of the orange juice the Pranksters liked to mix with their LSD.

But Plank Town wasn't that kind of brewery. They made an honest lineup of traditional ales and lagers and they did it well. It was a straightforward place—a friendly place, a comfortable place, but also a very Springfield-y sort of place, which perhaps explains why Ken Kesey didn't become *Kesey,* didn't usurp his own literary creation to become The Chief, until he left for California and realms beyond, places where he could finally let his freak flag fly free.

WHALES AND ALES: HIGHWAY 101

Back in the 1970s, a sperm whale the approximate size of Furthur washed up dead on the beach near Florence, Oregon. The sight was fascinating at first, a wonder of nature to assuage the monotony of life on the continent's lonely rim. But soon enough that whale got ripe. *Really* ripe.

A huge decomposing sea mammal poses quite the problem for a small town. After all, you can't bury the thing, as the sand is far too shallow, and while you probably could cut it up and haul it off, good luck finding anyone crazy enough to wade in with a chainsaw. So what solution did the good people of Florence finally settle on?

They decided to blow it up, naturally. Let the birds and crabs handle the mess.

Prudence suggested an engineer be consulted, and this man did freely admit, in an interview prior to the big day, that he wasn't exactly sure how much explosive to use, as he'd never dynamited a whale before. Twenty tons sounded about right. Tons, that is, not sticks.

The resultant spectacle, memorialized in grainy news footage, makes that ludicrous shark explosion at the end of *Jaws* look like a firecracker. After a tremendous boom, the gathered crowd found itself instantly covered in atomized flesh. A quarter mile away, a parked sedan was smashed flat by a door-sized slab of falling blubber. In the gore-covered reporter's own bemused words, "The blast blasted blubber beyond all believable bounds."

Kesey, who stayed in Florence for a few months while researching *Sometimes a Great Notion*, driving the logging trails by day and hanging around the bars at night, writes of a similar whale demolition—one so smelly it sickens the townspeople for a month—although this would predate the real-life events in Florence, which exceeded even Kesey's baroque imagination. Truth once again proved herself stranger than fiction, as she's wont to do. I considered the unpublished novels I'd written. Why had I ever believed anyone would bother reading made up stories in a country where sperm whales are detonated with TNT and a reality TV star with a bottle-blonde bouffant can secure the Republican presidential nomination?

As I neared the coast, however, I wasn't thinking about dead whales or Donald Trump's hairdo, but Jonathan Bailey Draeger, the labor organizer who travels my exact route in the opening pages of *Sometimes*. Draeger feels little affinity for this stretch of Oregon mud wallow, as the chronic damp has left him with a bad case of athlete's foot. The man is so depressed by the landscape and weather that he's hardly surprised so many natives take a "one-way dip" to escape the gloom of the rainy season. Unlike Mr. Draeger, however, I had the good fortune to pass through on a lingeringly warm summer day.

I parked alongside the docks, tasting the ocean on the wind. The inlet waters were crowned by lush hills and sailboats bobbed in neat rows. Gulls lazed in the rigging and the breeze whiffling their feathers smelled of mud. Bay Street's restaurants had white linen on the tabletops and served oily baskets of fish and chips. Trinket shops dotted the walk, selling saltwater taffy and coastal bric-a-brac. There was even a "working" birdhouse museum, and in the waters beyond it stood a piling filled with special birdhouses meant for purple martins, cormorants, and kingfishers.

In short, it was difficult to imagine a more charming, serene, idyllic coastal town than Florence, Oregon. Then again, if you happened to grow up in Florence, chances are you'd either develop a nasty drug habit or fall into a cloud of alcohol-induced despair, because nothing ever happens in Florence and nothing ever changes in Florence and every interesting person you might ever hope to meet would merely be passing through. And so one day you'd just pack up and leave for somewhere faster and harder, like Portland or Seattle—a place you could hate without a shred of guilt—and that way, with Florence safely in your rearview, it could remain the charming, serene, idyllic coastal town of your memories.

Not far from the birdhouse museum was the Beachcomber, the "Oregon Coast's Headquarters for Craft Beer" according to the banner. But to reach said headquarters, I had to bypass the geriatric motorcycle gang parked right outside the front door. While they weren't quite as wild as the 60's-era Hell's Angels that Kesey and the Merry Pranksters dropped acid with, these geezers were decked out in the full regalia: black leather vests emblazoned with skulls-and-crossbones, badass muscle-tees, and that particular style of red and blue bandana that for most people functions not as a sign of rebellion, but a snot rag.

Inside the bar was an even sketchier bunch—a party of Texans hell-bent on drinking the Beachcomber dry of Bud Light. I reminded myself to give strangers the benefit of the doubt, but the bartender was slow and the Texan to my right wouldn't stop mooing over the injustice of having to pay property taxes on the mansion he'd purchased back home on the range for the kingly sum of $200,000. I considered how much real estate that would purchase in the Puget Sound area (a parking spot, *maybe*), frowned, and then fled the Beachcomber while the bartender was still busy cracking open another round of Bud Lights.

After weaving once more past the Knights of Medicare, I crossed the street and treated myself to an unusually long lunch at the Traveler's Cove. On the deck overlooking the water, nursing a few bottles of ale, my thoughts returned to Kesey. The fishing scene in *One Flew Over the Cuckoo's Nest* is set in Florence and reads in a vivid rush, almost like something from Kerouac, as mad men shout and bleed and salmon strike in the blue murk and a girl shows her lovely breasts while wrestling a fish. In fact, the novel's hero, Randle Patrick McMurphy, reads a lot like Dean Moriarty / Neal Cassady: the same manic goodwill, the lustiness and bonhomie, even the same habit of scratching his belly while sounding off on this or that. A literary inheritance from the Beat Generation to the Acid Generation.

I picked at my lunch, sipped my beer, and took a little break from the world. Finally, I recalled an observation Kesey makes near the end of that fishing scene. It's one guys like Kerouac and Cassady (and even Robert Burton) could sympathize with: "Because he knows you have to laugh at the things that hurt you," Kesey writes, "just to keep yourself in balance, just to keep the world from running you plumb crazy."

#

Soon I came to the Oregon Dunes.

The dunes were why I'd felt compelled to linger over a so-so lunch and poke fun at harmless motorcyclists and Texans in my head. The dunes are why I had that second bottle of ale, even though I hadn't really wanted it. The dunes are also the first thing one sees after leaving Florence. Towers of sand jut between the sea and Coastal Range, huge and ghostly and lunar against the green and blue backdrop, forever shifting in the sea winds and rain, gathering and bulging, piling and disintegrating.

Buggies can be rented to explore the area. In fact, I'd done that very thing the summer before. My ex-girlfriend's mother was ill with cancer then, and she wished to see the dunes a final time, as it'd been something her family enjoyed in the past. But she was in those withered last days when even a few steps became exhausting, let alone jouncing over five-hundred-foot sandbanks in a buggy with an unforgiving suspension. The people who ran the rental outfit kept us waiting for two full hours in their flyblown parking lot, despite our having made a reservation and informed them they had a very sick and delicate customer on their hands. But they already had our Visa card numbers, so they didn't really care. All was nonrefundable.

Between trips inside to uselessly berate the useless manager, my girlfriend rubbed sunblock on her mother's shoulders, but the woman didn't seem overly concerned with the sun. She just sat there and sweated in the cool wind off the sea. As for the buggy ride itself, she swallowed her anti-nausea medication and somehow managed to smile through all thirty jolting, jarring minutes of it. Throughout the ride, I couldn't stop thinking of the winter before, when this woman had called me late one night—a surprise, as I hadn't realized she had my number—to say that she'd received a worrisome text from her daughter. She'd had to call me, she explained, because my girlfriend had recently moved into a boarding house and I was the only one who'd actually been there and knew where it was.

I drove in a rush across Seattle, thirty minutes, maybe more, and climbed the darkened steps. I found her unresponsive. Beside her bed, a suitcase lay open on the mauve carpet amidst a spill of prescription bottles. A 911 call turned from panic to farce when I realized I didn't know the address, either. I looked everywhere for a piece of mail—nothing but mildew and cobwebs. Then I burst into the room across the hall and found a teenage boy playing video games. His mother rented the adjacent room, but she was gone at work. I shouted for help finding the address, for help somehow, but the boy just stared at me, a plastic controller loose in his hands.

I ran outside, searching for a house number—too dark, too rainy, nothing. So I rushed back in and gathered her in my arms—she seemed to weigh nothing at all, as if some essential part of her had already fled—and hurried back down the creaking and half-finished spiral staircase and through a kitchen piled with the mess of transient people and across a sopping blue yard. An ambulance met us at a nearby bank. Across the street was a convenience store, people buying potato chips and beer and lottery tickets as the EMTs shrouded her face with an amniotic mask and swabbed the soft pale skin of her inner arm.

For three days and nights she lay with a tube down her throat and a machine inflating her lungs. Her mother was there constantly, very sick even then, although that remained her secret. The overdose had been accomplished with a mix of pharmaceuticals, some of which were quite dangerous. The doctors spoke in probabilities: she could recover completely, or there could be brain damage, perhaps slight, perhaps not so slight.

In the weeks following her discharge, she seemed okay, if fragile, but every moment we spent together was freighted with the knowledge that I now had to distance myself, that by trying to end her future, she had effectively ended ours. We talked about that night, of course, or tried to talk about it, rewound and dissected the hours leading up to it, looking for some explanation we might yet give each other as to why it'd happened and what it meant. But no matter how much we talked, there just didn't seem to be a key to the puzzle, which was perhaps the most upsetting aspect of all. A bad reaction to hormonal medication, she said. What she'd done that night wasn't her, wasn't real; there was no reason, no meaning behind any of it.

Burton teaches us that love is blindness and slavery, and I sank into just such a silence. Before I could find the courage to say what I knew needed said, came news of her mother's diagnosis. And in the months to follow, it was witnessing the girl's unflinching devotion to her fading mother that finally brought me deeper and hopelessly into love with the girl, even though from the moment I set foot in that darkened boarding house a pall lingered over us, to borrow an image from Kesey, like the rain-swollen winter clouds that blow in from the Pacific and rebound off the face of the Coastal Range like floating gray lakes.

#

As with melancholy in general, Burton writes that the love of women primarily affects the liver, but there were miles to go before I could abuse my own any further. The road climbed and the Pacific shimmered far below. I passed a sign advertising sea lion caves (the world's largest, supposedly), which sounded smelly and boring. Next, Heceta Lighthouse, which in the nineteenth century housed the coast's brightest light, but now housed tourists, having been retrofitted into a bed and breakfast. Then came Neptune Beach.

I parked and left a trail of size fifteen Nike footprints in the wet along the shore, imagining what Robinson Crusoe would've made of those suckers. On a slice of sand hedged by wind-worn cliffs, paper-white Oregonians lay sunburning themselves. I sat on a rock and watched the waves roll in. The most peculiar color lived in the curl of those waves, but only in that moment just before the break. This color might've been described as seafoam, although that wasn't quite right. The shade was mostly gray—gray merely hinting at green, whispering of green. Up the beach and across the road loomed a stand of wind-bent pines. Could the curious color be a distant reflection of the trees, land coloring sea?

Back on the road, I passed Cook's Chasm and Cape Perpetua, an inlet named for and a jutting promontory named by Capt. James Cook on his expeditions to locate the Northwest Passage. While Cook wasn't the first European to see the Northwest coast (that honor goes to the Spanish), he was the first to accurately map its contours, and so he gets the lion's share of the credit. Cape Perpetua overlooked a headland with views of the rocky coastline for fifty or sixty miles. The scenic area of the same name contained another nearby inlet known as the Devil's Churn, along with a tide-driven saltwater fountain called Thor's Well. With so many colorfully named sites along 101, I was tempted to stop every five minutes and snap a photo. Originally named after Teddy Roosevelt, the highway comprises hundreds of miles of winding cliffside pavement, soaring deck bridges, and tunnels through the mountainside. In a region full of amazing roads, it's one of the very best.

Eventually I reached Yachats (the "Gem of the Oregon Coast") but it was just more seaside shacks and unambitious restaurants—until I came to Yachats Brewing, that is. The place was half brewery, half farm store. The taps poured mostly guest brews and kombucha, but they had a few beers of their own, too. So I approached the bartender (who looked like a fifth-grader), stooped so she could hear my voice, and asked for tasters of everything brewed on sight. The most intriguing element of these samples were their names—Tears of the Innocent sour ale and Thor's Thumbnail IPA (or something like that)—which seemed fitting, as I was in a strange little town along the Oregon coast which itself had an unpronounceable name.

I asked the child-barmaid for a little clarification, and she wrinkled her rabbity nose and shoved her glasses back into place. "YAH-hots."

"Yachts?" I said, although I'd heard her just fine. "Like the boat?"

"No," she said, clearly fighting the urge to cup her hands and yell—"*YAH-hots.*"

"One more time, please?"

Her eyes grew enormous behind her thick glasses. "*YAH . . . Hots!*"

My walking tour of said town led past a series of homey bungalows. Who can pass by one of those without daydreaming about living there? The lazy summers—strolling to the beach with a cup of coffee before easing into an utterly tranquil day, and later watching the sun fold beneath the waves—then brisk autumn shading into the long winter. Tourists gone, neighbors huddled inside against the rain, soup on the stove and tea burbling in the pot.

Planted in the yard of one of these bungalows was a sign:

WHAT'S THE HURRY?

GO SLOW

ENJOY!

#

Beyond Waldport ("Where the Forest Meets the Sea"), I passed Seal Rock and a series of stores selling antiques, homemade fudge, and chainsaw-carved lawn statuary. Driving by Lost Creek State Park, I again wondered about the bounty of evocative names along Oregon 101.

Take where I grew up for the opposing example. Midwest settlers weren't quite as ambitious as the Oregon variety, let alone English sea captains. Imagine how it must've went. Those future Midwesterners packed up all their earthly belongings in Pennsylvania or Virginia or wherever, and then said tearful goodbyes to friends and neighbors before trundling up and over the Appalachians in search of a better life, only to make it a few hundred miles along the desolate prairie, take a look around, and think: *Well, guess this'll have to do.*

By contrast, the Oregon settlers endured a two-thousand mile trail of hardship up the Missouri through Blackfoot country and over the Rockies to the Columbia, risking cholera and starvation and scalping, while James Cook spent his life sailing from one uncharted place to the next, risking scurvy and monsoons and a diet of tinned English pig. But after going to such trouble to finally reach the Northwest, those settlers and that sea captain felt obligated to put some honest effort into naming things. Had my Midwestern ancestors made it all the way to the Oregon Coast, they'd have named Cape Perpetua something humble and aw shucks. Tall Ledge, maybe. Or High Point. Neptune Beach would've been named after some future Shriner (Bob's Beach) and the roiling and explosive waters of Devil's Chasm and Thor's Well would now be known as County Inlet #6b and Ed Duncan's Blowhole.

At Newport I turned off 101 just before the Yaquina Bay Bridge. I was headed for Rogue Ales, my former employer who'd screwed over my friend Max—at least according to Max. But I didn't entirely share his harsh feelings. Yes, Rogue's takeover of the Green Dragon diminished what could've been an iconic Southeast Portland taproom, but it was ultimately just another business decision—predictable, quotidian—and better bought out by Rogue than Anheuser-Busch. Plus, Rogue makes some really good beers.

A huge banner, reminiscent of the Beachcomber back in Florence, stretched across the front of the brewery: ROGUE NATION WORLD HEADQUARTERS EST. 1988. Was it a coastal Oregon thing to proclaim oneself the headquarters for craft beer? If so, Rogue had the far stronger claim. The parking lot was packed, and hundreds of kegs were stacked and waiting outside the shipping bay. Past a maze of fermentation tanks, I found myself in line with the other tourists, awaiting my turn to go upstairs and have a pint. As the minutes ticked away, the hostess distracted the crowd with a series of trivia questions. When I called out "Charlotte!" in response to a question about the author of *Jane Eyre,* people turned and gaped in Bobby Fischer-like wonderment, as if I'd divided 31,447 by 14.23 in my head.

Finally, I was led upstairs. The bar, while it had forty taps, had no available seating—but there was a bench beside a small window. A young woman scooted over to make room. She was tall and slender and dressed in cut-off denim shorts. Long blondish hair hung in curls halfway down her back and a silver nose ring gleamed in the soft light streaming through the windows. Not wanting to be rude, I said hello, and when she turned, her eyes were that exact shade of not-quite-seafoam green from back at Neptune Beach.

After traveling alone all summer, I'd miraculously found myself face-to-face with a true beer goddess—a living, breathing Ninkasi—and so I did what came natural: I confessed. I talked and talked. I asked thoughtful questions and then tried like hell to remember her answers. I smiled and laughed and regaled her with pithy, charming quips.

Her name was Danya and she was from Eugene.

"I'm here visiting Newport with my family," she said. "They're checking out coastal real estate, and I've been doing some surfing."

"A little cold for that around here, isn't it?"

"I've surfed all my life," she said. "But I got started in Florida. That's where I'm originally from."

This was easy enough to believe. On love, Burton opines that a well-proportioned leg hath an excellent lustre, and he was right, especially when said legs are suntanned to the rich hue of an amber ale. But I was too distracted musing over Neptune Beach and the twists of fate to catch all the details of Danya's background. By the time I'd ordered a beer—actually a sweetly potent concoction called a braggot[5]—she'd begun talking about art. She painted and sketched and even showed me some of her work on her iPhone's spidercracked screen. Then she recounted her travels. Despite her youth, Danya had been everywhere— India, Peru, Columbia, on and on. Iceland was next. She told me about the cities and sites she planned to visit.

"My first love is the mountains, though," she said. "I spent the last year in Jackson Hole." Then she described her adventures bartending and ski-bumming there.

"I've spent time there, too," I said, and told her about a summer I lived in the shadow of the Tetons and poured fancy wine for wealthy tourists.

Then—while I sipped another beer, an utterly fantastic IPA which I cannot remember a damn thing about—Danya

---

[5] Braggots have been around since Chaucer's day. They're a loose combination of mead, ale, and herbs and spices—a drink that, like gruit beer, predates the widespread use of hops. Rogue's interpretation used honey from their own bee farm, along with Oregon-grown marionberries.

told me how she'd gotten an MBA but quickly tired of the corporate world and decided to follow another path.

"I did the same thing with my law degree," I said. I left out the part about shotgunning bourbon instead of studying for the bar exam, but Danya didn't need to know about all that. We were finding such wonderful commonalities here.

Next, she asked how tall I was—she was six-feet herself—and, laughing, we ran through the inevitable Tall Person Conversation. Yes, I played basketball. No, not professionally. Yes, it's hard to find clothes. No, I don't hit my head on doorways or know earlier than others when it begins to rain. And so on.

Danya was describing a frightening climbing accident in Thailand, a fall, fractured vertebrae, when the server brought over a sack of takeout food and her bill.

We both looked at the sack. "My parents sent me out for dinner," she said.

I took a deep pull from the IPA. Strangely, the hops, which a moment before had seemed bright and lovely, were now intrusive and abrasive. I wanted to go back to the earlier, softer braggot.

"By the way, what's with the little notebook?"

I glanced down at the green pad covered in my scribbles. I'd forgotten I was even carrying it. "I'm writing a book about the Pacific Northwest," I said, and explained how I'd been exploring beer country. Of course, it's foolhardy to try to impress a woman by telling her you're an aspiring writer, but Danya seemed artsy enough to be intrigued. And besides, I occasionally have to get the weight of my ambitions off my chest. It's like lugging around a heart-shaped and piss-stained purple love seat everywhere you go. Between us, the takeout sack stood as impassively as the hourglass on *Vanitas,* the dour painting on the cover of the *Anatomy.* We both looked at the sack, then at one another, the ticking seconds a reminder of our earthly transience, of *memento mori.*

"But beer can't be all your book's about," she said, and fished her credit card from the back pocket of her shorts. "It just sounds like a very ambitious pub crawl."

I admitted this was possible, but then outlined my theory that the terroir of the Northwest, if not the very heart of the region's culture, could be experienced in no better way than through the character of its beer. I talked about Robert Burton and Ken Kesey and how beer and travel and literature are ways, tools, for setting aside, however briefly, the sepia tint of consciousness. How these things are all experiences, sometimes even spiritual experiences, and deserve to be approached with a certain reverence.

"Or maybe drinking just helps people forget their worries?" Danya said.

"Tomayto, tomahto."

She smiled.

"I've also found that beer people tend to be good people," I said.

"So what we drink improves us?"

"Well, it's more like a moths to the light sort of thing."

"I can't wait to read your book."

I told her that hopefully she'd get the chance someday, if only I could catch a break.

"I'll keep a lookout. What's the title?"

When I told her, she raised her dark eyebrows.

"Beer is the one thing that seems to help," I said.

She smiled once again but then grabbed the takeout sack. "I'm sending so many good vibes your way, I really am. But this food's gonna get cold if I don't get moving."

Outside, the sun was busy setting behind the arches of the bridge, banding sky and sea in lavender and gold and conjuring the very romantic moment that apparently wasn't meant to be. I cursed the damned sunset, smiling at Danya all the while.

"How far away do you live again?" she asked me.

I did some quick mental arithmetic. It was at least six hours, probably seven in traffic, maybe eight (or nine) if there was an accident on I-5, which there always was.

"About four hours," I said.

"That sounds pretty far, but who knows"—and then she gave me a long, lingering hug—"maybe we'll run into each other again someday?"

#

While Robert Burton advises against any maiden a man happens upon in an alehouse, he wasn't in the Rogue Alehouse that evening. Then again, the Oxford don is generally pessimistic on matters of the heart, as evidenced by his comparing romantic love to an infectious disease and concluding—after three-hundred pages of mulling it over— that the only realistic hope is for a deaf and dumb man to marry a blind woman. Although he lived a monastic life ("What have I to do with nuns, maids, virgins, widows?" he wonders, with characteristic modesty, before extolling at length exactly what he thinks of nuns, maids, virgins, and widows), Burton did seem to understand certain hazards and fallouts of love. For example, he notes that bachelors in sight of twoscore years often feel compelled to lie about their age, which is a lie I might've been tempted to voice myself, had Danya bothered to ask. Furthermore, as previously mentioned, he hypothesizes that love melancholy is a condition of the liver—*cogit amare jecure* (the liver compels to love)—for which weeping tears into one's beer provides ample support, although he also acknowledges the more practical wisdom of Gordonius, who "will have the testicles an immediate subject or cause, the liver an antecedent."

Regardless, love brooks no delays, and after Danya scooted off in her little car, I was left to contemplate a night alone in the fishing village-turned-tourist trap that is Newport, Oregon. After wasting a few hours in the bars and chowder houses along the historic fishing district—somehow resisting the urge to tour the waxworks museum and Ripley's Believe It or Not!—I paid a visit to the local sea lions. They lounged on slabs beneath the dock, stretched like obese corpses amidst the green murk, their rubbery barks echoing along Bay Boulevard. Each time a new lion swam up, his fellows did their best to keep the newcomer off the dry slab. They pushed and bullied, using their thick necks like battering rams, occasionally showing teeth in a halfhearted and comical way. And always that weird echoic barking—*Nope! Nope! Nope!*—which, as I stood listening, came to seem an oblique commentary on the likelihood of securing respectable lodging in Newport at my price range.

A beer-traveler has to rest his head somewhere, though, and so I left the docks with my eyes peeled for a 24-hour adult video store. But this wasn't for the tawdry reason you're probably thinking. It's actually an expedient shortcut for the budget-conscious, because once an adult video store has been located, one merely has to look across the street or alley and presto!—there's usually an affordable motel. Sure enough, after finding just such a video store and checking into just such a motel, I performed a *beer near me* . . . but the results only would've steered me back to Rogue Ales.

I'd just set out walking in hopes of finding a convenience store when, as luck would have it, I bumped into a little taproom called Bier One. Inside, however, were a bunch of woefully drunk men with strangely reptilian goatees. A few of these hairy dewlaps had reached sufficient length to actually tickle the wood of the bar. Observing these guys, with their loose manner and crude gestures, their cocky laughter and grandstanding, I realized they truly believed their facial hair looked *good*. This outrageous misapprehension was reinforced by their fellow goatee aficionados, and by the voluntary presence of women—although these ladies were no beer goddesses. As always when entering a locals bar, I was given a good staring down. But with Newport being a tourist trap, I was soon forgotten. Hours passed in a haze of pints. Finally, stomach grumbling, I asked the nearest local about Newport's late-night food options. Was there a decent sandwich shop nearby, or all-night pizza delivery? Tacos? Teriyaki? Something?

"Hey, you'd best just listen up a minute buddy . . ."

As the man's jaw moved, his foot-long goatee dipped into his pint. The scraggly gray tips glistened with foam. Distracted, I blanked on whatever else he might've said.

"Hey, where you from anyway?"

"Hey," I said with a smile, "up near Seattle."

This, of course, was exactly as he'd hoped.

"Seattle? *Seattle?*" Then he and his companions launched into a predictable diatribe about the shortcomings of the Emerald City. The clusterfuck traffic and sky-high prices, the gang-bangers and snotty chicks, and—worst of all—the bleeding-heart liberals with their cappuccinos and electric cars and Robin Hood taxation schemes. Although these men were clearly trying to anger me, and perhaps even hoping I might say something which gave them an excuse to try to slug me, I merely smiled and nodded, encouraging their every word and sentiment. After all, what did it really matter if some beery clowns used my presence as an excuse to tell themselves excuses for never having found the guts to leave home?

Eventually, I felt compelled to politely interrupt. "So you're telling me a person can't find anything whatsoever to eat at eleven at night here in historic Newport, Oregon?"

They conferred, grumbled, and said yep, pretty much, to which I replied that a person could always find something to eat in Seattle, no matter how late it was.

"Well, ain't that just lucky for you?" one of them said.

"It is lucky," I said. "And it's also how you know Seattle is a *real* city."

\#

I woke up feeling uncharacteristically optimistic, because my Newport digs featured both an in-room coffee maker *and* a continental breakfast. Now I was glad my unshorn friends from Bier One hadn't steered me in the direction of midnight cuisine, because sleeping on an empty stomach had plummeted my blood sugar and honed my hunger to a fine edge. Thoughts of reheated pastries and powdered eggs had me salivating, and a big cold glass of orange juice (from concentrate) sounded like ambrosia.

I loaded the two-cup coffee maker and hopped in the shower, imagining the day to come. The beautiful coastline, more good beer, more weird locals—who could guess what curious sights and shenanigans I might come upon? But after slipping into a pair of fresh boxers, it turned out my in-room coffee tasted like thinly warmed potting soil.

Still, I had a continental breakfast to look forward to. I'd stuff myself. I'd eat until they had to roll me out the door. After dressing and stepping outside, however, I found a world gone to water. Coastal winds swirled and tossed what might've otherwise been a misty shower into a gray maelstrom. Cold droplets saturated my face and hair, zoomed down the neck of my shirt and simultaneously up the hem of my shorts, as if planning to powwow somewhere in the vicinity of my bellybutton. Water hit me fore and aft, starboard and leeward. I shuffled through the soupy mud, bent and shivering. By the lobby, I was soaked.

Worse, my continental breakfast was a flop. Three varieties of high-fructose cereal—Faux Loops, Frosted Cocoa Smacks, and Carcin-'O'-gens—stood in plastic tubes beside a broken waffle iron coated in clay. My fellow motel-goers had gathered to stare at this morose scene, as if the cold iron were a dog stuck under a truck tire. Finally, the fruit basket contained either small, pale oranges or shriveled and blanched grapefruits, assuming they weren't in fact the month-old lemons they most closely resembled.

The hour wasn't even remotely decent for a beer, but after leaving the motel I noticed a bar I'd somehow overlooked the night before: Moby Dick's. Neon lights in the dark little windows made Day-Glo stripes on the flooded sidewalk. The sign above the door featured the requisite whale and also promised a sports lounge, night club, karaoke bar, live music, a game room, *and* a big screen TV! In short, I was compelled, perhaps even obligated.

Inside, a Miller Lite flag big as a sail hung from the ceiling above a bank of Oregon Video Lottery machines. Sad-faced people sat pumping dollar bills into these machines, frowning as each push of the button failed to return the windfall promised by the spinning cherries. Between their weathered countenances and tatty blue and gray clothing, these folks really did resemble sailors ashore from a whaling tour, although they'd seriously neglected their deck-swabbing duties. Moby Dick's was filthy. The walls were festooned with a paisley of greenish mold and buckets dotted the floor to catch the drips, a patina of dust covered everything (except the buttons of the lottery machines), and the bartender—no long goatee, but bushy muttonchops—wore an undershirt that must've already been yellowed back when Eddie Vedder and Kurt Cobain were thinking of starting bands.

This bartender did pour me a Widmer Hefeweizen, though, which was on special. The Widmer Brothers, Kurt and Rob, were instrumental in establishing Portland's early reputation as a microbrew haven. Their hefeweizen, while run-of-the-mill by today's standards, struck late '80s beer drinkers as very different—and much tastier—than Bud Light. But in 1997 the brothers struck a deal with Anheuser-Busch ($18 million for a percentage of common stock), which allowed them access to A-B's worldwide distribution network. Now their hefeweizen can be found at every grocery store in the western hemisphere, although ironically enough at many Portland bars you're more likely to find Pabst Blue Ribbon on tap. Why? Because Kurt and Rob Widmer sold out to corporate America, and for Portland's fedora and skinny jeans and indie music crowd, this means they are officially uncool, and thus so is their iconic beer.

I wiped the rim of my glass with a gummy slice of lemon the bartender had stuck on it, hoping the old citrus might still retain some antimicrobial properties. Beyond the window, rain fell gray and blowing. "Give me some rain," thinks the bartender in *Sometimes a Great Notion*, "some bad weather, and watch me roll the dollars. Give me a dark smeary shiny night full of rain. That's when the fear starts . . ." Constant rain and constant brew in the Pacific Northwest. Gloom and grain, hops and misery. Might the one more or less explain the other?

Heading up the coast, I passed through Otter Rock, a community named for a cute but easily duped sea mammal whose pelts were so valuable that today there are no otters to be found anywhere near Otter Rock. Next was the town of Depoe Bay, which holds claim (according to Depoe Bay, at least) to having the world's smallest navigable bay. The sea was horned in by a great swirling bowl of fog, but just beyond the town limits sign the fog parted to reveal evergreen hillsides veiled in mist. Past a whale museum and a few shacks offering whale watching tours, I parked beside a whale statue along a low stone wall. Far below, lugubrious tides slopped over black rock and sheeted off in milky rivulets.

The surrounding area, spooky and rugged, was the setting for the film adaptation of *Sometimes*. Rumor has it, Paul Newman liked the fish and chips at the local diners across 101. And while the fishing scene in *Cuckoo's Nest* takes place at Florence, the scene in the film was shot right there in Depoe Bay. Kesey likely approved, as he understood the rain. "For this land was permeated with dying," he writes, "this bounteous land . . . was saturated with moist and terrible dying." This echoes Burton's take on weather, where he advises the melancholy to avoid thick, cloudy, foggy airs—basically, all of his native England as well as the Pacific Northwest.

Down the stone wall was a memorial to a pair of local fisherman, who perished in the bay in 1936 on a dark and foggy night. IT IS NOT TRUE, their memorial read. LIFE IS NOT SLAIN BY DEATH. THE VAST, IMMORTAL SEA SHALL HAVE HER OWN, SHALL GATHER TO HER THIS EXPIRING BREATH, SHALL REAP WHERE SHE HAS SOWN.

With these elegiac words in mind, I stood in the drip and watched sea and fog churn, hoping to catch a glimpse of a whale or perhaps a particularly cagey otter. But no such luck. May as well have waited for the ghost of Paul Newman to emerge from the misty pines—or better yet, for Kesey and the Pranksters to come rolling down 101 in Furthur, a speedy Neal Cassady at the wheel, drinking acid-laced orange juice, freaking out the Hell's Angels, and tootling the masses.

HAYSTACK ROCKS, WILD ALES, AND JESUS MUSIC

Familiar throughout the Northwest, the McMenamins franchise buys up historical properties that have outlived their function—defunct schools, poor houses, old theaters—and rehabs them into Grateful Dead-inspired adult playgrounds complete with breweries and restaurants, distilleries and wineries, spas, whimsically Euro-style hotel rooms, and concert venues. So when a spontaneous *beer near me* suggested the McMenamins Lighthouse Brewpub, I was intrigued.

Thinking I'd stop for lunch and check the place out, I headed north past Boiler Bay, which is named for the boiler of a shipwreck visible at low tide, and entered Lincoln City, which advertises itself, "A Great Place to Try New Things." But the great place stretched for miles along 101, just one sea-scoured motel and low-end restaurant after another, as if Lincoln City weren't so much a city as a tapeworm grown long on tourist dollars and kitsch.

Furthermore, what does Abraham Lincoln have to do with anything? Why, for example, isn't Lincoln City named after one of the local tribes? Siletz City, say, or Chinook City. Especially considering Abe never set foot in Oregon, despite being offered first the secretaryship of the territory and later the governorship. But he turned both offers down in favor of practicing law back in Illinois, so that six score and some odd years later, fourth graders such as myself would have somewhere to go on field trips. Strangely enough, Lincoln City schoolkids are actually the ones responsible for the inapt name. A contest was held, for whatever reason, and because children are ill-prepared for tasks such as naming civic installations into perpetuity, they chose the first name recalled from those lessons sandwiched between lunch and recess.

Lincoln City still could've redeemed herself, though, as I was looking forward to lunch at McMenamins Lighthouse Brewpub. But while I'd anticipated a refurbished historic site, like the Edgefield property in Troutdale or the Kennedy School in Portland, a place where I might sip a fresh pint and nurse a steaming bowl of chowder as waves broke against the fog-shrouded foot of a quaint old lighthouse, instead I found a twelve-foot plastic lighthouse overlooking a busy intersection adjacent a Grocery Outlet and a Dollar Tree.

101 veered inland into the Siuslaw National Forest, the spruce swathed in moss and the ground carpeted with ferns. This was gorgeous old-growth forest, real Sasquatch country, and the diffuse light filtering down through the canopy lent all an eerie cast. I lowered the windows to let the clean air whip through the cab and soon turned off for the coast and Pacific City. A few miles to the south, a massive boulder loomed offshore, its crown busy with seabirds. I followed Cape Kiwanda Drive toward this big rock and, coincidentally, toward Pelican Pub and Brewery.

Pelican had a stunning beachfront view. It was also packed. So much so that the hostess handed out those tacky flashing discs that light up when a table finally comes available. This is the sort of humiliation family men suffer—the need for a massive, coffin-sized table, high chairs, cartoonish bric-a-brac—

but being a lone beer traveler I simply headed straight to the bar. There, I lurked until a seat came open and then slid deftly in, nearly brushing against the backside of the person vacating the valuable real estate. Wooden plaques touted Pelican's various beer contest victories. World Beer Cup Brewpub of the Year, Great American Beer Festival Brewpub of the Year, and so on. Beyond the large windows lay a stretch of beach bracketed on the north by a towering wall of sand. Perhaps a mile offshore loomed that massive boulder.

"That's Haystack Rock," the bartender said, when I inquired.

"Wait, I thought Haystack Rock was at Cannon Beach. It shows up at the end of *The Goonies,* right?"

"There's one up there, too. But that one's *our* Haystack Rock."

I sought to clarify the situation: was it really the case that there were two giant rocks, in two separate beach towns, and yet they shared the exact same name?

"Right," the bartender said.

"Okay, but why?"

"Beats me. Guess we're just not very creative out here on the coast."

Thinking of those schoolkids who named Lincoln City, I was tempted to agree, but then I hadn't yet tried Pelican's beer.

While sipping through a tray of tasters, I struck up a conversation with the woman beside me. She was married to a Swede, she said, apropos of (I can only suppose) my being a strange male who'd chanced to speak to her in a bar. Turns out, she'd managed to escape this husband and their half-Swedish brood for a much-needed beer and some leisure reading. The book in question was a sci-fi novel—one of the *Dune* series. I recalled that Frank Herbert, the author of *Dune*, was born in Tacoma and studied creative writing at the University of Washington. Rumor had it he was inspired to write his famous series, which is set on a desert world of shifting sands, after visiting those melancholy dunes near Florence.

"In my experience," I said, "beer people and book people are often one and the same."

"You know, that's probably true," said the Swede-marrying woman.

Then I noticed a still stranger confluence and pointed out the window at the real-life dune far down the beach. "Are people actually climbing that thing?"

She glanced over her shoulder at the smudgy little dots crawling up the face of the sand tower. "You should give it a try. The view from up top is really something."

"So you've climbed it?"

"Once."

I said it looked pretty difficult.

"It's not so bad." She paused to consider my extensive taster board. "So long as you don't drink too much beer first."

Later on, I walked down the beach past locals launching dory boats over the breakers. The dune was so big it took longer to reach than anticipated, and up close it was steeper than it'd appeared from the comfort of the pub. A number of people trudged up the huge thing, an expedition that didn't look even remotely pleasant, but I was in the mood for a little misery and so I kicked off my shoes and began to ascend.

Ten minutes later, maybe a third of the way up, I realized those people I'd seen climbing were all half my size and half my age. Being teenagers, they also probably hadn't been drinking quite so much beer. I bent over, lungs heaving, and spit up the remnants of my first sample from back at Pelican—a cream ale. Despite the name, there's nothing remotely creamy about this style. Traditionally, it was an ale lightened with corn additives to better resemble the day's popular lagers, but Pelican's take was all malt and barley. The result was light, crisp, and weirdly aroma-less going down. Mercifully, it came back up the same way.

I wiped the gory strings from my lips and resolved to keep going, but with each step up I slid two steps backward. I was buried to the ankles and sinking when a sudden belch brought back the Tsunami Export Stout, a beer that's rich espresso flavor made for a highly effective emetic. Some minutes later, concentrating on my breathing, I renewed my acquaintance with the best of Pelican's offerings: a "New-World" IPA brewed with Ella hops from Australia.

As I pushed for the summit—a summit which seemed to recede with each backsliding step—I thought of Burton, who notes that exercise is recommended by nearly all the ancient scholars, from Guianerius (gentle only, and after a good bout of frications), to Montaltus and Jason Pratensis and finally to Galen, who lauds how "nature's physician" expels sweat and other insensible vapours from the body.[6] But more than sweat was being expelled from my body, as I'd insensibly neglected

---

[6] Then again, the entire partition on cures is best taken with a grain of salt, especially considering Burton's concluding advice is to perform an enema with a chimney bellows to draw forth the flatuous melancholy.

the most crucial of Burton's advice—and this straight from the horse's mouth, no ancient scholarship required—"The fittest time for exercise is a little before dinner," Burton writes, "a little before supper, or at any time when the body is empty."

Finally, I managed to clamber atop the dune, woozy and sweating and pasted with sand. I collapsed in a lump, but the hard-won view really was great. The sea rolled blue to the horizon, punctuated by Haystack Rock, and a strip of beach curled south around Nestucca Bay. To the north, forested hills met Cape Lookout ten miles up the coast. But the splendor was dimmed by an incessant barfiness. Maybe my Cistercian beer fasting wasn't as healthy as I'd been telling myself?

Sometime later, I managed to stumble back down to sea-level. Resting in the Honda, I was queasy and my clammy t-shirt was glued to my ribs, but I did have something to look forward to: de Garde. Back at Hair of the Dog, Colin had told me how this brewery's founder—in order to locate the very best microbial terroir in all of Oregon—placed batches of wort up and down the coast, only to determine the finest place to spontaneously ferment beer was in the unlikely town of Tillamook, which was just up 101 from Pacific City.

#

Unlikely because Tillamook is a rinky-dink dairy farming community in the middle of nowhere—although it's possible, if not even probable, that all that zesty cow flop actually creates the world-class yeast profile which so elevates de Garde's beer.

The taproom was austere, but a trip to the john revealed a warehouse full of foeders and other large-volume casks, and the smell—of the beer, not the john—spoke of funky bugs and mystical happenings in oak. I found a table made from an old barrel, placed my backpack on the bare concrete floor, and sampled a wild ale called the Pas (sounds like *paw*). It poured a lush gold and tasted so improbably tropical that I asked the bartender if they'd aged it over fruit.

"She's all grain all the way," he said, and then launched into a delightfully geeky explanation of fermentation science. While listening, however, I couldn't help but notice the book he'd been reading—*Astoria,* by Peter Stark—as I'd recently read this same book in preparation for visiting the so-named town, which was still a couple hours up the coast. I commended the bartender on his literary taste, and we ended up discussing our favorite parts of the lively narrative. Once again, beer people shine. Craft beer is such a boon, such a bellwether of all that's thoughtful and decent. It's difficult to imagine life without it.

"Could I please do tasters of everything?"

"Actually . . ." the bartender said, and then explained in the gentlest of terms that de Garde didn't actually *do* taster-sized pours, because everyone wanted them, or at least thought they wanted them, and if they *did* do them they'd end up spending all day filling and washing itty-bitty taster glasses, and not talking beer and spreading the gospel of wild ales. "But I'm more than happy to pour you a *glass* of everything," he added.

Which is how I ended up ordering five beers at once and carrying the whole gorgeous menagerie back to my barrel-table. Having thus dedicated myself to a full day in Tillamook, I sipped from one beer after another, traversing from the tartness of a foeder-aged Berlinerweisse to a wild ale aged in French puncheons over boysenberries, to a wonderfully musty farmhouse blend. All the while I read, taking breaks every so often to simply stare out the rain-spattered window at the quiet road and empty fields. As the hours passed, the beers warmed, and as they warmed, the more intricate the flavors I was able to taste and the more thoughtful and reflective I became. Strange, or so it seemed, that this rural community—a place that due to its location between the coast and mountain passes was nearly as isolated and backwater as my hometown—could produce and support such an offbeat product. Could it be that while Oregonians make craft beer, craft beer is remaking the Oregonian? Might taste and creativity ultimately transcend the provincialism that typically makes rural living unbearable?

Hours later and happy as a smoked clam, I paid up and left. But de Garde isn't the only business in Tillamook offering up tasty morsels. A visitor may also tour the world famous Tillamook Cheese Factory—although *why* anyone would tour a cheese factory remains a mystery. I've done any number of brewery tours, and while those get dull after a while, at least you get to drink beer. A complimentary plug of Muenster just isn't sufficient motivation.

101 brought me to Bay City and then Garibaldi with its massive lumber barges just offshore and finally to Rockaway Beach. I pulled into the purported visitor's center, which was located in the caboose of an old red-painted railroad car. Inside, some chamber of commerce types debated how best to procure the necessary Mexican cuisine to see them through the rainy season now that the summer was winding down and all the restaurants would be closing. Could they stock up on burritos? Freeze a load of tamales? I stood eavesdropping in the cramped caboose—I'm six-foot-six, by the way—for an improbably long

time, and yet my looming presence distracted the chamber members from their enchilada emergency not one bit.

Then I walked down to Rick's Roadhouse where the patrons were all watching Family Feud on the TV and, strangely enough, eating nachos. Maybe Rick had 86'd the chamber of commerce for some reason? Whatever the case, Rick's regulars were really into the show, shouting answers between shoving gobs of half-melted Tillamook cheese in their mouths. The current subject was, ANOTHER WORD OR EXPRESSION FOR KISSING. Making out and smooching were already off the board.

"Locking lips!" yelled the portly woman on my left.

Her boyfriend dunked a fistful of chips in sour cream. "Snogging!"

"Sucking face!" said the martini-slurping elderly woman along the back wall.

"Tonsil hockey!"

"First base!"

"Swapping spit!" said the bartender. Then she turned to me. "Drink, handsome?"

Thoroughly distracted, I ordered a bottle of something or another.

"Frenching!" It was the portly woman again. She elbowed me, without ever taking her eyes off the TV. "That's an easy one."

"Necking?" offered the quiet man to my right.

"Whoa there, Dave," said another man, two stools down, and then explained that, at least in his experience, to *neck* implied more than just a kiss.

In back of the place, people played video lottery, losing money with each push of the glowing red button. It could've been worse, I suppose, as some of that cash gets funneled back into civic needs, swapping disability and Social Security to fund education and whatnot. Still, I wondered about the state sanctioning this behavior. Didn't placing those machines in bars encourage people to pile a gambling addiction atop their drinking problem? Wasn't this, in the words of Danæus, *Fons fraudum et maleficiorum,* (the fountain of cozenage and villainy), or was video lottery simply practical—the Oregon legislature having determined, after weighing all the relevant facts and figures, that a certain portion of the citizenry could only benefit from having its money reallocated?

"Tongue wrastlin!" the martini-slurping woman offered. "Come on, you stupid ijits! It ain't that hard."

"Good call, Sheila"—this from Dave the necking man— "I was just about to suggest tongue wrestling."

A couple blocks away was the Rockaway Beach Rock Garden. It was hard to miss, between a raggedy mini-golf course, a busy soap bubble machine, and a boom-box blasting Christian pop. Not a soul was around, although a posted sign declared the following rules:

1. PICK SOME ROCKS

2. PAY THE BOX (AN AMOUNT YOU FEEL IS FAIR)

Bubbles spattered against my jacket and rocks lay everywhere—not polished stones, just plain old rocks. Then a godlike voice from the boom-box interrupted the heavenly power chords: "FIVE ROCK DAILY LIMIT!"

I lowered the volume and sat on a wooden bench. I stayed there for quite a while, scribbling notes and watching the gulls float by, creaking on the sea winds, as iridescent bubbles sank and popped on the dusty rocks. No one else came to visit the Rockaway Beach Rock Garden in my time there, although I kept hoping someone might. It seemed strange enough for something noteworthy to occur. A place where a guy in search of an elusive peace and happiness just might find it. But that was only the movies talking, and so I finally tucked the notepad in my pocket, returned the Jesusy stereo to full blast, and continued on my way—after I selected a rock and paid three dollars to the box, that is, an amount I felt was fair.

#

After Nehalem and Manzanita, I passed the 1,661-foot summit of Neahkahnie Mountain, the highest point on the Oregon Coast. Neahkahnie is a native word meaning "home of the supreme being" and so it was: a view into forever, an endless blue framed far below by rugged offshore sea stacks and the vaporous coastline. 101 hugged the mountainside, unwinding along the precipice's edge, the view so sublime it actually constituted a hazard, as the touring motorist was apt to gawp himself right over the edge.

Later I rolled into Cannon Beach. Imagine a quintessential coastal community, the foggy streets, the sleepy bungalows, the seafood houses—but for the more sophisticated beachgoer. Patagonia. Sotheby's. A well-renovated theatre for the local thespians and GMO-free saltwater taffy. And of all the people strolling Hemlock Street, not one sported facial hair measurable with a yardstick. This was all fine by me, except that the price of eating dinner in Cannon Beach was on par with making a down payment on a Sotheby's property. Consider the $17.95 cheeseburger at Public Coast Brewing. This "Save Our Beaches Burger" involved a donation of one dollar to the Haystack Rock Awareness Program, an organization which I can only assume was in charge of coming up with a new name for one of those Haystack Rocks. Even accounting for the donation, the math troubled me. Seventeen-dollar hamburgers? What sort of world would this be for the grandchildren I was doing my best not to leave behind?

Just a couple blocks away, however, at Bill's Tavern & Brewhouse, I scored a hearty burger *and* a fresh schooner of Duckdive Pale Ale (brewed upstairs above the tavern), all for under $15, thank you very much. Not coincidentally, Bill's was packed with happy customers.

Satisfied, I trudged through the sand to have a look at Cannon Beach's famous Haystack Rock. It's much closer to shore than the one at Pacific City, and while it's definitely an imposing chunk, it's also just a big rock. I stood in the cold wind admiring it for what felt like five minutes, but was probably more like twenty seconds, and then trudged back the way I'd come.

A few miles up the road lay Seaside and the brewery named for it. The century-old building was formerly the town jail, and taps emerged from the wall cordoning off a cell block that'd once functioned as the drunk tank. Out in the beer garden, the waitress brought me a Blow Hole Hefeweizen that thankfully did not taste as if authentically spewed from a marine animal. I sat facing a brick fire pit and the heat radiating up from it caused the air to shimmer, casting the world beyond in that strange waviness reminiscent of how cartoons fade into dream sequences. And that's just how the Oregon Coast felt: dreamlike. Sleepy and kitschy. Quirky and full of things like saltwater taffy that are at once appealing and yet weirdly ominous.

Downtown Seaside was marred by a series of bland resort hotels which lorded over a tunnel of novelty shops and touristy crab shacks. Seaside was the spot for those who couldn't quite afford Cannon Beach, and it's important we poor folk have somewhere to vacation—but honestly, how many screen-printed t-shirt stores does one town really need? How many candy shops and arcades? Wasn't it possible that at least *some* visitors to Seaside, Oregon, although not wealthy, might fail to see the charm of junk marts peddling a hundred different specimens of Seaside shot glasses and Seaside cigarette lighters all made for pennies on the dollar in China?

The defense of all this is predictable. First, it's "family-friendly" and "for the kids." Second, it's crucial for local commerce. But as for family interests above all else, why? Why should we allow children—even if they actually do enjoy commercialized ugliness, which is hardly proven—to determine how things should be? Children, as already established, are unwise to the point of naming things incongruously after Abraham Lincoln, so why tune our environments to their interests? After all, no matter how much we infantilize, sanitize, and commodify our lives, we can't stop children from growing up, and we certainly can't be children again ourselves, which is perhaps the fantasy a place like Seaside is ultimately selling. And as for the preeminence of local commerce, why assume a little class would scare the tourists away—put more bluntly, why assume working-class people like stupid things?

I scowled at the happy families all the way down to the beach, where Broadway ended at a large circular promenade. In its center stood a statue in commemoration of Lewis and Clark's incredible journey. The explorers admired the sand and sea, brassy hips rubbing and shoulders pressed together. The old friends looked capable and proud, although maybe a little tired—especially Meriwether Lewis, who is mysteriously silent in the journals as to his feelings about finally reaching the Pacific after so much toil. William Clark famously scribbled, "Ocian in view! O! the joy." Yet Captain Lewis recorded not a word.

He was depressed, of course, which can make a man neglect his daily chores, but still. Just try to imagine his disappointment after traveling over 4,000 miles through hardscrabble *terra incognita*, after being chased around the Rockies in hair-raising fashion by pissed-off grizzly bears, after portaging raging rivers and wearing holes in all of his moccasins, after first running out of whiskey and then running out of salt to season the dogs he ate for dinner, after seeing himself and his crew laid low over and over by dysentery with only crude laxatives to treat their affliction, after getting shilled in barter time and again by hard-bargaining tribesman (and seeing his spoons and teapots purloined time and again by sticky-fingered tribesman), only to finally reach the cold and miserable Oregon Coast—already having realized the Northwest Passage was just a dream and President Jefferson's historic charge would go unmet—and find nothing there but chain hotels, trinket shops, and children and old folks having their potato chips burgled by gangs of thuggish seagulls.

Perhaps such disillusionment helps explain why, in the fall of 1809, just three years after his and Clark's celebrated return from the Northwest (a return which saw a nearsighted expedition member mistake Captain Lewis for an elk and plunk him in the ass with a musket ball), Meriwether Lewis, hounded by debtors and unlucky in love, beleaguered by alcoholism and inveterate melancholia—and, quite possibly, by the psychological effects of late stage syphilis acquired during the expedition—was finally overcome by the weight of his mind.

Traveling east in hopes of finally publishing the much anticipated journals, he stopped at Grinder's Stand, an inn and tavern along the Natchez Trail in the wilderness of Tennessee. There, after skipping dinner in lieu of a little whiskey, he shot himself in the head, then again in the chest, before opening himself up chin to toes with a razor blade.

DRINKING BEER WITH THE ASTORIANS

Night had fallen by the time I crossed the Youngs Bay Bridge into Astoria. My destination was Fort George Brewery, but first I needed to secure suitable lodging. I'd passed by the usual corporate dungholes and was resigning myself to yet another night of bed bugs and bodily fluids, when just across the street from the brewery I discovered the Norblad Hotel. With its terra-cotta doorways and tin awnings, the hotel's architecture resembled that of a big East Coast city, not a small town on the Northwest coast. In fact, what little I'd seen of Astoria in the dark and the drizzle was all reminiscent of some distant time and place. Downtown was full of tall stone buildings, while planted uphill from the Columbia were a number of eclectic Victorians with steeply-peaked roofs and intricate cupolas.

This sense of time warp only intensified in the Norblad's lobby, which was straight out of the 1970s. Stevie Wonder's *Inner Visions* spun on vinyl and the walls were lined with LPs. Springsteen's *Darkness at the Edge of Town*. The Ramones. Kool and the Gang.

The floppy-haired kid behind the front desk quoted a rate I couldn't really afford, and we commenced to politely dicker. "Love the music, by the way," I said. He agreed that the seventies were a tremendous decade in American music, and then admitted to having a marginally less expensive room available. Its slight inconvenience, a shared bathroom, was offset by the lower price. From there, we bargained some more, as it hadn't escaped my attention that the Norblad appeared nearly empty—Astoria's tourist season was winding down— and it seemed the town's collection of freshly-vacated hotels might be eager to compete for my valuable business.

The clerk admitted this was likely true. His honesty and matter-of-fact demeanor was so refreshing that I almost felt bad for haggling. Finally, he offered to shave off ten more bucks.

"Sold," was my reply, feeling deeply satisfied with our compromise—a satisfaction cemented upon discovering my discount room overlooked Fort George's barrel-aging facility.

Shortly thereafter, luggage dumped, I was seated at the bar with five generous tasters fizzing at my fingertips. Like Sam Bond's back in Eugene, Fort George was a converted auto garage. More notably, it also sat on the location of Fort Astoria, the first permanent American settlement west of the Rockies. Fort Astoria was a trading post founded in 1811 at the behest of John Jacob Astor and his Pacific Fur Company—a scheme intended to introduce pelts harvested from the Northwest into worldwide trade—but it became Fort George when the British took control during the War of 1812 and changed the name to flatter their king. The craft beer world being a small one, the brewery's founder previously worked for McMenamins at the Lighthouse Brewpub in Lincoln City and later at Bill's Tavern & Brewhouse back in Cannon Beach, slowly making his way up the coast, rather like myself.

A foot-long model Cavatica spider dangling from the ceiling dredged up fond memories of Cryptatropa in Olympia, where I'd enjoyed a pint of Fort George's arachnid-inspired ale. But I skipped the Cavatica in favor of the Optimist IPA. A lighter beer, at only around six percent, it felt just right for a melancholy traveler like myself. The nose was ripe with tropical fruits and floral spice. They say our sense of smell is deeply entwined with memory, olfactory and limbic systems in close accord, and optimism is a habit of mind born of a pleasant past—and since most of my pleasant memories involve beer in one way or another, perhaps my enjoyment of the Optimist was inevitable.

A group of young locals soon took the stools beside me. The girls were waitresses, their guy friend a commercial fisherman. I introduced myself and then asked them about life in Astoria—what it was like living so close to the Columbia and the Pacific, whether they enjoyed it, or whether the isolation and gloom could get rough—but for them Astoria wasn't really all that interesting. It was just home. All there was, all there'd been, all there'd probably ever be.

"*The Goonies* was filmed around here," one of the waitresses said.

"So was *Kindergarten Cop,*" the other waitress added, to which I replied that this particular film was, in my opinion, Governor Schwarzenegger's finest work.

"They made a few other movies around here, too," the fisherman said.

I asked which ones, but he couldn't remember. There were definitely others, though. Next, I asked about the beers they were drinking, and a pattern began to emerge.

"I'm not really sure what this is," the fisherman said, studying his pint. "I always get the same thing. The bartenders know what I like."

A few more questions revealed he was from the town of Chinook, just across the Columbia. A Chinook village at the same location predated the 1811 Astoria colony. The Chinooks had been friendly and helpful to the Astorians upon first discovering them stumbling around sopping wet and uncertain where and how exactly to build their new colony. I asked the fisherman what it'd been like to grow up there.

"In Chinook? Just regular, I guess."

"Were there still a lot of native people around?"

He said there were some, but not necessarily a lot.

"How did they like it?

"Like what?"

"Growing up in Chinook."

"Just fine, so far as I know."

I put similar questions to the two waitresses, who were from Astoria, and received similarly vague answers. Astoria was okay, the people were nice enough, it was a good place to raise kids, and so on. It occurred that these people came to this brewery at least a couple times a week, and had been doing so for years and in all likelihood would continue doing so unto the grave. They liked the brewery and they enjoyed the beer, and they were resigned to hometown life, but familiarity had rendered the details of that life more or less invisible.

We kept talking—they really were nice people—but they'd gotten me thinking of my own hometown, where I'd played basketball and read books and mooned over cheerleaders for eighteen long years. How much of my childhood had I missed due to the blindness of the familiar? What a strange thing: this paradoxical unfamiliarity with home.

Tasters finished, the bartender suggested I visit Astoria Brewing, and so I headed down 14th Street toward the

Columbia. But as I pushed through the door an employee came around the bar. He walked right up to me and for an odd moment I thought he meant to shake my hand. Instead, he neatly sidestepped me and flipped the OPEN sign to CLOSED. Keep in mind that he still hadn't spoken a word, despite my standing a foot away and having just walked through the door of his establishment. I remained there, smiling faintly, until he finally seemed to realize a response of some sort was necessary.

"Gosh, man, we just closed."

I glanced at the sign he'd flipped.

"You were wanting to try our beer?"

I admitted the thought had crossed my mind.

"Go next door," he said, "to The Chart Room. Our stuff's always on tap."

And so it was, although I can't recall a thing about Astoria Brewing's beer because The Chart Room rendered questions of taste more or less moot. All was dingy and tinged with a subtle but pervasive malice, the conversations simmering around me just slightly too loud, the content laced with innuendo not nearly clever enough to justify the crudity. The Chart Room was a dive bar, you see, not a brewery or a taproom, and dive bars are not necessarily full of good beer people, even if they happen to serve good beer.

A woman soon mounted the neighboring stool with a low grunt. Brunette and wiry and the owner of a pair of large and veiny hands, she reminded me of Carla Tortelli, the tough-talking waitress from *Cheers*. Without a word having passed between them, the bartender poured her a series of Crown Royal shots, which she quickly chased down with cola. She looked about my age, somewhere in her middle thirties, and considering we were seated all of eight inches apart, I felt it was socially proper to say hello. At the sound of my voice, she cut an eye my way, and seemed almost ready to return the greeting before she stopped herself. I smiled and faced forward, sipping my beer and waiting. A few minutes later, she finally began to grouse—in the coarsest and most unprintable of language— about the miseries of her job at a local pizza restaurant. Over her shoulder blinked a string of Oregon Video Lottery machines.

"I need a fucking cigarette," she said. "You got one?"

"Here's something interesting," I said.

"What—you don't got any cigarettes?"

"I knew you were a waitress before you ever said a word about it."

She inquired how this was possible, considering we'd never met before and she didn't know me from the next douchebag.

"Let's call it a sixth sense," I said.

"Call it whatever you want, but I'm done listening unless you go find me a smoke."

I watched her choke down two more shots, and wondered for exactly how many years she'd been dragging her weary bones into the dreaded pizza restaurant night after night, like a penury sentence handed down for doffing the old cap and gown at Astoria High. In fact, I got curious enough to inquire as to how long she'd been waitressing.

"Not more than a year or so," she said. "But I've just about had it."

I asked what line of work she'd been in before.

"Nothing much"—she gave me a shifty look—"I'm only twenty-three."

I studied her more closely. The light was oily and dim, but it simply didn't seem possible this weather-beaten and foulmouthed individual was that young. What were they doing to her at this pizza restaurant? In the Chart Room? In Astoria?

"I tell myself every motherfucking day that I ain't gonna drink when my shift's over," she said—then the men's room door swung open and I caught a whiff of something at once ammoniac and barnyard, as if the urinal pucks were made of toe cheese—"but then I think: fuck it, people suck and I gotta get my head right."

"You really do seem to like that Crown Royal," I said.

"Fuck you, asshole," the pizza waitress replied.

Colorful or otherwise, her demeanor set me on edge. Such naked hostility from a total stranger, even a diminutive one, served as a reminder that I was a stranger in a strange town with a rough-and-tumble reputation. Back in the late nineteenth century, before dams and overfishing decimated the salmon runs, Astoria thrived as a cannery town. But the crashing currents and shifting sands of the Columbia Bar—"one of the most fearful sights that can possibly meet the eye," according to Captain Wilkes, himself a fearsome man, in 1841—tended to attract fishermen who didn't worry too much about drowning while trying to hook a buck. Fatalists, in other words. Hard-drinkers. Brawlers. In fact, *The Oregonian* described the Astoria of this period as "perhaps the most wicked place on earth."

While the modern-day Chart Room crowd wasn't quite that intimidating, I assumed that, should I continue to drink and ask nosy questions, my chances of getting punched in the face by someone hovered north of twenty-percent, which didn't seem like particularly good odds. I hadn't been assaulted by a drunk in years, a streak I preferred to keep going. So after the pizza waitress finally managed to bum a fuckin' smoke and slip the fuck outside, I hiked straight back up the hill to Fort George for a couple more Optimist IPAs.

#

Morning found me sipping coffee across the street from the John Jacob Astor Hotel. A behemoth of whitish stone dated from the 1920's, it evoked the early modern architecture one sees in the historic districts of Seattle, but not usually in small fishing towns. The hotel's namesake was America's very first millionaire. Early in life, Astor realized the local tribes, lacking a sense of their niche in the global economy, would sell or trade valuable furs for mere trinkets, which he could then ship to Europe where the furs fetched big bucks. He leveraged this capital into a few forward-thinking real estate investments: namely, most of Manhattan before it was Manhattan. Astor later used this fortune to send two contingents of hand-picked men to the mouth of the Columbia—one by boat south around Cape Horn, the other overland along the old Lewis and Clark route—where they were to establish a series of trading posts along the Missouri and the Columbia, all leading to the hub at Astoria, whereby furs gathered from the interior and on the coast would be shipped along a global route of Astor's devising.

Although his fur empire didn't pan out—the Astorians had problems with the natives, problems with the weather, problems with each other, and problems with the British—

Astor later paid Washington Irving to pen a book about his Pacific Fur Company. The result, *Astoria, or Anecdotes of an Enterprise Beyond the Rocky Mountains* (1836), can be seen as akin to Donald Trump's ghost-written memoir *The Art of the Deal* (1987), insofar as both works were commissioned by capitalists who accrued fortunes by skinning the unwary. While the ghostwriter of Trump's book has since expressed regret at having contributed to Trumpism, Irving seemed genuinely impressed with Astor. "His genius had ever been in advance of his circumstances," Irving writes, "prompting him to new and wide fields of enterprise beyond the scope of ordinary merchants." While somewhat fawning, this is also accurate, because if Astor's plan *had* worked—if he'd gotten a fleet of his own ships trading cheaply-gotten Northwest beaver and otter pelts for Chinese esoterica that East Coast Americans would pay out the nose for—it's almost impossible to imagine how wealthy and powerful the man would've become.

Then again, it's clear neither Astor nor Trump bothered to read their Burton, in particular the subsect on covetousness, wherein we go from the apostle Paul's purported advice to Timothy on lust for money being the root of all evil and the cause of many sorrows, to the wisdom of the Roman poet Horace—"his wealth increaseth, and the more he hath, the more he wants"—which is a sentiment that unfortunately doesn't hold much water these days.

Nevertheless, between its fascinating history and striking architecture, Astoria was one of the most interesting places I'd yet been. I spent a long time wandering the streets of downtown (the Museum of Whimsy was closed, unfortunately), and then the neighborhood on the steep hill to the south, with its century-old ramshackle Victorians with darkly shuttered windows, leaf-choked koi ponds, and yards gone to jungle. These spooky houses made a passerby wonder who or *what* lived inside, although they were probably just full of surly pizza waitresses.

Down the hill, the massive Astoria Bridge spanned the Columbia, awaiting my return to Washington State. But there remained one last thing to see. So I headed back to the Norblad, retrieved the Honda, and followed a series of signs up to the Astoria Column. The monument is modeled after Trajan's Column and stands atop Coxcomb Hill, the highest point in Astoria, with panoramic views of Youngs Bay, the Columbia, and the Coastal Range. The Column's spiral frieze depicts various Northwest historical mainstays: beavers (still cute and lively, Mr. Astor not having made their acquaintance yet), Captain Robert Gray piloting the *Columbia Rediva* into the estuary of the mighty river that now bears its name, Lewis and Clark doing their thing, Chinook and Clatsop trading with white men, and finally the coming of the railroads.

I pulled in along a one-way, but was stopped by a boy and his beagle, both of whom wore yellow penny vests. The boy approached the window. Seeing as he was mildly disabled, the beagle must've been a service animal, and it was heartening to know the town of Astoria had seen fit to give the boy such a job, allowing him and his dog to greet the public at a historic site.

Then the boy politely informed me that the entrance fee was five dollars.

I dug out my wallet only to find it empty.

The boy explained, again with great politeness, that this lack of cash meant I had to leave. Normally, there was an adult in the booth who took credit cards, but today he was all by himself. He apologized profusely, although I kept assuring him it was okay. Even the beagle looked sad about my rotten luck.

"Thanks for letting me know," I said. Then I dropped the Honda into reverse and glanced over my shoulder.

"No, sir, wait!" the boy cried, and then explained how I couldn't turn around like that, but instead had to drive a loop all the way around the Column. It was very important to do it that way. The other way wasn't safe. He'd clearly been drilled on this point.

"Sure, I understand," I said, and thanked him again.

Seeming relieved, the boy again pointed out where I should go, while the beagle bounded in happy circles, eager to see another tourist follow the rules. So I drove around the loop, resigned to only the briefest glimpse of sea, river, valley, and town. The word "coxcomb" refers to either court jesters or (in later usage) to dandyish men, and the Column resonated with both. It was borderline silly-looking, and certainly vain, but impressive in its way, too. A hard thing to just drive right past. On the far side were a bunch of empty parking stalls, and it occurred that the boy and his beagle could no longer see me, as they were sitting in a patch of shade opposite the Column. Tourists climbed to an observation deck, but I would've felt guilty actually entering the monument after not paying my fee. Then again, it seemed a shame not to at least stop for a moment and stretch my legs, especially considering I might never pass this way again.

So I parked and got out. In the distance lay the Columbia Bar. It was here, amidst violently opposed tidal forces, that Astor's ship *Tonquin* first entered the western interior. Things did not go smoothly. Eight men drowned on the first attempt to pass the turbulent water. The ship's captain, a navy lieutenant named Jonathan Thorn, was described by Washington Irving as "a man of courage and firmness," but the captain was also determined to live up to his name. From the journey's outset, Thorn was incensed by his sailing partners' tendency to lounge around the deck all day, laughing and rolling smokes. In fact, on their very first night at sea he threatened to have them all put in irons. Later—after the captain was officially "nettled to the quick"—he attempted to maroon a few of these happy-go-lucky sailors on a deserted island in the Falklands. One can only imagine how energetically they'd rowed their skiffs once they saw the *Tonquin* raise anchor.

Thorn was also irked by a number of wannabe travel writers who'd infiltrated his crew—these young men of literary pretension were "a sore abomination for the captain." Finally, he couldn't even let his crew enjoy their stop in Hawai'i. Instead of pig roasts and hula, Captain Thorn insisted on seeing the spot at Kealakekua Bay where James Cook was beaten and stabbed to death by natives in 1779. As it turned out, this was foreshadowing.

Despite having received a letter from Mr. Astor which advised extra care in dealing with the locals, while attempting to trade with Clayoquots at Vancouver Island (humbly named by George Vancouver), Captain Thorn lost his cool with a cagey old chief named Nookamis. The chief had haggled more insistently—that is, more effectively—than Thorn would've preferred, and so the captain grabbed a sea otter pelt and rubbed it in Nookamis's face, as if he were a misbehaving dog. After Captain Thorn kicked all the Clayoquots off the *Tonquin*, the local interpreter suggested it might be a good time to leave, but the captain scoffed. There was no need to worry about a bunch of salmon-eating yokels.

The next morning, a party of Clayoquots returned for another round of trading. Once aboard, they seemed particularly interested in trading for knives. They also wore strange outfits—outfits so baggy one might've almost thought they were hiding something under their clothes. Soon enough, they commenced stabbing the *Tonquin's* crew with the knives they'd just bartered for and bashing in their skulls with the special skull-bashing clubs called *pogamoggans* which they'd had tucked in their waistbands. Captain Thorn was killed alongside most of his crew. Later, a handful of survivors tried to sneak away (they were caught and tortured to death), but one badly injured Astorian stayed behind with the *Tonquin*.

The following day, while the Clayoquots looted the ship, that lone crew member locked himself in the hold and ignited the entire magazine of gunpowder—all 9,000 pounds.

According to the interpreter, who was thrown clear of the blast, the *Tonquin* erupted in a thunderous fireball and a smoky rain of human flesh. For days afterward, torsos, limbs, and heads washed up on the beach. There's no footage of this explosion, of course, but if there were it'd put to shame both Galloping Gertie and that TNT whale demolition near Florence.

I'd gotten thoroughly distracted thinking of all this, when I heard a sound a traveler never wants to hear: not the enraged war cry of offended Clayoquots, but the hurt voice of a boy who realized he'd been lied to and swindled out of five dollars. I commenced a fast walk. Behind me, the boy bawled and the beagle chimed in mournful howls. Other tourists stared now, pack instinct kicking in, winnowing out the source of the boy's upset. Luckily, I wasn't wearing my backpack or I'd have surely been tackled on the spot. Take it from me that you really don't want to be stared at by fifty strangers in a strange town in that particular way. This is how ruinous arrest reports appear in newspapers. How mob beatings occur. How otherwise innocent beer-travelers get their skulls bashed in with *pogamoggans*.

I jumped in the Honda and squealed rubber. A pair of matching yellow penny vests shrank in my rearview, the boy waving his hands and the beagle baying as I zipped around the Astoria Column and down Coxcomb Hill.

IN THE LAND OF MELANCHOLY

After reentering Washington via the Astoria Bridge, I stopped at North Jetty Brewing on the Long Beach Peninsula for samples of their Starvation Alley wheat ale and Cape D IPA.

Starvation Alley was the historical road that ran through the peninsula's local cranberry farms, with cranberry farming having historically been somewhat less than lucrative, while Cape D was in reference to Cape Disappointment, a headland I'd just passed. The doleful name owes to the same John Meares who christened the Olympic Range and who in 1788 nearly became the first European to locate the mouth of the Columbia, only to miss it in the soupy fog.

Speaking of, a gray veil settled over 101 as I headed past Long Island Slough and the Willapa National Wildlife Refuge. Established in 1937 by FDR, the refuge houses a number of endangered species, including the spotted owl. In the 1990s, statutes enacted to preserve these owls and use them as a gauge for the health of old-growth forests became the focus of an economics vs. environment policy clash which contributed to the decline and depopulation of logging towns throughout the Northwest. But from what I could tell, both owls and loggers were now endangered.

Past South Bend was the village of Raymond, where Kurt Cobain played his very first gig—a kegger—back in 1987. According to the biographer Charles R. Cross, the band hadn't settled on a name yet. Instead of Nirvana, they were thinking of calling themselves Pukeaharrhea or maybe Poo Poo Box. Regardless, Cobain spent that first shy performance being heckled by mulleted Raymondites who demanded he cover old Black Sabbath and Led Zeppelin songs, and the gig ended prematurely when the bassist, Krist Novoselic, climbed atop the band's van and drunkenly urinated on the cars of those who'd come to see the show. But from the look of things, Raymond's brush with rock-and-roll history had done little to elevate the town, much as the rusty metal sculptures of Native Americans and deer decorating the roadside did little to alleviate the depressing vibe. This couldn't all be blamed on some funny-looking owls, could it?

The farther north I drove, the darker and wetter it got, and the more rundown things became. Coastal Oregon had been occasionally seedy, but also charming and quirky, whereas coastal Washington's foreboding landscape reminded me of Roethke's "The Longing":

In a bleak time, when a week of rain is a year,

The slag-heaps fume at the edge of the raw cities:

The gulls wheel over their singular garbage;

The great trees no longer shimmer;

Not even the soot dances.

Compared with Oregon, tourism was the obvious difference. The Oregon Coast has transitioned from a resource economy to one selling all-inclusive stays with a view, whereas Washington's coastline south of the Olympic Park has clung to the old ways, to logging and fishing, while simultaneously facing enormous pressure from white-collar Seattle to stop netting so many fish, stop cutting down so many trees, and keep everything wild and beautiful, sort of like how they do down in

Oregon. This tension made me wonder about the impact on the local people—not so much their limited job options and high unemployment rates, which has been well-documented elsewhere, but their thoughts and feelings. "Geography is destiny," or so Napoleon supposedly said, and people, just like beer, are the product of terroir. Like it or not, we are the sum of our ingredients, and those ingredients come from a specific place.

Passing the marshes along 105, Trump signs adorned the yards of rundown homes. "HILLARY IS LAWLESS" was painted on a crumbling barn. Herons footed the tidal flats and NO TRESPASSING and KEEP OUT signs greeted me as I rolled into North Cove. These signs were everywhere, adorning nearly every shed, shack, and shanty. Then I found myself being tailgated—dangerously so, not a yard from my bumper—by a lifted pickup truck with oversized tires and six-foot long CB radio antennae. The truck's paint job was sandy camouflage straight out of Desert Storm, a hard blend with the forest green. Eventually, the goateed and sleeveless pilots of this vehicle swerved into the oncoming lane and barreled past in a cloud of black smoke, but not before slowing to pause dead even, both of us locked in at sixty miles per hour. They stared down at me with what can only be described as murderousness in their eyes before revving their engine and roaring off. In the truck's back window was a faded decal of the Confederate flag.

Bizarre and pathetic as the encounter was, it left me wondering what I could've possible done to merit such hostility. Then I realized the obvious: in all likelihood, my crime was to be merely passing through.

Next was the little town of Grayland, where I decided to stop and see if the fear and anxiety was real, or just my imagination. But the only likely beer spot was called the Local Bar and Grill, and its parking lot was full of those same creepy pickups. In a place called Grayland, this was simply too much. I couldn't bring myself to venture inside.

The northern tip of the peninsula was a colorless wasteland, the forgotten tracts of the resource economy. Men passing in their trucks had skin the color of old notebook paper and stared me down, much as those other guys had done, with drained and empty blue eyes. Perhaps these were the spiritual descendants of that first great clear-cutter, Paul Bunyan, doomed to reap what that mythos had sown?

My phone eventually led me to Bogwater Brewing, although the place had no posted signage. I crossed an empty parking lot under swiftly lowering clouds. Upon first stepping inside, it seemed there were no employees present whatsoever, but finally a small man in a cook's outfit emerged from the back. "You're too late," he said, when I asked about beer, "the brewery burned down." He snapped his fingers. "Propane tank explosion."

"Wow, I'm sorry to hear that, I'll have to come back after the rebuild—"

"You should have a steak," he said, and shoved a menu into my hands.

The steak he meant cost $42. Besides the cook and myself, the place was entirely empty. There was nothing on the walls, no customers, and no music. Just the dimly-lit shell of a half-burned building. He stared at me expectantly, as if this desolation were somehow my fault. Feeling unaccountably guilty, I looked away and mumbled something forgettable. All things considered, it was one of the weirdest moments of the entire summer.

"It's a good steak," he said.

"I'm sure it is, but my stomach's feeling a little queasy."

"I'll pour you a glass of soda water and bitters. You'll feel better."

"Thanks," I said, backpedaling towards the door, "but I'm really not hungry."

#

HILLARY FOR PRISON read a huge sign in Bay City.

PUMPED 4 TRUMP read a sign in Ocosta.

MAKE AMERICA GREAT AGAIN read the signs in the village of Markham.

But in Aberdeen, the childhood home of Kurt Cobain, was a different kind of sign—a welcome sign which invited visitors to "Come As You Are" in reference to one of Nirvana's best-known songs. Clearly, though, the good citizens of Aberdeen hadn't listened to that song as closely as my high school friends and I did back in the Midwest, where Seattle's grunge scene had seemed the epitome of all that was cool and dark and forever beyond our reach. Because if they'd *really* listened to "Come as You Are" they would've surely recalled that haunting refrain which ends the song: *And I swear that I don't have a gun. No, I don't have a gun. No, I don't have a gun . . .*

Was it wildly bold black humor, or impossibly gross negligence, to welcome visitors to town with the suicidal ideations of the town's favorite son?

Situated between the old logging towns of Hoquiam and Cosmopolis, Aberdeen sits where the Chehalis River empties into Grays Harbor. It's the biggest city in the county, but feels utterly dwarfed by her surrounding nature, the thick dark forest and that powerful river emptying into a cold and leaden sea. Crossing the bridge into downtown, the sky drained of what scant color remained. As if on cue, dull drops broke against the Honda's windshield, while dark-bellied clouds bore down upon the brick-and-mortar skyline like a crown of gloom.

After parking off Wishkah Avenue and watching a longhaired man pose for a photo beside a bright red "ECIG" electronic cigarette sign, I took a walk around the city center. Nearly every building was in a state of neglect, with FOR SALE signs decaying in the boarded-over windows. The air smelled foul—a combination of algae, mold, and industrial waste dumped into the river by the umbrella corporations of absentee timber interests. Like Everett, Washington, and like the Lowell, Massachusetts of Jack Kerouac's boyhood, Aberdeen was an old mill town in decline. Nevertheless, people I've met who grew up there swear it was once a nice place. Some blame the economic woes on the previously mentioned spotted owl legislation, while others say Aberdeen and towns like it[7] would've gone down the tubes no matter what, due to the automation of an already faltering timber industry. Regardless of the cause or causes, those high-paying jobs cutting down trees are, like the rosy tang of fresh sawdust, just a memory.

I searched my phone for breweries, but not a single pin dropped on the map. Almost 20,000 people live in Aberdeen. In the Pacific Northwest, that's more than enough livers to support a few breweries. Yet not one. So I set out walking and soon enough came upon The Tap Room. It seemed my beer-luck was holding—until I stepped inside, that is.

The Tap Room's lone employee steadfastly refused to make eye contact. I tried smiling at her, clearing my throat, and I purposely chose a barstool directly in her line of vision, all to no avail. While I'm far from high-maintenance, her attitude seemed problematic for a service-oriented workplace. Finally, I decided to break the ice and asked what was good on tap.

Instead of answering, she pressed one fleshy hip against the counter and kept on texting.

"Are you not open quite yet?"

---

[7] Such as Forks, Washington, up on the Olympic Peninsula, which is the setting for the *Twilight* series of teeny-bopper vampire/werewolf romances. Who gives a hoot about spotted owls when an entire supernatural industry has popped up? *Twilight* tours cart fans around to locales fondly recalled from the books and films. But there's a problem with authenticity here that goes beyond vampirism and lycanthropy: the author of the series, Stephanie Meyer, didn't actually visit Forks until after the books became a hit.

Without even glancing my way, she spoke in a toneless voice, "What do you want?"

"Excuse me?"

"I said: What. Do. You. Want. It's a pretty simple question."

My initial instinct was to just get up and leave, which was clearly her preference, but then I thought I really should tell her off, although she probably would've enjoyed that. Instead, I took a breath and decided to start fresh. After all, it seemed Aberdeen wore its gloom outside its pants (in the immortal words of Towns Van Zandt) for all the honest world to see, and if this Aberdonian bartender could speak to me with such incredible bluntness, then perhaps I might do the same with her?

"If you don't mind my saying so, you seem terribly unhappy."

I'd expected this might disarm her a little, might force her to take note of my personhood and thereby notice how she was presenting herself, her cold distance and cavalier rudeness. Instead, she continued right on texting.

"Hello? Earth to bartender?"

"I'm pregnant, man." She *still* hadn't looked at me. "And I'm miserable."

"Oh, I didn't mean to—"

"And I've got a rotten molar."

"I'm sorry. Like I said, I didn't—"

"What," she repeated, "do you want?"

I slumped low on my stool and remained motionless, saying nothing whatsoever for a full minute or so. Surprisingly enough, however, The Tap Room featured a number of great beers, and so I finally asked if she might find it in her heart to pour me a Bone-A-Fide pale ale from Boneyard Brewing. According to the ledger, this beer cost only $3.50. Now a lack of jobs and a crumbling infrastructure and the calcium-leeching effects of pregnancy are all legitimate problems, but come on—Boneyard beer for $3.50? Aberdeen needed to look on the bright side.

After grudgingly filling my pint, the bartender went outside to vape. I remembered that longhaired man I'd seen posing beside the ECIG sign. Just like there was a strong correlation between good people and craft beer, perhaps there was a contrapositive for electronic cigarettes, much as with Bud Light and video lottery machines?

A few minutes later, the bartender returned. She had other customers now. The older couple who'd just wandered in were nicely dressed, but a little shaky on their feet. The woman leaned on her husband's elbow. "I'd like a cup of hot tea, please," she said.

"No tea here," the bartender said.

"No tea?"

"All we got is beer."

"Oh, I can't have beer," the woman said, and gave her husband a worried look. "How about just a cup of hot water then?"

The bartender paused in her texting, stumpy thumbs hovering over a greasy screen. "Sorry," she said, "I don't know how to do that."

The couple's jaws simultaneously fell open and hung that way. They briefly looked to me for help, for some semblance of normalcy or modicum of civilized behavior, but all I could do was shrug. Because here in Aberdeen was the ultimate triumph of discourtesy, the brass ring of lackadaisicalness, the *beau ideal* of fecklessness and scorn. Hot water in a cup? Please? *Sorry, I don't know how to do that.*

The couple left without another word.

A few minutes later, a guy came in and plopped down. He and the bartender began discussing the fate of a mutual friend who'd apparently been lying about being clean.

"Tommy's been buffaloing his folks for years," the guy said.

"That's always how it starts."

"But they don't wanna believe it."

"Would you?"

"He never can seem to hold down a job, either. That's a bad sign."

"Real bad."

"So I'm not surprised."

"Ain't nobody who knows Tommy surprised about Tommy."

"Someday he's gonna turn up cold and dead in a basement with a needle in his arm. That's what I'm afraid of."

Hearing this morose talk, I thought again of Kurt Cobain, who famously struggled with heroin addiction, seeming to use the drug to numb the pain leftover from a troubled adolescence. When he finally bolted Aberdeen for good, had he carried with him the macabre feel of his hometown, and hence his troubles, or would addiction have haunted his life regardless?

"But what's to be done about it?" the bartender said. "You answer me that. Go on."

"Hell if I know. An intervention?"

"Intervention my ass," the bartender said. "Does this look like a TV show to you?"

The conversation kept on like that, darker and darker, but I found myself wondering something darker still: how could anyone possibly *stay* clean in a place like Aberdeen?

Then the bartender fixed herself a salad. A few wilted leaves of romaine, slimy brown along the edges, a towering mound of chicken, and then approximately half a tub of barbeque sauce. She topped it all off with a fistful of shredded cheddar and began to shovel it down, chewing on the left side of her jaw to protect that failing molar.

"Any other places for craft beer in Aberdeen?" I asked.

"Nope," she said, and turned her back to me.

The fork raised to her mouth again and again, tines dripping barbeque sauce, as I swallowed the last of the pale ale and tipped heavy, if only for the sake of the next generation.

#

Taped to the door of a payday loan office was a flyer for Gray's Hostel, where a room could be rented for just $300 a month, utilities included—a price that seemed even more archaic than that $3.50 pint back at The Tap Room. I passed half a dozen abandoned buildings with still more FOR RENT and FOR SALE signs gathering dust in the grimy windows. But there was at least one business that still seemed to be doing well: Grays Harbor Guns.

On the sidewalk outside the store, homeless men loitered, like disheveled and chain-smoking advertisements for the wares sold within. As a teenager, Kurt Cobain and his friends propositioned Aberdeen's homeless to buy them alcohol (including one man so morbidly obese they had to push him around in a grocery cart). Later, Kurt dropped out of high school, grew estranged from his family, and ended up intermittently homeless himself, sleeping in the hallways of heated buildings and in the backseats of cars. Aberdeen was that sort of place. But down the block I finally stumbled upon an island of life other than the gun store.

Standing out front in welcome was a life-sized Jar Jar Binks and a bikini-clad alien. Just inside the door loomed Chewbacca, and beyond him—surrounded by erotically airbrushed photos of Princess Leia—was a Darth Maul mask made entirely of Legos. I glanced at the price tag and what I saw there was so stupefying that I actually blurted it aloud. "Eighteen-hundred-and-ninety-nine dollars?"

The gray-headed proprietor waddled over. "For today only," he said, with a wink, "everything in the store is half off."

The shop was packed with loose trinkets and dust-cloaked paraphernalia. There weren't aisles so much as tunnels carved through mounds of Star Wars junk. Obviously this was a hobby, a collection, long-ago spiraled out of control. I ducked beneath a $5,000 starship hanging from the ceiling and stepped over a table loaded with Ewok and Hans Solo Pez dispensers. But while weird, the place was also cheerful—at least compared to abandoned buildings and gun stores—and Aberdeen desperately needed some cheer. Nothing traditionally nice or even normal could possibly survive there. No trendy cafes or boutique clothing stores would last. Only a store selling deadly weapons or something like Sucher and Sons Star Wars Shop, a purveyor of fairytale, a merchant of make-believe, had any hope of shielding itself—much like an interstellar force field—against the all too real misery waiting just outside the door.

In the window of a nearby Catholic mission was an awareness poster—"Let's Talk Suicide;"—and below the semicolon were some practical suggestions for helping those who might be considering something rash. I ended up seeing many such posters throughout Aberdeen, and I don't doubt their necessity. Self-harm was in the air. You could feel it, almost taste it. As an eighth grader, Kurt Cobain and some friends were walking to school one day when they saw the corpse of a boy they knew swinging from a tree where he'd hanged himself. The boys stood and stared for thirty minutes before school officials finally noticed. Later, at age fifteen, Kurt made a movie titled *Kurt Commits Bloody Suicide,* wherein he acted out the cutting of his wrists with a torn pop can and fake blood. Add to this multiple suicides by gun amongst the males in Kurt's immediate family, and what was to come now seems almost preordained.

I kept walking, hoping to talk with a local or two and get their take on their gloomy hometown, assuming I could somehow breach the topic delicately. But it was the oddest thing—besides the homeless, there were no pedestrians. Zero. I walked the downtown streets until my feet ached, yet not a soul. Vehicles aplenty, whizzing past with waxen-faced drivers at the wheel, but even though it'd quit raining some time ago, the walkways remained abandoned.

I did find, however, painted on the wall of a store offering a carpet remnant sale, a mural titled "Nirvana and Aberdeen." It featured the twin images of Kurt as a boy and that floating baby from *Nevermind* along with a list of grunge bands: Soundgarden, Meat Puppets, Fitz of Depression, Dharma Bums, and so on. Here, fading in the gray weather on the side of a furniture store, was the official soundtrack to angst, a playlist for anger turned inward, the melancholy art of inertia, despair, and self-loathing. To the north, more gloaming clouds crept inland over a hillside dotted with houses, and I could almost hear that soul-hurt music playing beyond the shuttered doors, playing back through the decades, and see that pale and skinny and wildly talented kid locked in his bedroom with headphones clamped over his ears, having just smoked a little pot or maybe even dropped a hit of acid, the better to understand this dark place where he'd been born.

Having come this far, it only made sense to walk up Market Street to the little park dedicated in Kurt's honor. It sat along the banks of the Wishkah River—a derivation of a Chehalis word meaning "stinking water" or so a plaque claimed—at the Young Street Bridge, which is the bridge immortalized in "Something in the Way." Artists often make myths of their childhoods, transforming memory into something grander, into a lie which tells the truth. Jack Kerouac made myth of Lowell in *The Town and the City* and *Dr. Sax*, while in the legend Kurt constructed in song and interview, he actually lived under the Young Street Bridge for a time, although those who knew him best said he'd just hung out there. According to the plaque, some of Kurt's ashes had been spread into the stinking Wishkah. There was a statue of a guitar, and in the mud under the graffitied bridge lay a smattering of dirty needles.

#

The rabbit-spider-creature was chained up in a cage alongside a rusty utility box. Something about its shrunken pink head made me distinctly uncomfortable. Later, I realized that, intentionally or otherwise, it evoked microcephaly and fetal alcohol syndrome. It had human feet and a cigarette dangled from its mouth.

The Grizzly Hare.

Sure, Kurt once described Aberdeen as like *Twin Peaks* but without the excitement, and yes the downtown buildings did seem likely places for irradiated spider-monsters to spin their webs, but the city had apparently *commissioned* this thing. Much as with that ghastly welcome sign, they'd sanctioned its placement along a public street. I'd noticed a few other odd pieces of civic art sprinkled around, but this one stuck out: the Grizzly Hare *was* Aberdeen. Fascinatingly macabre, ugly although not devoid of interest, it seemed symbolic of what living in such a place might do to a person—the gallows humor, the morbidity and ominousness, the grotesquery, all right there in that sculpture.

Aberdeen was a smorgasbord of depression, a veritable feast of ennui. I've seen far more dangerous places in America, poorer places and places with less to offer—but if there's a *sadder* place than Aberdeen, I wouldn't know where to find it. And this sadness wasn't the reflective type described in the *Anatomy*. Not that quiet lucidity which encourages reflection. No, this was a sadness that led Kurt to tell a kid he grew up with that he wasn't concerned about what he'd do at age thirty because he wasn't ever going to *be* thirty.

I was a freshman in high school the day Kurt shuttered himself in the garage of his Seattle mansion with a syringe and a shotgun. Although my friends and I were thousands of miles away, news of his death still hit us hard. After all, here was a guy we felt we *knew*—an adult, sure, but one not so much older than us—a guy who had it all, who lived in a cool city and didn't have to listen to what anybody said and didn't have to work some shit job for money, a guy whose name was chanted by legions and whose sallow face and unwashed hair were a fixture on MTV. Kurt was the most famous rock star in the world, and he'd gotten that way by singing about how much it hurts to be alive, which is something every teenager knows about deep in their bones; but instead of enjoying this dream of a life, instead of basking in the adoration of his countless fans, Kurt jabbed holes in his arm and followed his own lyrics where they led. I hate myself and want to die. There's real fear in that for a kid, even if he cannot begin to express where that fear comes from or what it might mean.

It occurred to me then, standing alone on that street, that if I were to live in Aberdeen—to rent one of those $300 hostel rooms, say—I would either write a searing book marked on its every page with the resilience of the human spirit in the face of grinding misery, or (more likely) I'd give up beer for vodka, start hallucinating Grizzly Hares on the walls, and join the addicts and schizophrenics on the rain-slick pavement outside Grays Harbor Guns. Because after touring the state capitals of Washington and Oregon, and the de facto beer capital in

Southeast Portland, it seemed I'd found yet another capital: that of the Land of Melancholy.

GOOD ROADS AND GOOD BEERS: THE COLUMBIA RIVER GORGE

The Columbia River Gorge houses the densest concentration of high waterfalls in North America, and to get a look at them one drives the Columbia River Historic Highway, which begins east of the town of Troutdale at Chanticleer Point, an overlook on the Gorge's western edge now known (somewhat less mellifluously) as the Portland Women's Forum State Scenic Viewpoint.

The morning was cool and gray, the air laced with particles of water so fine as to be almost invisible. Far below, the foggy Columbia wended through green hills and patchwork fields.

A peculiar man named Samuel Hill was responsible for the historic highway, and a fifty-ton granite boulder (sculpted by a descendant of Meriwether Lewis, no less) commemorated Sam's achievements. A Harvard man and lawyer, an inveterate globetrotter and erector of kooky monuments, Sam married the daughter of railroad tycoon Jim Hill, the same industrialist who once flirted with naming Everett, Washington the terminus of his Great Northern Railroad. Sam spun this marriage into a profitable career, which allowed him to indulge his many eccentricities, one of which was an abiding love of roads and driving. "Good roads are more than my hobby," Sam once declared, "they are my religion."

Indeed, throughout his life Sam delivered upwards of 1,000 lectures to schoolkids on the importance of roads. And while this stretch of the Gorge had only dirt trails back at the turn of the century, Sam dreamt of a highway as beautiful as it was useful, a road that's gentle grades and graceful curves would spiritually rekindle those who traveled it—after all, what good was Manifest Destiny without good roads? Where would Kerouac and the Beats have searched for that ever-elusive American Dream without guys like Sam Hill dreaming up transcendent highways?

I soon reached Vista House at Crown Point. This stone observatory is perched some seven-hundred feet above the Columbia and was designed, in the architect's own words, to evoke "the ancient and mystic Thor's crown." Inside, all was marble and limestone and stained glass. I bought some fresh coffee and then read about Crown Point and the history of auto touring in the Gorge. In fulfilling Sam Hill's vision, the Columbia River Highway (completed in 1915) was designed not with efficiency in mind, but to show off the Gorge's most arresting "beauty spots." Here was a road for travelers, not just commerce. A road intended to edify as much as transport, a concept at once distinctly American—a country in love with automobiles and driving—but also influenced by the European, considering its inspiration owed to the mountain roads of Switzerland.

Outside again, the fog had thickened with rain. I drove down a long stone viaduct hugging the Columbia, wiper blades washing back a sum of water seemingly greater than its parts. All was greener than green, the stonework guardrails suited in moss, cedars and boulders and open ground all parcel to the same creeping sponge. The road's lush dip and rise allowed for a speed of about thirty, which felt just right.

At Latourell Falls, I parked and hiked up a trail, slipping and sliding in the muck. The rocks on this trail, as if selected with nefarious intent, were of perfect ankle-spraining size—too big to ignore, too small to step on—and so I spent the hike not admiring nature, but staring down at my feet. I was a basketball player growing up and can still recall the agony of sprained ankles. It's as if that tender flesh surrounding the joint has more nerve endings than anywhere else in the body short of the eyelids. This downward attention allowed me to admire the quickly accumulating mud. By the quarter-mile mark, my shoes were brown and wet, by the half-mile, my ankles the same, and by the time I gave up and turned around, I was muddy to the shins.

Past more handsome stone masonry lay Bridal Veil Falls. But as soon as I parked, the sky became a waterfall all its own. Nevertheless, the lot was full of Oregonians preparing to waddle and scurry about in the deluge. But while my credentials as a Northwesterner are impeccable when it comes to beer-drinking, they're iffy as to outdoorsiness. Sure, the landscape is dramatic and one-of-a-kind. But does that really mean I'm obliged to *hike*? Is it truly necessary to brave raging rivers in dinky little kayaks and, come Saturday, climb 14,000 foot volcanoes for no practical reason, preferably using crampons and ice-axes and other terrifying accoutrements?

I zipped past Wahkeena Falls without so much as a glance.

Back in April of 1806, the Corps of Discovery had reached the Pacific Northwest and Meriwether Lewis, always a colorful diarist, wrote, "we passed several beautifull cascades which fell from a great hight over the stupendious rocks . . ." The most remarkable of these was Multnomah Falls, which plunges six-hundred feet down the face of Larch Mountain. And it was at this postcard-worthy spot, exactly one century ago (in 1916, just like the Everett Massacre) that the Columbia River Highway was officially dedicated and ground broken at Crown Point.

This was the star of show, and I couldn't very well just drive past. So, after battling for parking—Multnomah sees about four million tourists a year—I dutifully went and got soaked. Approaching Multnomah was like being rained on in zero gravity, water evanescing from all possible angles, misting over me in a chilly cloud. Even the dogs had dressed for the weather, the Chihuahuas in waterproof four-legged jackets and the Labradors in hooded parkas. A short hike led up to Benson Bridge, a handsome stone span between the upper and lower falls. My fellow gawkers hustled out onto the bridge, turned their backs to the plunging column, turned their cold grimaces into Instagram-worthy smiles—click, click, click—and then hurried back down to the concession stand and restaurant fronting the parking lot.

I had more or less the same idea, but while headed back I noticed a scrap of dirty paper crumpled on the ground. This struck me as utterly unconscionable. What sort of heinous ingrate, upon witnessing the majesty of the Columbia River Gorge, after having laid eyes on those beautifull cascades falling from such stupendious hights, would possibly dare *litter*?

I bent and picked it up, a scowl on my face in case the litterbug still lurked nearby. Once I'd smoothed it out, I saw the paper was actually a receipt from Burgerville. Sadly, this made sense, with a taste for fast food and a lack of social conscience being part and parcel to one another. But just before

I stuffed the litter in my pocket, I realized something else: the order detailed on that receipt—deluxe chicken sandwich, small fries, chocolate milkshake—constituted none other than my own midnight snack from the night before.

#

Sam Hill's historic highway ended abruptly in a wash of light.

On the Columbia's north bank stood Beacon Rock, a nearly 900-foot column of basalt that was originally called *Beaten* Rock by Lewis and Clark (or *Beatin* Rock, in William Clark's scattershot spelling) when the Corps of Discovery camped there in the fall of 1805, a little over five months before Lewis so eloquently described Multnomah Falls on their return journey. A century later, another corps—the U.S. Army Corps of Engineers—made plans to blow Beacon Rock to smithereens for no apparent reason. Thankfully, an early greenie named Henry Biddle (a descendant of the original editor of Lewis and Clark's journals) bought the rock and then sold it to the state of Washington at a price of one dollar, but on the condition they spare the dynamite.

Beyond lay Bonneville Dam, the first of the New Deal-era's hydroelectric projects on the Columbia. Then I passed under the Bridge of the Gods—the modern one made of steel, not the legendary Native American land bridge caused by the Bonneville Slide—and entered the town of Cascade Locks, home to Thunder Island Brewing. It sat in a marine park, just past a little museum housing the Oregon Pony, a steam locomotive which had once hauled wagon travelers past the Cascade Rapids. While Lewis and Clark described these rapids as moving "with great velocity forming & boiling in a horrible manner," the dam had flooded and tamed them and provided a placid backdrop for the beer-drinkers on Thunder Island's patio. In the taproom, I sampled a citra pale ale and a saison, both of which proved fine beverages—so fine that Meriwether Lewis might've gladly traded a sack of dog jerky for a cold six-pack. The Pacific Crest Trail passed nearby, and Thunder Island provided customers the option of purchasing a charity pint for some future thru-hiker.

After resting up, I crossed over the Columbia on the Bridge of the Gods, the $2.00 toll into Washington State more than mitigated by a wonderful view of forest and river. A few miles to the east in Skamania County awaited Walking Man Brewing, but first I wanted to visit the Columbia River Gorge Interpretative Center.

Relieved of nine more dollars (a full ten had I not lied about AAA membership), I began the tour. Past a display of primitive baskets and stone tools was a statue of Sacagawea, who at fifteen-years-old and six months pregnant was conscripted into the Corps of Discovery as an interpreter by a rascally French Canadian husband who'd won her (along with another teenaged wife) in a bet. In February of the expedition's first winter, Captain Lewis pulled double duty by acting as Sacagawea's midwife. Considering this was "the first child which this woman had boarn," the delivery was long and painful, so Lewis took the advice of the locals and administered a cup of tea brewed from rattlesnake tail. While Lewis was skeptical of the treatment, not ten minutes later Sacagawea delivered a healthy baby boy.

The museum had an entire room dedicated to the goods—wapato root, dried salmon, hazelnuts, muskets—which the Corps of Discovery traded with the locals, although fifty years later, ninety percent of those locals would be dead from diseases carried by men just like Lewis and Clark. Distracted by replica canoes and stuffed cougars, an Interpretive Center visitor could easily miss this last detail. But why dwell on smallpox,[8] cholera, and syphilis when there are things like the McCord Fishwheel to see?

Fishwheels—basically windmill-powered spinning baskets—were erected over salmon corridors to catch the fish returning upstream to spawn. Churn, scoop, churn, scoop, all day and all night long. You'd think fishwheelers might've anticipated the obvious longevity problem with their business model, but no. The devices were eventually banned, but not before millennia-old runs were decimated. Standing in juxtaposition to the fishwheel was a native longpole dipnetter, scooping up his salmon inefficiently and sustainably with a homemade net.

Upstairs, framed under glass beneath a portrait of Abe Lincoln, was a set of Rules for Teachers, circa 1872. These rules included chimney-sweeping and hauling coal, ten hour workdays followed by Bible-reading, no marrying for female teachers (for fear they'd get pregnant and quit) and no drinking or visiting barbershops for male teachers (for fear that, drunk

---

[8] According to Washington Irving, one of the Astorians, fearing the local Indians after the destruction of the *Tonquin,* devised a sinister ploy: he claimed an empty bottle was filled with smallpox. "I have but to draw the cork," he said, "and let loose the pestilence, to sweep man, woman, and child from the face of the earth."

and freshly barbered, they'd tempt the female teachers to marry them and quit), all capped off by no retirement plans for anybody. While this echoes Burton on the miseries of scholars, the list was just a fabrication intended to make us modern wimps feel coddled and guilty.

Nearby was another fake rule: a 1969 Skamania County ordinance declaring Bigfoot officially a person; therefore, to shoot Bigfoot would constitute a homicide. And with this mysterious proto-man of the forest in mind, I left the Interpretive Center and headed for the little town of Stevenson, where I soon found Walking Man Brewing. Their logo is the descent of man from lower primates—with the final humanoid having evolved from a dangling crouch to stride upright with a pint of beer clutched in his opposable digits. I parked out back and entered through a tucked away beer garden. On the porch, a codger played "Amazing Grace" on a set of bagpipes. The bar was small, trimmed in natural wood and forest green paint. A bunch of beer festival medals dangled from the muscular neck of—you guessed it—an ugly stone Sasquatch.

I took a window seat, better to enjoy the lugubrious bagpiping, and the waitress pulling taps smiled at me like an old friend. After evolving through tasters of Pale Strider Ale, the astringently bitter Knuckle Dragger IPA, and finally the old-growth-cedar-tasting Homo Erectus Double IPA, it was time to slouch onward to the Gorge's most prolific beer town: Hood River.

#

Sam Hill once described the Gorge's western edge as "Where the rain and sunshine meet." And so it was. Driving this stretch was like going from Ireland to Arizona in a few blocks—from rainforest to high desert, just like that.

Hood River, which sits at the confluence of the so-named river and the Columbia, was reminiscent of Astoria down at the river's mouth. The streets sloped up a steep hill, the resource economy was in transition, and the towns were about the same size. But unlike Astoria, Hood River never aspired to empire. It was a laid-back place. In fact, judging by all the folks playing on the water, recreation seemed to be the number one industry. The winds that whip through the Gorge are world-class, and so Hood River has become a destination for windsurfers and kitesurfers. Those winds also inspired the town's oldest and best-known brewery, Full Sail, whose facilities took up an entire downtown block. Formerly a fruit cannery, the warehouse's windows displayed an extensive bottling line, a matrix of conveyor belts, stainless steel gizmos, and plastic-wrapped crates of beer loaded onto forklifts. While a huge operation by craft brew standards, much of this space was dedicated to Full Sail's Session line.

Like Mickey's malt liquor, Session beers come in stubby grenade-shaped bottles. They're inexpensive and easy to drink, being relatively low in alcohol and hop bitterness. Session is an attempt to cadge a little of Anheuser-Busch's "lawn mowing beer" market, and although nothing in the Session lineup rivals the better beers of the Northwest, I can get behind the product.

Imagine you're a young windsurfer who, after years of trying, has finally managed to flunk out of college and deeply disappoint your parents. No more living in the basement, father said, and no more free meals, mother said, and therefore you had no more reason *not* to chuck it all and move to Hood River. One day you find yourself at the grocery store. You're hankering for some cold beer, as you've spent all day catching air in the blow and working up a righteous thirst, but selling nose putty part-time in the board and kite shop only pays a nickel over minimum. As a craft beer booster, I'd much rather see you buy a six-pack of modestly priced Session ale and keep your money in the local economy, rather than tip a Bud.

Founded in 1987, Full Sail was a pioneer in the early bottling of craft beer, and this contributed much to the spread of their brand. It's the second largest craft brewer in Oregon by barrel volume (a little bigger than Rogue out in Newport but behind Deschutes Brewing in Bend). But despite its splendid view of the Columbia and all those happy kitesurfers, Full Sail was family-friendly to a fault. Children scurried around, creating noise and bashing each other over the skulls with *pogamoggans.* All that separated the bar area from the kid zone was a flimsy railing. Call me puritanical, but I don't really enjoy drinking around minors. It's a tonal thing. Besides, children are happy just being children, and teenagers all have iPhones nowadays, so can't we save our brewpubs for those of us a little further down the pike—those who've watched their springy knees and baseless optimism erode?

After a quick Hop Pursuit IPA, I was outside again basking in the quiet, but only then did I realize the hour had grown late—or at least late for Hood River.

Logsdon, closed.

pFreim, closed.

Big Horse, closed.

I checked the time, shook my head, and added this to my list of reasons to never again live in a small town. Last call at 8:15? Thankfully, one of the finest breweries in Hood River, Double Mountain, was still open—although only for a few minutes more.

"But your posted hours say you close at ten," I pointed out.

The waitress shrugged, as if time were a flexible concept this deep in the Gorge.

"Better bring me tasters of everything then."

"Everything?"

"Besides Full Sail, which is actually full of minors, you're the only game in town."

"Tonight's been busy," she said. "Always is when we've got live music."

Sure enough, in the next room a man did his best to evoke Cat Stevens circa 1971. Hood Riverites swayed to "Peace Train" with that flaccidly drugged look which overtakes a crowd anytime anyone plays a Cat Stevens tune. How many times did "Moon Shadow" and "My Lady D'Arbanville" play over the loudspeakers in the People's Temple at Guyana? My critical mood was ruining the Double Mountain experience, though. I felt unduly rushed. Last Call cannot be outrun or bargained with; it's a solemn nightcap on the possible. And why drink beer at all if it can't lead anywhere new?

Just then, as I sipped a well-executed oatmeal stout (touch of coffee, smidge of chocolate, delicate nitro bubbles), a young woman at the next table over slipped from her chair and went thump on the floor. Spraddle-legged, cross-eyed, and flush-faced, she babbled out a list of complaints: her (wholly oblivious) friends had let her down yet again; she was sick and tired of getting plastered in the same old shitty bars and there wasn't anything to do and they needed to get the hell out of this stupid brewery and go find some greasy food before the whole goddamn night was flushed down the toilet just like every other goddamn night in Hood River; and so on.

I leaned down closer to her and asked if she were okay.

"Okay?" the young woman said. "*Okay?*"

Then I asked if she might like some help up.

"This floor feels awfully hard . . ." she said, splashing at its dusty boards with the flats of her hands. Then she narrowed her eyes and asked me why I'd pushed her off her chair.

"But I didn't push you off your chair. You fell."

"Are you *sure?*"

"I'm positive. I saw it happen."

Then she clamped her hands over her ears and shouted, "Damn it, that old hippie music sucks!"

Moments later, I managed to catch my waitress's eye and made the universal scribbling motion which means, *Check, please.*

#

The Columbia churned green in the morning light, as if disturbed by memories of her former passage. I was parked along Highway 14 on the Washington side, overlooking the spot where Celilo Falls once was, where the river had narrowed to just forty feet across and the rapids had dropped eighty feet in half a mile. Lewis and Clark portaged these falls in late 1805, and then passed through again on their return journey the following spring. Celilo Falls was the ancestral fishing ground of the local tribes—one of the oldest human settlements in North America, inhabited continuously from the end of the last ice age to the completion of The Dalles Dam in 1957. Celilo was the sacred place Chief Bromden's father sold out from under his own people in *One Flew Over the Cuckoo's Nest*, and the falls were where that longpole dipnetter from the Interpretive Center would've caught the salmon leaping upstream to spawn; Northwest tribes had gathered here to trade and socialize with tribes from as far away as California and the Great Plains—witnessing this, William Clark referred to Celilo Falls as "the Great Mart of all this Country."

But the Great Mart had gone out of business. A placard claimed the tribes were awaiting enactment of a 1988 congressional order that would allow them to fish between the Bonneville and McNary Dams, to "guarantee the way of life for the Indian fisher." It took until 2012, but eventually those sovereign fishing sites, thirty-one all told, were completed. That's slim comfort for the Indian fisher, though, because with fourteen hydroelectric dams disturbing the Columbia's natural flow, there just aren't enough wild salmon left to catch. Today's reality would've seemed like science fiction even in the nineteenth century, let alone 11,000 years ago: the mighty Columbia, that 1,200 mile surge that crashes and booms into the Pacific at the deadly bar which had so terrified the ferocious Captain Wilkes, a monster river discharging a quarter-million cubic feet of water a second, now flows at the whim of Diet Coke-sipping civil engineers.

Past deeply striated cliffs, I drove into the dry heat and rock of the eastern Gorge. The hills were dotted with ranch homes, many of which advertised a desire to MAKE AMERICA GREAT AGAIN. But considering the splendor of their backyard—the flood-cut hills and majestic river, Mt. Hood snowy and pyramidal in the shimmering distance—it was hard to imagine what more these people could want. Then again, there are those who can never be satisfied, people for whom the concept of "enough" is anathema. Take Sam Hill, for instance.

In 1907, not long after being dismissed from the Great Northern by his father-in-law—either because of Sam's frosty relationship with the tycoon's daughter, or because Jim Hill felt his son-in-law was mentally unstable—Sam purchased 7,000 acres and built a home intended to overlook his own personal utopia. Maryhill, as Sam called the place, was to be a Quaker agricultural community and modern-day Eden situated amidst the natural beauty of the Gorge.

Circling down to the bluff, however, it appeared Sam had built not a home, but a castle. "I expect this house to be here for a thousand years after I am gone," he once said, and from the looks of its square-shouldered architecture and thick concrete walls, it may well be.

Maryhill stands on a table of basalt eight-hundred feet above the river, with water and hills laid out like a Hudson River School painting in the distance. A number of sculptures adorned the grounds. A deer welded from old tools and gears recovered from an abandoned mine. An abstract sunbather in yellow. A metal pine tree flattened by the winds roaring through the canyon. Sam named the place after his daughter, who was profoundly depressed all her life. As was typical back then,

Mary's melancholia was spoken of as a purely physical disorder, one best treated with exercise and fresh air. So it's likely Sam built Maryhill, at least in part, in hopes that the Gorge's beauty might heal his troubled child.

Whatever his motivations, Sam Hill was a man of vision. At the time of construction, there were no paved roads so deep in the Gorge, and yet the castle contains a big parking garage. Stranger still was the construction of ten miles of wildly expensive experimental roadway that began nowhere and led to pretty much the same—although these looping roads did later prove useful as trial runs in building the Columbia River Highway. Maryhill was also wired for electricity from day one, even though the grid wouldn't reach it for twenty years. But even the grandest of visions bump into reality, and Sam's farming community faced one insurmountable problem: the spot he'd chosen, while breathtaking, was a few miles east of where the rain and sunshine actually met.

So, in 1926, getting older and surely embarrassed by Maryhill's failure, Sam took the advice of the world-famous dancer Loïe Fuller, who was a close personal friend, and dedicated his half-finished home and grounds to the public. *Time* once called Maryhill the world's most isolated art museum, which it must surely be. Just to the right of the entrance, a plaque commemorated the dedication ceremony, which was conducted by another famous friend, Queen Marie of Romania, who Sam met while selling railway bonds overseas. "THERE IS MUCH MORE IN THIS BUILDING MADE OF CONCRETE THAN WE SEE," the Queen said. "THERE IS A DREAM BUILT INTO THIS PLACE."

After paying a modest fee, I headed downstairs to the space Sam had meant for his automobiles, but instead I found a collection of Rodins. In the middle of the Columbia River Gorge: Rodin. Maybe two dozen sculptures under glass, with as many sketches and watercolors. One sketch was an 1882 self-portrait. Dour and brooding, the great artist had worn a melancholy face, and his work reflected this. The collection included casts from what would become *The Gates of Hell,* an intended relief based on *The Divine Comedy.* Rodin spent twenty years working on this project at the behest of the French government, only to see that government eventually decide to build a railway station on the proposed museum site. The sculptures seemingly reflect Rodin's feelings about bureaucracy and civil patronage. *Despair* (1880), *Sorrow* (1887), and, of course, *The Thinker.* Studying abroad as an undergrad, I'd had the opportunity to view a full-size bronze of this last one, and while Maryhill's *Thinker* wasn't quite as impressive—he was just a foot tall and plaster—it was still a curious thing to stumble upon.

Leaving the castle, I'd thought my capacity for disbelief exhausted, but no. Because a few miles east, past a vineyard and atop a steep hillside dotted with mobile homes, was Stonehenge. Yes, *that* Stonehenge: a full-sized recreation of the famed Anglo-Saxon ruin.

Around the same time I'd visited the Rodin Museum in Paris, I crossed the channel and toured the ruins of Stonehenge on Salisbury Plain. I remember feeling hesitant to go near the eerie monoliths. But the feeling was different at this Stonehenge, because they weren't ancient stones quarried, transported, and carved by a pre-technological society, but sixteen-foot towers of concrete. If I felt remiss to approach them, it was only because they looked a little silly.

Placards on the pillars carried the names of Klickitat County veterans killed in World War I. The story goes that while visiting England, Sam was told (inaccurately) that Stonehenge was the site of druidic rituals of human sacrifice, and this had somehow conflated in his mind with the slaughter occurring in Europe, and therefore he'd built an American Stonehenge to revise the narrative from blood rites to honoring war dead. But I was unconvinced. No, this Stonehenge reeked of Sam's unique brand of manic optimism. Looking at the stone towers—in perfect shape, not in ruins—one suspects Sam's reasons for building them were more personal and obscure than patriotism or even some dementedly pharaonic impulse. It was like he woke up one morning with an itch to go see Stonehenge, only to recall the ruins were across the Atlantic, and so, over eggs and coffee, he decided to just build one in his backyard.

This kind of impulsivity, along with his daughter's melancholia, has led some to speculate that Sam lived with mental illness himself. Consider his chronic restlessness. He made countless trips abroad at a time when trips abroad were not easily made, touring Western Europe and Russia and Japan again and again. Ostensibly, these trips were to spread the gospel of good roads, but Sam just couldn't sit still. His butler claimed he kept dozens of suitcases stashed at hotels around the world, each outfitted with identical clothes and toiletries, while a companion said he was utterly miserable unless he worked and traveled sixteen hours a day, every day. But when you're as rich as Sam Hill, the nutty things you do are considered merely eccentric, and so long as the checks keep cashing nobody minds. Then again, maybe Sam was one of those rare souls able to see the world, or at least a little corner of it, in a way unique unto himself. Queen Marie put it best: "Sometimes the things dreamers do seem incomprehensible to others, and the world wonders why dreamers do not see the way others do."

Sam's tomb overlooked the river. I picked my way down the sundrenched boulders to pay my respects. A modest tomb (so far as public tombs go), it wasn't really his style. No, Sam had built his own monuments *during* life. The Columbia River Highway, a castle full of Rodins, and American Stonehenge: taken together, these constitute Sam's real memorial. A few families milled around, snapping photos and struggling to spread picnic blankets against the wind. While the day was bright, the Columbia turned a darker green as it flowed west, as if her waters yearned for the shadows of that mossy forest Sam was so keen to show the world. To the north, high atop the Klickitat Hills, churned a series of wind turbines. Stark white against the sky, they stood tall as redwoods, and in their graceful silence and with their trinity of clock-like blades, they might've been alien monuments with a meaning now lost to us.

#

Driving back west along I-84, a sign warned that littering carried a max fine of $6,250.

Good thing I found that Burgerville receipt that'd fallen from my pocket back at Multnomah Falls. The sign also reminded me of my childhood. Specifically, the trips we took each summer to visit my paternal grandmother, who lived seven hours away in deepest, darkest Missouri. Much drive-thru fast food was consumed on these sweltering road voyages, as my father wouldn't dream of allowing his wife and son to actually sit down and eat in a restaurant, for fear we'd grow partial to air-conditioning and free soda refills, thus increasing the likelihood of our falling prey to other subversive leftwing ideas, like regular dental checkups.

After swerving all over the highway in his cussing and ham-fisted attempts to apply mayonnaise to a double bacon cheeseburger at sixty-miles-per-hour, my father would inevitably crank down the window of our family jalopy and chuck the empty food bag out. He would frown in his peculiarly slat-browed way as he performed this misdemeanor, as if a clean environment somehow insulted him. I thought little of the old man's littering at the time, although I did notice no other families seemed to eject garbage onto the roadway.

But three decades on, the memory brought a smile to my face. In fact, I enjoyed a full-blown cinematic fantasy of being nine-years-old again, stuck in the hot and miserable back seat, having watched my father slobber down another Whopper and fries, wad up the greasy wrappers, and chuck the whole shebang out the window—only then, in my fantasy, a police cruiser appeared in the rearview, whirligig takedown lights flashing red and blue.

"Mr. Hurst," the officer would say, having inspected my father's almost certainly expired driver's license, "do you realize littering is a crime?"

"Littering? Speak English, you fool."

"Sir, you threw a sack of trash out the window of your automobile."

"The hell you say."

"I witnessed you do it."

"Can't you see you're wasting my valuable time?" my father would say. "We're on our yearly family vacation. Daylight is burning and meanwhile here you are impeding our progress."

At this, my mother's eyes would roll behind the paperback novel she read to combat boredom and car sickness.

"Answer me this, officer—are you a civil servant, or just another government leech?"

"Sir, I'm going to have to write you a ticket for littering."

"I'm a taxpayer, goddamnit! I'll have you know I voted for *Ronald Reagan!*"

And so my fantasy ends with that Oregon patrolman handing my red-faced father a ticket for $6,250, or approximately five times the value of our family car.

My father was forty-four when I was born. Burton (quoting Scoltzius) writes that "old men's children are seldom of good temperament" but are instead "wayward, peevish, sad, melancholy sons." If that's true, it's not due to mysterious bodily humours, but to the simple fact that older men have already lived so much disappointment that they often can't help but cast a gloomy shade. That and, like Burton, my father was an *aquæ potor,* and never have I encountered an individual who more desperately needed a cold beer.

All this reminiscing had left *me* needing a beer, too, and so I exited at The Dalles.

Due to the Gorge's steep walls, The Dalles had marked the end of wagon travel on the Oregon Trail, leaving pioneers to choose between a treacherous float down the rapids of the Columbia—the water "agitated Gut swelling, boiling &

whorling in every direction," according to William Clark—or a brutal trek across the Cascades. Lucky for me, however, Clock Tower Ales was just off the main drag. A hard place to miss, with the eponymous three-story pile of bricks lording over the business district.

Inside, when I asked about the building's history, the bartender proved a font of information. She leaned close and in a near-whisper asked if I minded a bit of scandal.

Intrigued, I said not all, that I actually considered myself something of a connoisseur of scandal.

"This building right here," she said, and I knew from her tone exactly what was coming, "was the very first *bordello* in all the Pacific Northwest."

"No kidding? So where does the bordelloing happen these days?"

Her face instantly dropped, but I decided to wait and see what might come of the awkwardness.

"Well," she finally said, "it was also the site of the last hanging in Oregon."

"So where do you hang people now?"

This time she almost smiled, but not quite. I asked her what else the building had been, half afraid she'd claim it was once an insane asylum.

"It was a mortuary, too," she said. "The mortician was the one who turned it into a bar. And it was the town jail for a while. The old Wasco County Courthouse. That metal door over there"—she pointed toward the toilets—"was the holding cell."

Feeling good about this stop, I ordered a pale ale from Barley Brown's, the brewer of that terrific stout I'd drank at Sassy's back in Portland. Barley Brown's was out in Baker City, another three hours into the desert along I-84. But if one were to hook north on I-82 into Washington, they'd soon run into the Hanford Nuclear Site, the former employer of the whistleblowing former owner of Old Schoolhouse Brewery up in Winthrop. Today, Hanford is home to nine decommissioned reactors and a number of double-shell million-gallon tanks, some of which are leaking radioactive waste. Scary news considering Hanford has over fifty million gallons of this poison stored underground. Call me Chicken Little, but it's probably worth remembering that Hanford sits along the Columbia— the most important water source west of the Rockies—and that this river irrigates all those orchards in the salad bowl of eastern Washington, while the sludge left over from weapons-grade plutonium production is just about the deadliest stuff on the planet. Radiation levels downwind from Hanford occasionally "burp" into the Three Mile Island, Fukushima, Incredible Hulk range. Cancer scares make the papers. Workers get sick. People shake their heads.

But Baker City was far enough away that Barley Brown's beer probably wouldn't mutate my DNA, and the first cold sip was just the thing after all that wind and sun and inexplicable art.

"The Freemasons meet upstairs, too," the bartender informed me.

"As in the secret society? The ones from *The Da Vinci Code?*"

"They wear suits and sneak in through the employee entrance by the back stairs."

"Lewis and Clark were masons. They took it pretty seriously, I guess."

"Well these guys are all about seventy and grumpy as can be," she said. "They drink beer at their little meetings, too, even though they're technically not supposed to."

"Know what's stranger than this place having once been a bordello and a mortuary?"

When she shook her head, I said that just a few miles away there was a basement full of original Rodins. But by the way she looked at me, I could tell she needed a hint.

"French guy, bigtime sculptor." I propped an elbow on my knee, stuck a fist under my chin, and glowered. "*The Thinker* is his most famous one."

"You're trying to tell me that thing's *here*—in the Gorge?"

"Sure is. A cast of it, anyway."

"Guess I hadn't heard about that . . ." the bartender said, and then eased down the rail and busied herself washing glassware. She'd clearly lost interest in talking about the colorful history of Clock Tower Ales, having decided her latest customer was either a liar or a drunk.

BEER TOWN, USA

Mere days remained of summer. Soon I'd find myself back in the classroom, charged with saying pithy things about writing and punishing teenagers for failing to cite their sources in MLA format. Despite having decided to build a class around travel literature that might be at least somewhat enjoyable for all involved, summer's end was bittersweet—but not like a good IPA. No, the grind's inevitable return was simply bitter, like an IPA past the sell-by date. So much exploring remained undone. So many beers as yet undrunk. In short, my last trip had to really count.

Thus: Bend, Oregon. Beer Town, USA. Home to more craft breweries per capita than anywhere else in America. But it wasn't just the unparalleled beer density which called me to Bend, it was the quality. Here was my chance to quaff straight from the source, to taste and feel this finest of American ale towns—and to put my assorted ideas about the terroir of beer, people, and the soul of the Pacific Northwest to the final test.

But first I had to get there. Bend is nestled along the dry shoulder of the Cascades, east from the Willamette Valley and Eugene, but I was coming from Portland and so I took the Mount Hood Scenic Byway. The mountain itself, the highest point in Oregon at a touch over 11,000 feet, is named after Samuel Hood, an English naval officer who—just like Mount Rainier's namesake—fought against the good guys during the Revolution. As with Denali in Alaska, Hood's name should be changed to something which honors the Northwest's indigenous heritage. Because despite what Ohioans might argue, William McKinley had absolutely nothing to do with Alaska, and therefore his name does not belong on a 20,000 foot Alaskan mountain—and if it's stupid to randomly stick a president's name on a certain peak, what about a martial enemy sworn to shed American blood?

Moreover, consider what Washington Irving had to say on this question of naming. In *Astoria*, he writes of the overland party's encampment on the Grand River in present day South Dakota, just before they diverged from the old Lewis and Clark trail. Now "Grand River" is certainly no feat of geographical designation, but back in the early 1800s it was known as "Big River." The sheer laziness of this launched Irving into a scathing critique of the "stupid, commonplace, and often ribald names" attached to the landmarks of the West. Irving argues that the more euphonious tribal names could easily be salvaged, and that in addition to being "more sonorous and musical, would remain mementoes of the primitive lords of the soil, of whom in a little while scarce any traces will be left." But wait—while touring the Oregon Coast didn't the author comment on the superiority of the western naming tradition as compared to the Midwest? Sure, but that doesn't mean western names are uniformly great. They're just better, by and large, than those of the prairie states. After all, what would Washington Irving have made of a journey to Windsor, Illinois that saw him cross Flat Plain before fording County Stream #7 on the way to a round of Bessie Bingo? No, Irving was right: restoring the Indian names could save the country from—in his words—"the wretched nomenclature inflicted upon it by ignorant and vulgar minds."

That said, rechristening landmarks is only a good idea if those in charge of the renaming *have* good ideas, and Obama's term was almost up. While it seemed all but inevitable that Hillary Clinton would win the upcoming November election, it wasn't impossible things could go the other way . . . and that Obama's successor might prove very, very enthusiastic about just such a renaming project. Mount Trump. Trump Mountain. Trump Peak. Imagine how Washington Irving would feel about all those billboards slapped on the glaciers.

Later, I followed a turnoff that led up Mount Hood to Timberline Lodge. One of FDR's Depression-era projects, the lodge was used for the exterior shots of the haunted hotel in Kubrick's *The Shining*. It's a skier's paradise come winter, a summer base for hikers and sightseers, and an active volcano with a decent chance of erupting someday soon, a prospect considerably more frightening than ghostly twins and possessed fire hoses. In the lobby, massive timbers radiated from a chimney so huge it contained three separate stone fire pits tall enough for a guy to step inside. Old mountaineering gear was on display. Wooden skis, pickaxes, snow goggles of leather and glass. At the Ram's Head bar up on the mezzanine, I ordered an IPA (from Mount Hood Brewing, no less) but let it go warm, content to simply look out the windows at the snow-tracked trails leading up to Palmer Glacier.

Back in the Honda, Warm Springs Highway led southeast past the 45th Parallel, the halfway point between the Equator and North Pole, and the land turned ochre and sere. After the green of the Cascades, the palette of the Oregon Outback was startling. Rocky canyons carved the roadside and the high desert sprawled toward spaghetti western hills gone blue in the distance. Then the highway crossed over the Deschutes River.

Bend was still an hour away, but the town sits on the Deschutes and is named after a funny curve in the Deschutes and its best-known brewery calls itself Deschutes—so the sight left me in a state of pleasant anticipation, as I meant to visit as many Bend breweries as time and my liver would allow for, and the water in all that beer came primarily from this winding and picturesque river.

#

On October the twenty-first of 1805, Lewis and Clark had a truly prophetic experience while traveling through central Oregon: one of the expedition members, a rabblerousing private named John Collins, discovered that some camas root they'd procured upriver from the Nez Percé had gotten wet and gone moldy and sour.

In the words of William Clark, "Collins presented us with Some verry good *beer.*"

The next day, the party came upon a large river known by the locals as *Towarnehiooks*, which emptied into the Columbia. This, of course, was the Deschutes, thus making it likely that the Corps of Discovery were the first Americans to enjoy a brew along this beeriest of American rivers. In fact, they were so pleased that Meriwether Lewis bought a dog from the local Paiutes (along with some firewood to cook it), and Clark later gave the river an altogether different name—Clark's River—although that one obviously didn't stick.

More modernly, I found myself at Bend Brewing Company, just off the Deschutes at the lazy stretch known as Mirror Pond, the result of a dam that powers the city.

Established in 1995, Bend Brewing was the second oldest brewery in town (after Deschutes Brewing: 1988) and seemed like a good place to kick off my summer finale. I took a seat on the deck and my taster board arrived just as the last shreds of light faded through the trees. I really would be back in the classroom soon—the nip in the air insisted this was true—but I couldn't help feeling my travels were incomplete, and that even a trip to Beer Town, USA probably couldn't remedy that.

But whatever. I got my nose down into a palate-opening sour called the Razz Tafari, made with Oregon raspberries and lemongrass. Next, a 9% Baltic porter that tasted of licorice and went down smoother than its ABV might suggest. A dry beer brewed with lager yeast—think imperial stout for those who take their coffee black—Baltic porter is wrongly neglected. Historically, it derives from the English porter shipped up to the cold climes of Russia and Poland, but the style remains obscure in America, in part because of Cold War trade restrictions, but also simply due to the name—*Baltic*—which is a morose-sounding sea that most Americans have little hope of locating on a map. If this wonderful beer were simply called dry porter, or maybe imperial dry porter, its popularity would soar.

After a dessert of Wicked Medicine, a Belgian-style strong ale that evoked rum-soaked banana bread, I asked for my check.

"Just visiting?" the waiter asked.

"Sort of," I said, and briefly explained what I was up to, how Bend was the culmination of a long summer's beer travel.

"Sounds like you'll be needing this," he said, and handed me a Bend Ale Trail map.

I thanked him.

"Silver Moon," he said, while dragging his finger along the map, "is just up Greenwood Avenue. They were the third brewery in town after us."

Simple consecutiveness seemed reason enough to go, and this proved a good decision. First, it was half-price night, and my generous taster board cost under $5. Second, Silver Moon's vibe was perfect. Peaceful, beer-loving Bendites huddled around a mishmash of tables as a trivia emcee did his thing onstage. Everyone was happy. You could feel it in the very air and light of the brewery. Painted on the bricks above the stage was a mural. The Cascades cut warm and brown against a dusking sky, with three gleaming Silver Moon tap handles jutting out like metal glaciers. Beer flowed into a massive pint glass that stood on a ledge, tipping, the beer tumbling down into the blue waters of the Deschutes that flowed into the foreground, past dams and bridges and spruce, toward the town of Bend itself. The colors were primary and dreamlike in a lovely way. While I'm skeptical of the afterlife, if it turns out I'm wrong, I wouldn't mind spending eternity in a place like the one evoked by that mural.

As for Silver Moon's beer, a standout was IPA 97, which walked a fine line: any more malt sweetness or any less hop citrus and it would've tasted like canned pineapple juice. Instead, it was just right. '97 was also the year of my coronation as prom king of Windsor High School. A somewhat dubious honor, the crown had looked suspiciously like an old ice cream bucket wrapped in sparkly paper, and—despite giving the prom queen a healthy snuggling when Whitney Houston belted out that high C in "I Will Always Love You"—the whole thing was pretty embarrassing. But despite its limited resources, my high school wasn't a bad place, because there were a lot of good people there, much like it wasn't the beer that made Silver Moon such a fine brewery. I could easily find beer this good around Seattle, but I'd be hard pressed to find a communal space like this with such easy togetherness.

"Know of any can't miss beers to try while I'm in town?" I asked the friendly hippie dude at the next table, whom I'd begun chatting with.

"Ale Apothecary," he said, with no hesitation whatsoever. "That's the one for you, man."

"Oh yeah," his girlfriend said. "That stuff is bomb-diggity."

"Bomb-diggity bodacious brew!" the dude said.

"Excuse me a moment," I said, and pulled out my notepad. *Ale Apothecary,* I scribbled, and then, *Bomb-diggity . . .*

Although tired from the longish drive, I wanted a nightcap. First, I elbowed my way into Deschutes, which is not only Bend's oldest brewery, but one of the most successful craft breweries in America. It was packed, and the vibe wasn't nearly as mellow as back at Silver Moon. This was tourist central, a sense of anxiety and crush, of money changing hands without much pleasure. I liked Deschutes beer—loved some of it—but after waiting ten minutes for a seat to open along the bar, jostling with thirsty strangers and bumping into stressed-out servers, it was a relief to leave.

Across Bond Street—which in Bend's early timbering days was a hotbed of gambling and prostitution, much like Hewitt Avenue back in Everett—stood White Water Taphouse. I bellied up to ponder a few connections. Because early twentieth century Bend saw a temperance movement that mirrored Everett's own, even down to visits from the dry tent show evangelist Billy Sunday and, in turn, the wet lawyer Clarence Darrow. What strange jobs these men had: traveling from town to town and debating whether it was okay for people to drink beer.

Ultimately, however, Oregon went dry. In fact, this happened exactly a century before, in 1916, the year of the bloody Everett Massacre and the same year Sam Hill's Columbia River Highway was dedicated. What a year 1916 was for the Northwest: socialists got shot to pieces for exercising their free speech rights in a muddy lumber town on Puget Sound, one of the nation's most beautiful roads opened to the public, while Oregonians simultaneously voted away their right to have a cold one. But progress is always two steps back for every one forward.

Above the taps hung a photo of Jack Nicholson of *The Shining* and *Cuckoo's Nest* fame, along with a quote of his: "Beer, it's the best damn drink in the world."

#

Come dawn, I enjoyed a roasty cup at Palate Coffee in old town Bend. On the walk there, the high desert sun gently baked the residual alcohol from my system. Quite a change from west of the Cascades, where the lack of sunlight can be hard on those of us whose disposition is already a little dark. As far as environment and melancholy goes, Burton spills much ink struggling with whether the condition originates in the bodily humours, from circumstance, from the mind and spirit, or some combination thereof. And while all his talk of choler and bile, of cold livers and hot stomachs and moist brains, is gibberish, he clearly sensed the connection: despite the potent illusion of consciousness, that sense of body as mere wheelbarrow for the brain, all is hopelessly entangled. As for me, I'd lived on a private Hawaiian island prior to Seattle, and so it's possible my brain soaked up too much equatorial light and flooded itself with dopey chemicals, thus preventing my thinking clearly about the prospect of life in the land of ale and gloom.

But it was *sunny* in Bend, gloriously so, and these worries could wait for the gray of the coming school year, when student essays sprouted up around me like prehistoric mushrooms in the dankness of my studio apartment and beer gave way to dark liquor.

Later, I visited Crow's Feet Commons, where rumor had it I might find one of those bomb-diggity bodacious brews my friends at Silver moon had spoken of. Turns out, The Ale Apothecary was actually just a guy named Paul (formerly a brewer at Deschutes), with a one-barrel system. Paul was up to some amazing things, though: smaller than small-batch brewing, Old World methods, wood barrel aging *and* wood barrel dry-hopping, lacto and brett and proprietary yeast strains cavorting with the local bugs, bottle conditioning à la champagne, and a facility closed to tours out of respect for the neighborhood. A nice touch of mystery, that last bit.

The Sahalie came in a 750 ml bottle. Uncorked, funky notes of citrus and oak breathed from the neck. The fermentation apparently took place in a tun cut from a two-hundred-year-old spruce. Here was a unique living beverage, a beer my friends back in Illinois would've bet their last five bucks of beer money wasn't really beer at all. Delicious and interesting as it proved, however, finishing that big bottle would've endangered the day's ambitious tasting schedule. Still, it seemed criminal to abandon such a nectar to be put down the sink.

"Hi there," I said to the couple at the next table, "I've got a lot of breweries to visit today, and if I drink all this I'll never make it. Care to help me out?"

Normally, such an offer would arouse suspicion, but the couple accepted the Sahalie without hesitation. On my way to the door, I glanced back and saw them happily pouring the remainder into their cups.

Then (after brief stops at Immersion Brewing and the Atlas Cider Company) I made my way to Crux Fermentation Project, which sat on the edge of the Old Mill District down a dirt lane. Hop bines climbed a looming trellis in DNA-like helixes. Touching the buds, their spines clung tenaciously to the sun-bleached wood. Ripe with resinous oils and so green they almost glowed, they were beautiful and intricate little things. Burton actually recommends the *Lupulus* plant as good medicine, saying it purifies melancholy blood and purges it of choler, much as the plant's bitterness balances out what would otherwise be overly thick and fulsome brew.

Crux's beer garden was huge. Three food trucks bordered a football field of grass, with happy folks reading and chatting, tossing Bag-O and playing on a giant Connect Four board. I passed a tin man statue welded from old kegs on my way into the spacious bar, where more sculptures made of copper piping and gauges twinkled in the clean light streaming through the high windows. When my taster board arrived, it had a T-shaped copper handle affixed to a bowed blade of wood that curved gently up and over the tabletop, much as the bridges spanned the river downtown.

First up was Sezóna, a farmhouse ale. The name is Czech for "saison" and it was brewed with Czech malts and a Belgian yeast and finished with a touch of dry-hopping. On the nose, the Sezóna was like raunchy gym socks, but it tasted earthy and good. All the way to the bottom of the taster, sip after sip, bad smell, delicious flavor, back and forth, until finally I just had to call it *curious*—a descriptor, much like *interesting,* that far outstrips "good" or "tasty" or even "excellent." This was followed by a pale ale brewed with a new hop strain called Denali (a cross, apparently, between Nugget hops, Zeus, and a variety known only as USDA 19058), and then a tart and musky Flanders Red aged in Oregon pinot barrels. From the layout to the vibe, from the funky art to the funkier ales, Crux seemed not so much an experiment in beer brewing, but in creating the type of adult happiness so many of our towns and cities lack.

Last came a bourbon barrel-aged Russian Imperial Stout called Tough Love. What a complex aroma: bitter roasted malt and chocolate, the warmth of the alcohol itself, and that bourbon sweetness like vanilla extract. As the bouquet continued to unfold, it deepened into something strangely familiar. In full beer geek mode now, I spent a long time just sniffing and furrowing my brow. This ought to be embarrassing, of course—a grown man mooning over a little glass of beer and scribbling precious notes—but I was beyond caring.

And then came the answer: the Tough Love smelled exactly like the maple donuts my mother used to bring home from the grocery store on Sundays. This wasn't just the smell of baked goods, though, but of being nine-years-old again. A fourth-grader in love with the simple pleasures of his life.

As I sat ruminating, the couple from Crow's Feet Commons walked in.

"Sniff this," I said, and handed the guy the taster. "Remind you of anything?"

He smiled, having taken a moment to recognize me. "Smells like trouble to me."

We chatted while they waited in line. As it turns out, they were headed up to Portland next, and so I told them about Hair of the Dog and Cherry Michael, how it was one of the most compelling beers I'd had the good fortune to try over a long summer of beer-tasting.

"We'll look for it," the guy said.

"Thanks so much," his girlfriend said. "Thanks again, I mean."

"Hey, no problem. Beer people have to stick together, right?"

"That we do."

The waitress returned, having noticed my empty taster bridge, and asked how I'd liked the samples. Perhaps a bit overexcited, I told her how the Tough Love had taken me back to my childhood, and it wasn't until her mouth dropped open that I realized how this must've sounded.

"That didn't come out quite right," I explained, "but a few beers might've done my old man some good."

"What kind of beer does he like?"

I admitted my father didn't seem to enjoy any kind of beer.

"Your *dad* doesn't like beer?"

"No, but neither did Robert Burton. Although he did admit that beer was better for us than carp."

"Look, no offense," the waitress said, "but this Burton guy and your old man wouldn't fit in very well around Bend. I can tell you that much."

I couldn't help but smile, picturing Robert Burton and my father strolling together along the sunny banks of the Deschutes, Burton dressed in his canonical robes and pontificating upon this or that philosophical point, my father sporting his patented socks-and-sandals combo and tossing hamburger wrappers into the river, both of them soberly frowning at all the happy goings on. Burton probably would've liked Bend just fine, actually, but he'd have overanalyzed everything and ruined the fun, whereas my father would've believed himself surrounded by pinko commies and un-American activities.

"Those are some nice selections you made," the waitress said, and grabbed the empty tray by its copper handle. "Our best pours, right down the line."

I gobbled this praise right up, feeling totally in the know. But I hadn't just made some lucky choices. Instead, I'd noticed a number of Crux's beers had the word "experimental" in the name, and ordered those. After all, what had my summer of beer-traveling and odd-book-reading been, if not an experiment in hope?

#

While finding Boneyard on draft had gone a long way toward elevating my otherwise miserable tour of Aberdeen, when I finally located their taproom in Bend—it was hidden in a residential neighborhood—I was surprised to find it small as a shoebox. A handful of taps lined the back wall and merchandise lined the rest. "NO PINTS!" was scribbled everywhere in magic marker, so nobody would take a notion to linger.

Boneyard had cultivated a skater punk vibe. Cypress Hill blasted from the stereo, and with their Dickies workwear and flat-brimmed trucker caps and tattoo sleeves, the dudes working there reminded me of the years I'd lived on the beach in San Diego. While I tried a few samples, these guys filled crowlers for the tourists streaming in. As the name implies, a crowler is a canned growler. After the big can is filled with beer, it's sealed by a nifty machine that spins a top down onto the aluminum. Crowlers are great. They allow people to take draft beer home as with a growler, but without having to lug around those bulky glass jugs. They're also half a standard growler's size, a more civilized size, and one conducive to drinking craft beer at its freshest. Plus, it's just fun to say. Go ahead, try it. Crowler. *Crowler.*

Post-Boneyard, I stretched out on a sunny patch of grass in Pageant Park. The Deschutes twisted by, her tranquil waters dotted with ducks and geese, and people biked along the riverside path and sat under fir trees reading books. My impressions from the day before were confirmed: Bendites were a happy lot, a town of sunny and well-adjusted folks with bellies full of handcrafted beer.

After rousing from a brief nap and leaving the park, however, I was startled to discover I'd somehow failed to realize that particular weekend was Bend Oktoberfest. German flags were being unfurled along Oregon Avenue and grills wheeled in for brats. They'd even erected a stage for oompah music (sponsored by OREGROWN recreational marijuana) and the requisite yodeling contest. Down the street stood two large beer tents featuring the usual suspects: marzen and doppelbock, kölsh and hefeweizen. Finally, a banner promised both "absurd games of sport" and "wiener dog races."

The festivities hadn't quite kicked-off, though, so I decided to try visiting Deschutes again. Oktoberfest would bring a crowd, and considering how overloaded Deschutes was with tourists already, if I didn't get a beer there now I might not get one there at all—and to visit Bend without having a beer in its oldest, biggest, and best-known brewery simply would not do.

On the way I passed Tin Pan Alley, which featured a painting titled *The Millworker*. The subject was a grizzled logroller with the fingers amputated from his right hand. Nevertheless, the painting's bright colors and light-washed style conveyed an unmistakable cheeriness. I reflected on my experiences in Everett and Aberdeen, both of which were old mill towns. Had Tin Pan Alley been in one of those downtrodden cities instead of Bend, *The Millworker* probably would've not only been missing fingers, but had alien tentacles jutting from his scapula and a face like an octopus beak. But which rendering would've held more truth about blue-collar life? Could a man whose work quite literally tore the flesh and bone from his body still remain happy, were he simply fortunate enough to live in a sundrenched river town full of great beer— are we truly such simple creatures?

Once at Deschutes, an irritated teenage hostess seated me at a little table between a restroom and the broom and mop closet. The next thirty minutes were loud, jostling, and full of maniac children. When my beer finally arrived—Chasin' Freshies, an IPA made with Oregon-grown Centennial hops fresh off the bine—the glass had sticky crap on the rim, as if the bartender had been making a margarita, but instead of rimming the glass with lime juice and dunking it in salt, he'd rimmed it with grape jelly and dunked it in cat litter. To her credit, my waitress quickly rectified the mistake, and when the new (clean) beer came, it proved very drinkable. The Public House itself, however, was simply too popular for its own good. I placed a ten-dollar bill under my glass, shoved a few children to the ground, and left.

Lingering by the river in Drake Park, peaceful vibes soon returned. Ducks bobbed for dinner, tipping their feathery derrieres to the sky, and what from a distance had looked like a war memorial cannon turned out to be a high wheel log skidder, a relic of Bend's lumbering history.

But there was one discordant note. Just after I'd crossed the bridge and reached my next destination, 10 Barrel—the brewer of that sour ale I'd enjoyed at Brews Almighty back on the first day of summer—a guy came toward me on the sidewalk. He was dressed in a ratty t-shirt and blue jeans, spiritual kin to the logroller from Tin Pan Alley. We were at a distance where it would've been rude to step past him, as he would've had to break stride, but at the same time it felt awkward to just stand there waiting. But wait I did, because rude I endeavor not to be, and as this man shuffled past, I noted that he still had all his fingers. He also carried two distinct items: in his left hand, a twelve-pack of Coors Light; in his right, a family-sized bottle of antacid.

#

The next morning greeted me with a crushing headache, which had a certain poetry to it, considering I'd spent the evening prior drinking 10 Barrel's Crush lineup of fruit sours. Cucumber Crush. Black Currant Crush. Apricot Crush. These beers were so light and refreshing that I'd consumed them under the assumption it was okay to have two or three of each, although that may have been presumptuous. Along the way, gathered around a fire pit, I met Alex and Elisabeth, a young married couple with a great story.

They'd been living near Philadelphia and commuting to corporate jobs when they awoke one day and confessed their dissatisfaction to one another. They decided to quit those jobs, ditch those commutes, buy a camper trailer, and actually do what they'd always dreamed of doing: travel the West. They'd been on the road for a few years now, working seasonally and living for adventure—river rafting and mountain biking, hiking and climbing. While new to Bend, the town seemed promising. They were thinking of staying put for a while.

"It's lovely here," Elisabeth said. "And everyone's been incredibly kind to us."

"Bend really is a great town," I said. "Plus, there's just so much good beer."

"*Great* beer," Alex said.

"It can't be a coincidence," I said.

"There's no such thing as coincidence," Elisabeth said. She was petite and blonde and calm of demeanor, just the right kind of girl to live out of a camper trailer with.

Alex studied my face. "She's right. I never really got it before we began living on the road, but synchronicity is as real as anything else. As real as that miserable job I worked for so long. As real as getting older."

"You've just got to let go," Elisabeth said, "and what you need will find you."

"Cheers to that," I said.

A few beers later, after I'd admitted to being an English teacher, Alex fessed up to writing poetry. He was bearded and dark, a little older than Elisabeth. Clearly a dreamer type, just like me.

"Ever read *Utopia* by Sir Thomas More?" Elisabeth asked.

I took another sip of sour ale and admitted I hadn't, though I'd recently been thinking of the book because Burton mentions it a few times. Specifically, he cites More's advice on how we shouldn't work ourselves to death like horses. Half the day, it is argued, should rightly be dedicated to work, the other half to honest recreation—in this case, traveling around in a camper and taking the time to enjoy being young and in love.

"The book had a big influence on our decision to give up our old life," she said. "You should give it a try."

I promised I would, followed by pints, pints, pints, a blurry cab ride, and then—with virtually no transition whatsoever—the morning sun spilling through the motel window. After a blistering shower, I dragged myself into Thump Coffee downtown, where the counters gleamed and the baristas were all slinky twentysomethings with tattoos and smoky eyes.

At first, the words of the *Anatomy* swum on the page. I was now deep into the final partition on religious melancholy, which meant that after so many years I'd finally caught Burton by the tail. I felt I'd also at least caught a glimpse of what the old scholar had known, the insight which led him to spend decades writing and revising his incredible book: that melancholy wasn't really a disorder at all; that the symptoms, while troublesome to endure, while difficult or impossible to alleviate, while potentially fatal, were ultimately symptomatic of our being so mysteriously alive, of our yearning for a meaning that wasn't necessarily there and an authenticity that more often than not proves elusive. The reason the *Anatomy* was so preposterously long and dense and circular was because its subject attempts to embrace all the world. In all of its forms, melancholy boils down to a grappling with consciousness, an awareness painfully confused by itself. Or, as Burton would have it, "Melancholy in this sense is the character of mortality."

I jotted a few notes, memories of the night before bobbing to the surface like carbonated bubbles, and readied myself for one last day in Bend.

A short drive east brought me to Worthy Brewing, where I found an elaborate greenhouse dedicated to Dr. Al Haunold, Hopmeister. Behind that, a large grain bin declared "Balance, Not Bombs" with the 'o' in the last word substituted for a hop bulb. Inside, the brewery was cathedral-like, the towering brick walls cut with massive glass windows to show off a number of enormous fermentation tanks.

Rumor had it there were plans underway to build an observatory on site and install a NASA-type deep space telescope so that Worthy visitors could look for supernova over a few pints. Apparently, the guy who founded and funded all this was an attorney who'd struck it rich filing class-action lawsuits on behalf of the victims of asbestos poisoning. Although our learned guide declares lawyers mere wranglers of no esteem, after seeing Worthy's setup I couldn't help but wonder if I'd erred by surrendering to the siren call of writing—typically accompanied by a backbeat of menial jobs, eviction notices, and jalopies—and missed a golden opportunity to secure a tort windfall and then go buy myself a brewery.

At the bar I noticed yet another framed photograph of Jack Nicholson, this one a screenshot of the actor from *Cuckoo's Nest*.

"That's twice now I've seen Jack Nicholson in Bend," I said to the bartender, who'd graciously offered to prepare me a taster board.

She rapped her knuckles on the bar. "The wood came from the old insane asylum where they filmed that movie."

"In Salem. Oregon State Hospital. I toured the museum there."

"That's odd," she said.

I asked her what else a guy was supposed to do in Salem.

"Not odd that you went there," she said. "Odd that it's there at all."

"Piece of advice," I said, and then sipped from an excellent polish smoked wheat ale. "If you ever visit, resist the urge to answer the old-fashioned black phones."

The bartender promised to keep this in mind. And she was right, of course—the Museum of Mental Health was odd—but not so much odder than building a bar out of the asylum's castoff wood. Such unexpected patterns were emerging. Maybe Elisabeth and Alex were right about synchronicity after all?

On that same bartender's suggestion, I next headed north to Bridge 99 Brewing, where above the bar hung yet another sign: HAPPINESS IS NOT A DESTINATION, IT'S A WAY OF GETTING THERE. The place was tiny, really just a garage with ambition. The couple who ran it were sweet people. She poured the beer, he brewed, and they both loved to chat. The brewer, Trever, spoke fondly of all the local breweries. In fact, he said Deschutes had given him a lot of help getting started, sharing ideas and even supplies.

"My goal here," he said, "is to grow until I can hire maybe eight guys—"

"Or girls," his wife said.

He smiled. "And then we'll all just work hard every day and make good beer and have fun. That's all I want out of this—all I want out of life, really, you know?"

Listening to Trever's philosophy, I pondered my writing, the years spent working hard to make books which in all likelihood no one besides myself would ever read. A situation much like brewing beer, soberly tasting it, and having to admit that for whatever reason—a poorly conceived recipe, faulty ingredients, bacterial infestation—it was flawed. Therefore, the whole batch of beer, the entire sheaf of pages, had to be flushed down the sewer.

As if sensing my pensive thoughts, his wife poured me a taste of citrus IPA. "The Oregon Beer Angels peeled the grapefruits for this one," she said.

"Beer Angels?"

"For every pint sold, we donate a dollar to the animal shelter. The Angels raise money for a lot of different charities. They're a great group of gals. And they're all about the beer, too. They know beer and talk beer just like the boys."

"That's terrific," I said.

Even though historically women were the first brewers (recall the beer goddess Ninkasi), as brewing was traditionally a domestic chore, guys tend to dominate the craft beer scene these days. While the gender dynamics are definitely changing, and while I've met many women who know and love craft beer, chances are if somebody's talking about bottle conditioning and proprietary yeast strains, that body has a Y chromosome—not to mention a beard and a potbelly. But apparently not so in Bend, Oregon.

#

Driving back along Highway 20, however, I couldn't help but feel a little bummed. This was my last day in Bend, the last day of summer, and the last day of my travels through beer country. It'd gone by in a sudsy blur, and I hadn't seen or tasted nearly enough. So, in a mood of superstitious optimism, I performed one last *beer near me* . . . which brought me to RiverBend Brewing.

After months of searching, after countless hours of lonely driving, my final query had brought me here. This was a lot to live up to, but based on what I'd seen of Bend so far, I felt confident the brewery could bear the weight of my expectations.

Inside, however, my heart filled with choleric black bile. Because RiverBend Brewing—like Cash Brewing out on the Kitsap Peninsula—was a sports bar.

TVs blared football and the waitresses all wore jerseys. People ate fried food and the air stank of grease. I told myself this couldn't be happening, that my summer's travels simply could not end this way, that my hopes mustn't die this particular death. In the men's room, I splashed cold water on my face and examined my baggy eyes in the mirror. Maybe I really could just pretend this hadn't happened—get back in the Honda, drive a little more, do another search?

But no. If this place, this *sports bar*, was where my road ultimately led, then so be it. Maybe such bitter disappointment was the real sign I'd been looking for all along: it was high time I started seeing this world for the crass and bottom-feeding place it truly was, cull the romantic notions from my soupy head, and start living like a grownup—like a bitter, cheated, soul-crushed grownup.

Back at the bar, I decided to take my medicine fast. I'd drink one lousy beer, watch some football, scream a few choice obscenities at the TV, and leave.

"Oh, there you are!" the waitress said. She was cute and young, spritely in a snug-fitting Oregon Ducks jersey. "Saw you come in, but then you disappeared on us."

"Just pour me a pint of whatever."

"Well, what kind of beer do you like?"

"I'm almost afraid to say."

When she asked why, I assured her that I'd drink whatever she brought me, and that I'd tip well no matter what. Seeming a little concerned, she spun around with ponytail whipping and returned a moment later with a frothy pint. "This is our fresh hop," she said, and placed a coaster on the bar. "Straight Outta Crosby."

I buried my face in my hands and groaned.

"What's the matter, honey? You told me to go ahead and pick for you . . ."

"Yeah, and you chose a beer named after a *hockey* player."

"Hockey?"

"Sidney Crosby. You should probably know who he is, considering this is a sports bar and you guys name your beers after athletes."

"Crosby," she said, "is the name of the farm where we source our hops."

I raised my face from my hands. "No kidding?"

"No kidding."

"I apologize."

"Apology accepted."

Upon first sip, the din of TV football and clamoring people faded to a low slush. The Straight Outta Crosby was definitely interesting—bright and chewy with Amarillo—as well as satisfyingly curious—dry-hopped on the nose but without a bitter palate—and while this wasn't the best beer I'd encountered over the summer, or even the best beer I'd had in Bend, it was almost certainly the best beer ever brewed in a sports bar, anywhere, ever.

Turns out, RiverBend's head brewer came over from 10 Barrel, having first cut his teeth at Deschutes.

#

Oktoberfest was in full swing on Oregon Avenue.

After wading through the beer line, I ordered a pint of the goofily-named Bruno Märzen from Silver Moon. Märzen is an amber lager named after the month of March, when this beer was historically brewed in Bavaria. Because lagers need a few months to condition, and because bacteria was more likely to infect and spoil beer during the hot months, brewers brewed in the cooler air of March and let the beer rest until fall—hence, Oktoberfest.

Sipping, I moseyed over to the wiener dog race and pulled my notebook from my pocket. The contestants milled around the starting line, tubular bodies wiggling, teats and peckers dragging the well-swept pavement. As the dogs were chuted and readied, the announcer cracked a series of groaning jokes about diets and training regimens. "On your marks," he finally said, ready to toss a tennis ball down the track and commence heat #1, "get set—"

But then the wiener in chute five took off in the wrong direction, wiener number eight followed, and they had to reset the whole thing. I took a sip of märzen. Five minutes later, they finally managed to complete the first heat. Mona was declared the winner, although it was unclear whether any of the dogs actually crossed the finish line. Being too slow to follow the tennis ball, they'd just milled around, panting and looking anxious.

Heat #2 saw the gate lift and all the wieners immediately run into the crowd. This diaspora was the fault of the wiener in chute three that'd been dressed in a hotdog outfit, whom the others seemed to view as a leader. The reset took a long time. Finally, Basil managed to run the correct way down the track— if not quite all the way—and was declared the winner.

Dexter zipped across the finish line to take heat #3, while a few minutes later heat #4 saw a wiener in a Superman costume lead a protest, as all the dogs except one (Lucas, who was declared winner by default) simply sat down and stared at their owners.

A half-hour had passed by then. People had tired of the announcer's quips and would've surely faded away to the beer tents, if not for a charitable politeness. When heat #5 finally commenced, none of the dogs finished. The tennis ball was thrown and retrieved again and again, with Yuri eventually crossing the line, although some raised doubts as to whether Yuri was actually a wiener dog at all. Some minutes later, the dogs burst from the chutes for heat #6 and immediately circled around behind their masters' legs. When the wiener from chute three actually ran in the correct direction, the crowd cheered so loudly that the startled animal turned tail and retreated. Another ten minutes passed.

Then a tattooed Humane Society volunteer took the mic. "Looks like we'll have to run that heat again, everyone . . ."

"You gotta be kidding me!" said a man to my right, and then, amidst a chorus of similar sentiments, the volunteer importuned the crowd to please remain calm, as the noise was frightening the athletes and making the races take even longer.

Eventually, Frankie (wearing an American flag bandana) was coaxed across the finish line.

Heat #7 included a dog so fat that it had to stand in front of the chutes, which caused yet another delay as it was debated whether the head start constituted an unfair advantage. None of the dogs ran, anyway. More tennis balls were thrown. Eventually, the obese dog's owner baited it with a meaty treat and it perked up and waddled a couple yards before collapsing in the street.

"Heat stroke," said the guy beside me, before taking a sip of his brew.

"Looks like we'll have to do another restart, folks," the announcer said.

I glanced at the time. The good people of Bend had endured an unbelievable fifty minutes of this. Finally, Heat #7 was declared a wash and the previous winners readied for the finals. Mona was in lane one, yipping and yapping. She was so jacked up that the guy beside me hollered out for someone to test her for amphetamines.

The announcer pretended he hadn't heard this and held the mic to Mona's snout: "Who's gonna win the race, Mona?"

"Yip! Yip!

"Isn't Bend a great town, Mona?"

"Yip! Yip-yip!"

"Trump or Hillary, Mona?"

"Yip!"

He kept this routine up for far too long, basking in his cleverness, until the crowd ceased its polite laughter and Mona's owner stepped out of mic range. Meanwhile, Basil and Dexter

THE LAND OF ALE AND GLOOM

and Lucas milled about lanes two, three, and four, and Yuri and Frankie took lanes five and six.

"Here we go, folks! Now for the finals of the 2016 Bend Oktoberfest Wiener Dog Races!"

The crowd rallied to produce a hearty applause.

"Let's give a big thanks to our volunteers from the Central Oregon Humane Society!"

More applause.

"And let's give another big round to all the other volunteers who helped put the race together today!"

The applause fell to a smattering.

"And lastly, don't forget about all our tremendous athletes!"—he pointed at the wieners—"Let's hear it for them!"

But the most applause was earned by a sweaty woman who cupped her hands to her mouth and shouted, "Just throw the damn ball!"

The finale proved a classic photo finish. So much so that five minutes later, the organizers were still talking it over and a winner had yet to be declared. The crowd had finally seen enough and a mass exodus made for the beer tents. Walking back down Oregon Avenue through the Oktoberfest crowd, I was glad I'd come. Bend was a special place, the perfect town to end my summer. The oompah music picked up steam. A cannabis dispensary raffled off joints. A pretty girl in a snug blue t-shirt looked me dead in the eyes and smiled so openly that I felt twenty again. Then, while passing the tents, I saw a man sharing his beer with an old gray-faced Labrador. He held the cup low so the dog could get his nose into it, the long pink tongue lapping streamers of froth onto the pavement.

"Is he an ale or a lager man?"

"Dogs just love beer," his owner said.

With the man's permission, I scratched the old lab behind the ears. His neck was thin, the skin loose under his coat. His tongue slathered my wrist and he closed his milky eyes and tilted his face to the sun like a blissed-out Ray Charles.

While Meriwether Lewis often made a lunch of dogs, Jack Kerouac could afford a little more sentimentality, and once wrote, "Dog is God spelled backwards." That's a silly thing to have written, of course, but I almost repeated it to the man then. Doing so would've seemed a little strange, though, and there was no way to explain my admiration for Kerouac's tenderheartedness. As a boy, Jack watched his beloved older brother Gerard die a bad death of rheumatic fever. Soon afterward, the family moved across town, their new home sandwiched between a funeral parlor and a cemetery. What do such experiences do to us, or even for us?

I put these thoughts aside and focused on the old dog under my hands, the bony skull and long carious teeth, the knobby growths on his snout and along the ridges above his eyes. But despite the sunshine and festivities, I couldn't help thinking of the relatively few days he and his owner had left together, of the unfairness of the one hourglass running out so much faster than the other. Old or not, though, this dog and I were both alive and drinking beer on a sunny day in Bend, Oregon. What more could we rightly ask?

Down the block and around the corner on Brooks Street, a smattering of orange and yellow leaves littered the sidewalk, and as I stepped into the elm shadows the air turned crisp and blue. The breeze changed, shifted, the coming winter trickling into the seams. But between Bend Brewing Company and Crow's Feet Commons stretched the Deschutes, and she was beautiful, her slow water painted with motes of sparkling autumn light.

LAST CALL: ALE COUNTRY

Come November, my travels finished in all ways except the longest of them, the writing of them, I was hunkered down against a tranquilizing gray rain while chin-deep in student essays on *The Oregon Trail*, when the cream-faced sycophants on TV announced in mock horror that Donald Trump had somehow won the presidency.

Beyond the windows, cold water blew through tree branches like exposed bone. Drops condensed on the panes and snaked along the sills in rivulets that finally dripped down to the flood of a leaf-choked drain. I tapped a pen against my teeth, struggling to digest the weird news. I thought of Zbigniew Brzezinski and that three a.m. phone call back in 1979, the year of my birth and the same year President Carter made the craft brew revolution possible. Then I considered the date—November 8, 2016—which was very nearly a century to the day after the Everett Massacre. So the triumph of the robber barons was finally complete, as the same class of blue-collar workers who in 1916 stood on the docks of Port Gardner Bay and shot the Wobblies who'd come to protest on their behalf, had now voted for a man who nakedly schemed to further grease the skids for his billionaire cronies.

I put aside my glass of ale—now ash to the taste—and looked more closely at the essay I'd been grading. My student, writing about the frontier spirit, had quoted Rinker Buck on the famous showman Buffalo Bill Cody, a "braggart impresario who prospered by exploiting the gullibility of the American people, most of whom are so poorly read, so bamboozled by religion and the sensationalist, mogul-worshipping press, and so desperate for heroes, that they'll believe almost anything that a grand bullshitter like Cody shovels out . . ." This brought to mind all those MAKE AMERICA GREAT AGAIN signs I'd seen over the summer, which reminded me of AB-InBev scheming to sell Budweiser to my fellow gullible Americans by printing the word "America" on the cans, which in turn reminded me of how my beer travels began.

I'd gone to Brews Almighty to celebrate the end of the school year, when a pair of blue-collar and heavily-tattooed Thug Life Kowalskis had strutted in with their pit bulls, angling for Bud Lights. At the time, I'd attributed their fondness for corporate lager to a lack of taste born of their having been brainwashed by the modern-day svengalis of Big Beer, but what I'd failed to realize was that on the national scale such tastelessness could elect a Bud Light President.

Maybe I'd dropped the ball? Maybe instead of shrugging my shoulders at the Kowalskis and their predicament, I should've bought them some real beer and introduced them to all they'd been missing? Because the craft beer revolution clearly still has work to do: while it may have carved twenty billion out of Big Beer's market share and revived a host of near-extinct beer styles, it hasn't yet penetrated deeply enough to shield America from her own worst instincts.

In the hours to come, rain sizzled and TV news blared. Bent over the essays, spilling red ink, I found myself once again thinking of Robert Burton, bent all his life over that one bottomless and remarkable book. His final advice is to be wary of solitariness and idleness—and just then, I glanced up from my work and saw a pale and owlish face glowing in the darkened windowpane. The face was cut with deepening lines and, for the oddest of moments, I almost didn't recognize this person, this familiar yet alarming brother. In fact, had the same melancholy stranger passed me on the street, I doubt I'd have known him at all.

But then something else occurred to me: what if, as Kierkegaard argues, there's a distinction worth remembering—even for skeptics such as myself—between Burtonian melancholy and some deeper, and dare I say spiritual, form of despair? Between a mood, no matter how dark, and a sickness unto the very soul. Maybe feeling low, even if the feeling is inveterate and lifelong, is ultimately a hard but fair price to pay for an expansion of one's sense of what it means to be fully human—and just maybe, as that tornado-phobic old-timer from Sunburst, Montana tried to explain to me back in Mt. Vernon, that this life of ours is full of woe need not necessarily be the end of us?

#

The following spring, my birthday rolled around again.

I marked the dubious occasion with a return trip to de Garde, out on the coast in Tillamook, Oregon. After a few wild ales, I retraced my route of the previous summer and found myself at Bill's Tavern & Brewhouse in Cannon Beach. The plan was to haunt the bar, reading and drinking pints until midnight struck and I was, officially, a thirty-eight-year-old man.

"So it's your birthday today?" the bartender said.

This startled me, as I hadn't spoken a word to him yet, let alone revealed the occasion for my visit. Then I realized he wasn't addressing me at all, but the young woman to my left. I looked at her for a good long while (it was impossible not to, really), until she finally returned my gaze. I was riveted to my stool. Here were eyes to be trapped within—*aucupium amoris,* as our guide would have it, or fowling love. The sort of eyes that send out mysterious spiritual vapours to infect the spirit and blood. Finally, she blinked and sipped from her pint.

Amidst my efforts to compose myself, I once again caught a glimpse of my own face—this time reflected in the back bar mirror—and again I thought of Roethke ("The mirror tells some truth, but not / Enough to merit constant thought") only to realize this loneliness I'd been lugging around had over time become a thing entirely my own. I'd come to know it, earned it, owned it. And so perhaps it was also mine to set aside? All I had to do was turn to my left and find a few suitable words, chance having seen fit to send yet another beer goddess across my path—one whose birthday happened to fall upon the day before my own.

Hours later, after a sloppy game of pool and a long walk on the dark, cold, windy beach, she and I sat in another bar, warming ourselves and drinking more beer—but now with our hands clasped and our faces mere inches apart. "You realize," I said, "that there's going to come a moment, one second, a blink, when your birthday bleeds into mine?"

And when that moment came, love brooking no delays, I kissed her.

#

The following Halloween, we adopted a young black cat who'd been struck by a car and left to die alongside the road. Surgery saved his life, but left him with a crippled leg and a sauntering, John Wayne sort of limp. But despite such a melancholy beginning, he proved a spritely and fun-loving animal, almost as if the early brush with the grave had somehow wakened his feline soul to the inscrutable come what may of being so softly alive in this most indifferent of worlds.

As for the little cat's name, which I deliberated upon for days on end, Jack somehow just didn't suit him, Kerouac would've been laying it on way too thick, and it soon became clear that Lewis (let alone *Meriwether*) would never feel quite right. Considering the circumstances, this left but one other alternative: a burly, ruminative, old-school name—and a name which, at this late hour, having come this far, you surely don't need me to spell out.

ABOUT THE AUTHOR

Phillip Hurst is the author of a novel, *Regent's of Paris,* as well as a book of nonfiction, *Whiskey Boys: And Other Meditations from the Abyss at the End of Youth,* winner of the 2021 Monadnock Essay Collection Prize. His writing has appeared in literary journals such as *The Missouri Review, The Gettysburg Review, River Teeth, Cimarron Review,* and *Post Road Magazine.* He currently lives and writes in the Pacific Northwest.

Learn more at philliphurst.com.

ABOUT THE PRESS

Unsolicited Press was established in 2012 and is based in Portland, Oregon. The team produces poetry, fiction, and nonfiction by award-winning and emerging writers.

Learn more at www.unsolicitedpress.com.

9 781956 692037